Financial Crime and Corporate Misconduct

The Fraud Act 2006 presented a wholesale reform of the pre-existing deception offences under the Theft Act 1968 and Theft Act 1978. This edited collection offers a critical evaluation of fraud legislation and provides a review of the Fraud Act 2006 within the context of measures introduced within the previous decade to combat financial crime, fraud and white-collar offences.

The edited collection brings together contributors from a range of unique perspectives including academics, practitioners and a former member of the judiciary. It covers several related themes and provides the reader with a unique and original commentary on how the Fraud Act 2006 has been applied by the courts, the type of prosecutions that have taken place, the effectiveness of the Act, and other legislation which is used to prosecute financial crime and corporate misconduct. It covers procedural and evidential aspects relating to fraud trials, namely consideration of the composition of the tribunal of fact in complex fraud trials, and good character directions in fraud trials. It will be of interest to those teaching and researching in Financial Crime, Corporate Law, Criminal Law, the Law of Evidence, Criminology, Criminal Procedure and Sentencing.

Chris Monaghan is a Senior Lecturer in Law at the University of Worcester. He is the Research Lead for the School of Law and the Deputy LLB Programme Leader. His research interests include fraud and property offences, legal history and public law. Since 2009, he has published on the Fraud Act 2006 and the issue of criminalising parents who provide misleading information on school application forms. His research has been published in the *Criminal Law Review* and the *Journal of Criminal Law*.

Nicola Monaghan is a Senior Lecturer in Law at the University of Worcester. She is a member of the Honourable Society of the Middle Temple and teaches criminal law and the law of evidence. She is the author of *Criminal Law Directions* (Oxford University Press) and *Law of Evidence* (Cambridge University Press) amongst other books. Her research interests include juror misconduct and compensation for miscarriages of justice and she has published articles on these areas. The Law Commission of England and Wales and the Law Reform Commission of Ireland have cited her research on jury misconduct. She also co-founded the Blackstone's National Criminal Advocacy Competition and has taught advocacy to undergraduate students since 2002.

The Law of Financial Crime

Series Editor: Nicholas Ryder

Available titles in this series include:

For more information about this series, please visit: www.routledge.com/The-Law-of-Financial-Crime/book-series/FINCRIME

Financial Crime and Corporate Misconduct

A Critical Evaluation of Fraud
Legislation

**Edited by
Chris Monaghan and
Nicola Monaghan**

Routledge
Taylor & Francis Group

LONDON AND NEW YORK

First published 2019 by Routledge

2 Park Square, Milton Park, Abingdon, Oxfordshire OX14 4RN

52 Vanderbilt Avenue, New York, NY 10017

Routledge is an imprint of the Taylor & Francis Group, an informa business

First issued in paperback 2020

British Library Cataloguing-in-Publication Data
A catalogue record for this book is available from the British Library

Library of Congress Cataloging-in-Publication Data

Names: Monaghan, Christopher, author. | Monaghan, Nicola (Lawyer), author.
Title: Financial crime and corporate misconduct : a critical evaluation of fraud legislation / Chris Monaghan, Nicola Monaghan.
Description: Abingdon, Oxon [UK] ; New York, NY : Routledge, 2018. | Series: The law of financial crime | Includes bibliographical references and index.
Identifiers: LCCN 2018025198 | ISBN 9781138557093 (hardback)
Subjects: LCSH: Commercial crimes—Great Britain. | Great Britain. Fraud Act 2006. | Corporations—Corrupt practices—Great Britain. | Corporation law—Great Britain—Criminal provisions. | Fraud—Great Britain.
Classification: LCC KD8000 .M66 2018 | DDC 345.41/0263—dc23
LC record available at https://lccn.loc.gov/2018025198

ISBN: 978-1-138-55709-3 (hbk)
ISBN: 978-0-367-49847-4 (pbk)

Typeset in Galliard
by Florence Production Ltd, Stoodleigh, Devon, UK

Contents

Notes on contributors

Sam Bourton is an Associate Lecturer in Law and a PhD candidate at the University of the West of England, Bristol. She lectures on several undergraduate and postgraduate modules including, Foundations for Law, the Law of Financial Crime and Regulation, and International Financial Crime. Her research focuses on the law of financial crime, particularly tax evasion and money laundering, and she has written several articles on these topics.

Caroline Collins is a Visiting Lecturer in Law at King's College London. She has been teaching law since 1997 and specialises in criminal law and the law of evidence. Over the years, she has worked for various other universities and institutions as a Lecturer in Law and in other leadership roles, including; Birkbeck College, University of London, The Open University, Oxford Brookes University and London Metropolitan University. Her other interests include the law of theft and the law on corporate manslaughter.

Bill Davies is Head of Law at the School of Law, University of Worcester, which is a position he has held since the School of Law was established in 2016. Previously, Bill was Principal Lecturer in Corporate Law at the University of Greenwich where he was also the LLB Programme Director. Bill's teaching and research interests include Company Law, Banking Law and Commercial Law. Prior to Bill's career in academia, he was a professional violinist and played in the West End production of *Les Misérables* for 7 years.

Cecilia J. Flores Elizondo is a Research Associate at the University of Manchester collaborating on research projects on counterfeit alcohol and on food fraud. She has research expertise in international economic law and food law and regulation. Her research interests lie primarily in the interrelation between international, regional, national and sub-national laws and regulations with regard to trade, food integrity, food security and sustainable food systems.

Richard Glover is a Senior Lecturer at Wolverhampton Law School and a former practising solicitor. He is the author of *Murphy on Evidence* (Oxford University Press) which, currently in its 15th edition, is regarded as a work of authority in the common law world and is regularly cited in judgments and by law reform groups. He has authored a number of journal articles on issues in the law of evidence, criminal law and public order law.

His Honour Toby Hooper QC is an Honorary Fellow of the University of Worcester and was formerly a Circuit Judge and Honorary Recorder of the City of Hereford. In 2000, he was appointed Silk and was elected as a Bencher at the Honourable Society of the Inner Temple. In the same year he was appointed as a Recorder. He was appointed as a Circuit Judge in 2007 and from 2010 to 2013 he was a Member of the Parole Board.

Stephen Hurley is a Solicitor and Senior Lecturer in Employment and Equality Law at the University of Worcester where he is also Deputy LLB Course Leader. Stephen has previously worked as an Employment Law Partner in private practice and has extensive experience of advising employers and employees on disciplinary processes. He also sits as a Magistrate on the Worcestershire Bench (though writing here in a personal capacity). He teaches and researches in the areas of Contract Law, Disability Law and Employment Law.

Maureen Johnson is a Senior Lecturer in Criminal Law at the University of Hertfordshire. Her main interests focus on the meeting point of criminal law and the operation of the cyber environment, and she has presented conference papers and written articles on this subject for many years. Her chapter was written as a result of her PhD research into the role of inchoate offences in the cyber control society for Durham University. Her research interests include the history of criminality in the UK and the increasing application of possession and communication offences in the risk society.

David Kirk is a Consultant Solicitor at RS Legal Strategy. He has experience of working as a practitioner specialising in prosecuting and defending in high-profile fraud cases. After working for the Director of Public Prosecutions and the Attorney General in the early 1980s, he established the first fraud and regulation team at a City firm, Stephenson Harwood, in 1988. He was subsequently a partner at Simon Muirhead and Burton from 1994 to 2006, and during his time as a defence solicitor he defended clients in early Serious Fraud Office cases, most notably Guinness and Blue Arrow, as well as in many other complex fraud investigations. In 2006, he was appointed Director of the Fraud Prosecution Service, a division of the Crown Prosecution Service, and from 2009 to 2014 he was Chief Criminal Counsel at the Financial Services Authority. After leaving the Financial Services Authority he became a partner at McGuireWoods London LLP until 2018, when he joined RS Legal Strategy.

Nicholas Lord is a Reader in Criminology in the Centre for Criminology and Criminal Justice (CCCJ) in the School of Law at the University of Manchester. Nicholas has research expertise in white-collar, financial and organised crimes, such as fraud and corruption, and their regulation and control. Notable publications include *Regulating Corporate Bribery in International Business* (2014, Ashgate – Winner of the British Society of Criminology Book Prize 2015), *Corruption in Commercial Criminal Enterprise* (2018, Routledge, with Liz Campbell) and *Negotiated Justice and Corporate Crime* (2018, with Colin King).

Noel McGuirk is a Judicial Research Fellow, The Courts Service (Ireland) and a Doctoral Researcher at the University of Birmingham. Noel's research interest focuses on the practical usefulness of the criminal law in contemporary societies as a basis to manage offending in various contexts such as fraud, terrorism and counter-terrorism..

Chris Monaghan is a Senior Lecturer in Law at the University of Worcester. He is the Research Lead for the School of Law and the Deputy LLB Programme Leader. His research interests include fraud and property offences, legal history and public law. Since 2009, he has published on the Fraud Act 2006 and the issue of criminalising parents who provide misleading information on school application forms. His research has been published in the *Criminal Law Review* and the *Journal of Criminal Law*.

Nicola Monaghan is a Senior Lecturer in Law at the University of Worcester. She is a member of the Honourable Society of the Middle Temple and teaches criminal law and the law of evidence. She is the author of *Criminal Law Directions* (Oxford University Press) and *Law of Evidence* (Cambridge University Press) amongst other books. Her research interests include juror misconduct and compensation for miscarriages of justice and she has published articles on these areas. The Law Commission of England and Wales and the Law Reform Commission of Ireland have cited her research on jury misconduct. She also co-founded the *Blackstone's National Criminal Advocacy Competition* and has taught advocacy to undergraduate students since 2002.

Axel Palmer holds a PhD specialising in economic crime and is a Visiting Lecturer at the Department of Law, University of the West of England, UK. He is a former Head of Debt Management and Head of Litigation at a major UK bank. His research interests are in the field of economic crime, encompassing fraud, bribery and corruption.

Rhonson Salim is a Lecturer in Law at the Open University and a Part-time Research Fellow in Collective Redress at the British Institute of International and Comparative Law (UK). His research interests focus on collective redress, private international law and international commercial arbitration. Rhonson was a legal expert to DG Just, European Commission in a multinational research project 'Study evaluating national collective redress mechanisms in light of the implementation of the 2013 Commission Recommendation on Collective Redress'. He was also an EU rapporteur on collective redress to Deutsche Gesellschaft für Internationale Zusammenarbeit and a legal rapporteur to OHADAC on private international law in the Caribbean.

Jon Spencer is a Reader in Criminology at the University of Manchester and has a lengthy career in criminological research. His particular interest is in how serious crimes are organised and in particular the points of contact between legitimate and illicit markets. He led the ESRC Research project 'Supply network integrated systems analysis of Food Fraud' at the University of Manchester from 2015–2017 and he is currently developing, with colleagues, a model for identifying vulnerability to food fraud within food markets.

Foreword

The origin of this collection was a workshop which the School of Law at the University of Worcester convened in its inaugural year coinciding with the 10th anniversary of the Fraud Act 2006. The contributors represented various aspects of research and teaching at their respective Universities, and in David Kirk, the practising profession and in me, recently retired judiciary.

I believe that this combination of background and experience evidences two matters worth highlighting here. First, the public benefit of University research and teaching, exemplified in these studies of significant public interest legislation. Second, that law academics and law professionals work purposefully together; such was a founding precept of the Law Commission, and it was the Law Commission which inspired the Act.

The contributions which comprise this collection reflect in various ways the significance of the 10th anniversary of the Fraud Act 2006. Many cases charged under the Act have derived from the recession commencing within a year after the Act came into force. Many cases involve challenges of the digital age which the Act, with its origin in the Law Commission's recommendations, shrewdly anticipated.

Not only substantial undertakings have featured in cases under the Act. It was during these 10 years that Billy Burglar sold his van and bought a laptop. Fraud has been just one of the nefarious purposes to which Billy has put his new technology.

This collection contains contributions from Sam Bourton, Caroline Collins, Bill Davies, Cecilia J. Flores Elizondo, Richard Glover, Stephen Hurley, Maureen Johnson, David Kirk, Nicholas Lord, Noel McGuirk, Chris Monaghan, Nicola Monaghan, Axel Palmer, Rhonson Salim and Jon Spencer.

Drawing all forms of fraud together, Maureen Johnson cites in this collection research which Experian currently publishes on its website to the effect that the annual cost of fraud to the UK economy is £193 billion. I observe here that the NHS website currently reports that the NHS budget for 2015/16 'was around £116.4 billion'. It is an arresting reflection that the cost to the UK economy of offences of fraud exceeds the NHS budget.

Examples of the way in which contributions in this collection consider how Parliament has moved with the times in addressing these challenges are the following.

For example, Maureen Johnson shows how the definition of 'representation' in section 2 of the Act readily catches 'phishing' and its various emanations, and conduct by use of a device, and averts any defence that a representation cannot be made to a device.

The public interest is particularly represented in the examination to which Cecilia J. Flores Elizondo, Nicholas Lord and Jon Spencer subject food fraud. They identify opportunities under the Act for greater prosecutorial initiative in the interests of the vital well-being of everyone which food fraud potentially threatens. They show that breach of food safety can and should often be prosecuted for fraud, with the opportunities for severe sentencing which the Fraud Act 2006 facilitates.

In their respective contributions Sam Bourton and David Kirk examine legislation following but evidently inspired by the Fraud Act 2006. Sam Bourton considers the new strict liability offence relating to offshore tax evasion enacted in the Finance Act 2016. David Kirk draws on his work as a practitioner in prosecuting and defending in high-profile fraud cases when examining legislative and procedural activity relating to fraud since 2006. He considers the normative potential of recent complex prohibitory and punitive measures for improving commercial conduct while at the same time reducing the risk of serious damage to the economy and consequential further recession.

Associated developments in the common law are addressed. The landmark case on dishonesty of *Ivey v Genting Casinos Ltd trading as Crockfords* [2017] UKSC 47; [2017] 3 WLR 1212 takes hold in a number of contributions. Sam Bourton considers the difficulties encountered pre-*Ivey* in the prosecution of tax evasion offences. I consider directions to the jury post-*Ivey*. On an issue of potential adverse impact on defendants in fraud cases, Richard Glover examines the restriction on 'good character' directions to the jury after *Hunter* [2015] 1 WLR 5367.

I respectfully believe that these and the other contributions in this collection represent individually and together an appropriate and useful marker of the 10th anniversary of the Fraud Act 2006. I convey my sincere congratulations to my fellow authors for the value which they add to the theory and practice of law in these serious public interest matters.

His Honour Toby Hooper QC
Hon. Fellow, University of Worcester
Formerly a Circuit Judge and Honorary Recorder of
the City of Hereford
29 April 2018

Preface

The Fraud Act 2006 came into force in January 2007 and presented a wholesale reform of the pre-existing deception offences under the Theft Act 1968 and Theft Act 1978. *Financial Crime and Corporate Misconduct: A Critical Evaluation of Fraud Legislation* seeks to place the Fraud Act 2006 within the context of measures introduced within the previous decade to combat financial crime, fraud and white-collar offences. The edited collection is based on a one-day workshop, *The Fraud Act 2006: Ten Years On*, which we convened at the University of Worcester in January 2017. The contributors are drawn from academics who research in criminal law, the law of evidence, corporate law, employment law, and criminology, one contributor who has extensive experience as a senior circuit judge, and one who is an experienced practitioner specialising in fraud.

Financial Crime and Corporate Misconduct: A Critical Evaluation of Fraud Legislation brings together a number of related themes and provides the reader with a unique and original commentary on how the Fraud Act 2006 has been applied by the courts, the type of prosecutions that have taken place, the effectiveness of the Act, and other legislation which is used to prosecute financial crime and corporate misconduct. It also covers procedural and evidential aspects relating to fraud trials, namely consideration of the composition of the tribunal of fact in complex fraud trials, and good character directions in fraud trials. *Financial Crime and Corporate Misconduct: A Critical Evaluation of Fraud Legislation* is intended to offer a critical review of the Fraud Act 2006, other fraud offences and issues relating to white-collar crime. It will appeal to a wide readership including legal academics, criminologists, postgraduate and undergraduate students, practitioners, and professionals working in fraud prevention.

The contributors to this book provide a range of unique commentary based on original empirical research, critical commentary, and practitioner and judicial experience. In his chapter, *A critical commentary on the Fraud Act 2006*, **Chris Monaghan** provides both a doctrinal and theoretical critique of the Fraud Act 2006 and considers the implications of the Supreme Court's decision in *Ivey v Genting Casinos Ltd trading as Crockfords* [2017] UKSC 47. **Axel Palmer** considers the impact of the enactment of the Fraud Act 2006, in *The Fraud*

Act's 10th anniversary: time to celebrate? Not quite? and considers whether the Act has proved an ineffective deterrent in light of the increase in fraud to £193bn. In *An empirical review of the use of the Fraud Act 2006 and other criminal offences within the school application system* **Chris Monaghan** draws upon his empirical research on the school application system and whether deliberately misleading or fraudulent applications are a real problem and whether local authorities treat this conduct as falling within the criminal law. **Cecilia J. Flores Elizondo, Nicholas Lord** and **Jon Spencer** in their chapter, *Food fraud and the Fraud Act 2006: complementarity and limitations,* explore the issue of food fraud and why they believe that the Fraud Act 2006 better informs how we understand, investigate and ultimately prosecute food fraud.

In *Fraud in the twenty first century: is the criminal law fit for purpose?* **Caroline Collins** and **Noel McGuirk** provide a comparative analysis of measures to prevent and record instances of fraud. Their chapter explores Australia, New Zealand and Canada and considers the effectiveness of each jurisdiction in combatting fraud. **Maureen Johnson** in her chapter, *The Fraud Act 2006 – a decade of deception?,* considers three academic concerns relating to whether the Fraud Act 2006 could cope with the use of new technology by criminals, how the inchoate nature of the offence would impact on prosecutions, and the impact of the importance of dishonesty. In *Criminal fraud legislation since 2006,* **David Kirk** draws upon his extensive experience of prosecuting and defending in high-profile fraud cases to evaluate the addresses the merits and the impact of the legislative programme intended to combat fraud.

Sam Bourton considers the Finance Act 2016 and how it will impact on prosecutions for offshore tax evasion in *Revisiting dishonesty: the new strict liability criminal offence for offshore tax evaders.* In her chapter she considers the strict liability nature of the offence and whether the safeguards and defences under the Finance Act 2016 are effective. In *Brexit and financial crime* **Rhonson Salim** considers the impact of Brexit on how the United Kingdom will fight financial crime. He considers how Brexit may impact on the operation of the European Arrest Warrant, confiscation regimes and the financial penalties that can be currently imposed. In his chapter, *Do we need a failure to prevent fraud offence?,* **Bill Davies** considers whether there needs to be such an offence in the Fraud Act 2006. He analyses the operation of the failure to prevent bribery offence under the Bribery Act 2010. Finally, he also examines the duty imposed on directors under section 172 of the Companies Act 2006 and the extent to which this has brought about cultural change at board level. In *A judge's perspective of the impact of the Fraud Act 2006* **HH Toby Hooper QC** draws upon his experience as a circuit judge. His chapter considers the procedural aspects of a fraud trial, the role of sentencing and how it compares to other sentencing for other offences, and the impact of the Proceeds of Crime Act 2002.

In his chapter, *The fraudster at work: the interaction of the criminal justice process with the operation of an employer's disciplinary procedures,* **Stephen Hurley** demonstrates the link between the substantive offence of fraud under the Fraud Act 2006 and the procedural requirements that employers must follow when deciding to dismiss an employee on the basis of fraudulent conduct. This shows that different areas of the law do not exist in isolation. **Nicola Monaghan** considers the debate surrounding the use of juries to try complex fraud cases in *Who should try 'complex fraud trials'? Reconsidering the composition of the tribunal of fact 30 years after Roskill.* She argues that more research is needed before we remove the jury from trying such cases and that much more can be done to ensure that these types of trials are conducted effectively. Finally, **Richard Glover**, in *Good character directions: some implications of Hunter for Fraud Act 2006 prosecutions,* criticises the Court of Appeal's decision in *Hunter* [2015] 1 WLR 5367 which restricts the circumstances in which a good character direction will be given. He argues that this has particular significance for those who are charged under the Fraud Act 2006 as the defendant's character is central to the offence.

We would like thank our colleagues who helped with *The Fraud Act 2006: Ten Years On* workshop. Professor Sarah Greer, Deputy Vice-Chancellor, and Bill Davies, Head of Law, at the University of Worcester for supporting the workshop and providing funding. We would also like to thank Janey Robins, the Senior Departmental Administrator, for helping to organise the workshop and for ensuring that it was a success. We were fortunate to have the support of HH Toby Hooper QC, who kindly agreed to deliver the keynote address and provided considerable encouragement during the planning stages. We would also like to thank Professor Nicolas Ryder, the series editor, Alison Kirk, Brianna Ascher, Alex Buckley, Chloe James, Tamsyn Hopkins and the production team at Routledge, and the academic reviewers, for their help with turning the workshop proceedings into a published book. Finally, we would like to thank the contributors. It goes without saying that without the willingness of the contributors to turn their workshop papers into chapters, there would have been no book.

This book is dedicated to Katherine and Rebecca.

Chris Monaghan
Nicola Monaghan
Worcester, May 2018

1 A critical commentary on the Fraud Act 2006

Chris Monaghan[1]

1.1 Introduction

The Fraud Act 2006 was a product of the Law Commission's proposed reform of the deception offences that were contained within the Theft Act 1968[2] and the Theft Act 1978.[3] The Fraud Act 2006 was enacted by secondary legislation on 15 January 2007 and had its origins in the Law Commission's consultation paper in 1999[4] and the Law Commission's report in 2002.[5] In 2004, the then government launched a consultation in response to the Law Commission's report and in 2005 a Bill that would become the Fraud Act 2006 was introduced into Parliament.

1.2 Background to the Fraud Act 2006

Prior to the enactment of the Fraud Act 2006 'fraudsters' were prosecuted under the deception offences, the offence of false accounting under section 17 of the Theft Act 1968 and the common law offence of conspiracy to defraud. The deception offences were notoriously difficult to prosecute and were 'overly technical'[6] and created 'a hazardous terrain for prosecutors'.[7] Professor Edward Griew had criticised the deception offences, observing that '[n]o one wanting to construct a rational, efficient law of criminal fraud would choose to start from the present position'.[8] The Law Commission had noted that the complexity of the existing offences meant that defendants could be charged under the wrong offence and this could 'result in unjustified acquittals and costly appeals'.[9]

Other problems included the requirement that the victim was *actually* deceived into handing over the item to the defendant. The case law on this was complex and involved examining the defendant's conduct in order to ascertain whether the victim had been deceived.[10] Finally, in cases involving a computer or a machine, it was difficult to argue that the defendant deceived the machine. This point was addressed by the Law Commission, as '[a] machine has no mind, so it cannot believe a proposition to be true or false, and therefore cannot be deceived. A person who dishonestly obtains a benefit by giving false information to a computer or machine is not guilty of any deception offence'.[11] The Law Commission identified the impact of modern technology on prosecuting fraud and was of the opinion that 'this gap in the law will be increasingly indefensible'.[12]

1.3 A positive reception?

Whether the Fraud Act 2006 was to be welcomed as an improvement on the deception offences is a moot point. Writing at the time that the Act came into force, Victor Tadros has been resolute in his criticism of the new legislation: '[n]o-one seriously doubts that this compromise solution was inadequate, not least because it created a number of practical problems that should not bedevil the new offence, including comprehensibility to jurors and difficulties in deciding which offence to charge'.[13] In 2007, Professor David Ormerod, observed that:

> General fraud offences offer many *practical* advantages ... [However] [t]hese practical advantages must not ... be allowed to produce a general offence that is overbroad, based too heavily on the ill-defined concept of dishonesty, too vague to meet the obligation under Art.7 of the ECHR, and otherwise deficient in principle. It is certainly questionable whether the Act has secured these practical advantages at the cost of undermining important principles.[14]

David Kirk, who was the then Director of the Fraud Prosecution Service at the Crown Prosecution Service, expressed similar reservations:

> Although the aim has been to keep things simple, there must be a risk that the provisions will in fact give rise to a new rash of cases in which the elements of dishonesty are picked over. Furthermore, the underlying specifics are by no means as simple as the legislators would have us believe.
>   . . .
> The new offence(s) of fraud will lead to more difficulties than they solve.[15]

However, other commentators were clear that the Fraud Act 2006 should be welcomed. Carol Withey observed that, '[t]he main offence of fraud by false representation is a welcome development that goes a long way to rectify the problems associated with the former deception offences'.[16] Withey concluded that, '[o]verall though, [the section 2 and section 11] offences are a vast improvement on the former offences of obtaining property by deception and obtaining services by deception, bringing some clarity and a welcome simplification to the law'.[17]

1.4 The general offence of fraud

The Fraud Act 2006 created England and Wales' first general offence of fraud, even though the common law had developed tortious liability for fraudulent or deceitful statements. Whilst fraud is a commonly understood word and the person on the street could come to a reasonable definition of what it meant, it had proved difficult to come to a clear legal definition of what behaviour is *per se* fraudulent. This was a point addressed by Longmore LJ in *Cavell USA Inc v Seaton Insurance Co*,[18] where he observed that 'the concept of fraud is notoriously difficult to define'[19] and that '. . . great judges have had similar difficulties in defining fraud'.[20] These great judges included Lord Hardwicke who wrote that '[f]raud is infinite . . . [and if the court were] to define strictly the species or evidence of it, the jurisdiction would be cramped and perpetually eluded by new schemes . . .',[21] and Lord Macnaghten who observed that, '[f]raud is infinite in variety: sometimes it is audacious and unblushing; sometimes it pays a sort of homage to virtue, and then it is modest and retiring; it would be honesty itself if it could only afford it'.[22]

1.4.1 Fraud by false representation

Under section 1(2)(a)-(c) of the Fraud Act 2006 the offence of fraud can be committed in three different ways. The first is under section 1(2)(a), fraud by false representation. Under section 2(1) the defendant must '(a) dishonestly make a false representation, and (b) intends, by making the representation – (i) to make a gain for himself or another, or (ii) to cause loss to another or expose another to a risk of loss'. Section 2(2) states that '[a] representation is false if – (a) it is untrue or misleading, and (b) the person making it knows that it is, or might be, untrue or misleading'.

As the prosecution no longer have to adduce evidence of operational deception, it is dishonesty that is crucial in determining whether the defendant has committed fraud. The maker of the representation must intend to make a gain or to cause loss to another. There is no requirement that the victim was actually deceived, or that the gain or loss occurred. The intention to cause these is sufficient. The subject matter of this intended gain or loss must be property, which is defined by section 5(2) of the Fraud Act 2006.[23] The definition of property is the same as in the Theft Act 1968.[24] This can be problematic for a number of reasons. First, the gain or loss might not equate to property as defined under section 5. Second, how remote does the intended gain or loss have to be in order to fall within the definition of property? Remoteness is problematic and Ormerod and Laird have argued that the decision of the Court of Appeal in *Kennedy (No. 2)*[25] (a manslaughter case in which the issue of remoteness was also raised) has left the question of remoteness uncertain as '[t]he Court of Appeal seems reluctant to impose clear rules of remoteness in criminal law contexts'.[26] Ultimately, the question of remoteness is left to the tribunal of fact to decide, and as Roderick Evans J stated in *Gilbert* 'it is a matter for the jury on the facts of each case whether the causative link between the intention and the making of the false representation, required by this section, is established'.[27] This could mean that where fraud is tried on indictment there could be scope for uncertainty, as different juries might reach different decisions as to whether an intention to gain, or to cause loss, is too remote.

Section 2(3) states that a representation can relate to fact or law, or the state of mind of the defendant or a third party. Subsection (4) states that '[a] representation can be express or implied'. Reflecting the concern that the previous statutory offences were out-dated and unable to be used efficiently against fraudsters using modern technology, subsection (5) states that a representation can be made to 'any system or device designed to receive, convey or respond to communications (with or without human intervention)'.

As the *actus reus* of the section 1(2)(a) offence is relatively straightforward (in comparison to the old deception offences), the *mens rea* is the key element of the offence, as the factual determination for the jury (or the bench, when tried summarily) is whether the tribunal of fact believe that the defendant was dishonest.[28] Whilst the prosecution are required to establish that the *actus reus* is satisfied, section 1(2)(a) appears to be a dishonesty offence.

There has been academic debate over the breadth of the offence. Professor Victor Tadros had argued that the offence captured 'misleading advertising puffs' and even if this was wrong, that these were 'only a very minor wrong, and not something that should result in a criminal conviction'.[29] This criticism was rejected by Professor Jeremy Horder, who argued that whether something is a '"very minor wrong" depends on matters of fact and degree' and that 'English law has no *de minimis* principle' and legislation already criminalised the making of a false representation in certain situations.[30] Tadros was clear that, '[w]hilst general fraud offences have had their advocates, the offence as drafted is very broad, demonstrating a failure to take the concerns that lay behind the Theft Act seriously at all'.[31] However, Horder defended the new offence, as the 'criminalisation of such breath centres on the cumulative consequences of tolerating the reckless endangerment of others' interest' is justified as it requires individual to 'concern themselves with the truth of statements they make'.[32]

It is argued here that the introduction of such a broad offence was unwelcome in theory (if not borne out by reality, given the lack of general controversy surrounding the use of the Act over the past decade), as it was far too wide in scope. The argument that we should be responsible for statements that we make cannot be disputed, however, the forum to achieve this responsibility surely should not always fall within the ambit of the criminal law. The solution is not to say that such responsibility should be achieved through the criminalisation of such conduct, especially, when mere puffs are not actionable in civil law, but could possibly amount to criminal conduct under the Fraud Act 2006.

1.4.2 Dishonesty – is Ghosh still good law?

The safety valve under the section 1(2)(a) offence is whether the tribunal of fact believed that the defendant was dishonest. Professor Ian Dennis observed that 'the new Act contains no definition of dishonesty. Presumably therefore the courts will continue to apply the Ghosh test, and leave factfinders to apply whatever they conceive the current standards of honesty to be'.[33] The Fraud Act 2006 did not define the test for dishonesty that should be used to determine guilt.[34] Until recently it would have been sufficient to mention the two limb approach set out in the Court of Appeal's judgment in *Ghosh*.[35] In his judgment Lord Lane CJ had outlined a test that had both an objective and subjective limb.[36]

The *Ghosh* test had recently been applied by the Court of Appeal in *Hayes (Tom Alexander)*[37], where the court rejected expanding the objective limb to include evidence of the 'standards of the market'.[38] However, the *Ghosh* test has recently been criticised by Lord Hughes, who gave judgment for the UK Supreme Court in *Ivey v Genting Casinos UK Ltd (t/a Crockfords Club)*.[39] *Ivey* concerned contractual issues pertaining to a gambling contract and whether there was a term implied into the contract that required a player not to cheat. Lord Hughes considered the development of the *Ghosh* test, observing '[t]hat case arrived, as has been seen, at a compromise rule which is partly objective and partly subjective'.[40] His Lordship was critical of the need for a subjective limb, noting that 'the less the defendant's standards conform to what society in general expects, the less likely he is to be held criminally responsible for his behaviour'.[41] Lord Hughes was of the opinion that the subjective limb was contrary to how the criminal law operated in general:

> There is no reason why the law should excuse those who make a mistake about what contemporary standards of honesty are . . . The law does not, in principle, excuse those whose standards are criminal by the benchmarks set by society, nor ought it to do so. On the contrary, it is an important, even crucial, function of the criminal law to determine what is criminal and what is not; its purpose is to set the standards of behaviour which are acceptable.[42]

Furthermore, His Lordship viewed the subjective limb as confusing jurors as '[t]he idea that something which is dishonest by ordinary standards can become honest just because the defendant thinks it is may often not be an easy one for jurors to grasp'.[43] Lord Hughes preferred the test that had been developed in civil law proceedings by Lord Nicholls in *Royal Brunei Airlines Sdb Bhd v Tan*[44] and approved by Lord Hoffmann in *Barlow Clowes International Ltd (In Liquidation) v Eurotrust International Ltd*.[45]

Having reviewed the pre-*Ghosh* case law, Lord Hughes held that there are 'convincing grounds for holding that the second leg of the test propounded in *Ghosh* does not correctly represent the law and that directions based upon it ought no longer to be given'.[46] It is important to appreciate that the Supreme Court did not overrule the approach in *Ghosh* and resign the subjective limb to the legal scrapheap. Firstly, the appeal was not concerned with dishonesty for the purposes of theft or fraud, rather the meaning of dishonesty for an implied term in a gambling contract. Secondly, Lord Hughes' criticism and conclusion that the *Ghosh* test should not be used is *obiter*, as technically *Ghosh* is still good law, even if trial judges are now to be encouraged to follow the test preferred by Lord Hughes when directing the jury as to the meaning of dishonesty.

Ivey has been subsequently considered in a number of cases. In *Wingate v Solicitors Regulation Authority*[47] the Civil Division of the Court of Appeal considered the meaning of dishonesty post-*Ivey*. Rupert Jackson LJ offered guidance on what (for the purposes of the civil law) the law is now:

> Let me stand back from the kaleidoscope of the authorities and consider what the law now is. Honesty is a basic moral quality which is expected of all members of society. It involves being truthful about important matters and respecting the property rights of others. Telling lies about things that matter or committing fraud or stealing are generally regarded as dishonest conduct. These observations are self-evident and they fit with the authorities cited above.[48]
>
> . . .
>
> The general law imposes criminal and/or civil liability for many, but not all, dishonest acts or omissions. As explained most recently in *Ivey*, the test for dishonesty is objective. Nevertheless, the defendant's state of mind as well as their conduct are relevant to determining whether they have acted dishonestly.[49]

The Administrative Court's decision in *DPP v Patterson*[50] is crucial to understanding the impact of *Ivey* on the determination of dishonesty for the purposes of the criminal law. Sir Brian Leveson P's interpretation is key:

> These observations were clearly *obiter*, and as a matter of strict precedent the court is bound by *Ghosh*, although the Court of Appeal could depart from that decision without the matter returning to the Supreme Court . . . Given the terms of the unanimous observations of the Supreme Court expressed by Lord Hughes, who does not shy from asserting that *Ghosh* does not correctly represent the law, it is difficult to imagine the Court of Appeal preferring *Ghosh* to *Ivey* in the future.[51]

More recently in *Pabon (Alex Julian)*[52] the Criminal Division of the Court of Appeal considered Lord Hughes' criticisms of *Ghosh*. The appeal concerned the direction given by the trial judge on the test for dishonesty before *Ivey*. Gross LJ's observations are of considerable importance, as it implies that a trial judge should apply the test from *Ivey* in the future, as '[i]t is therefore apparent that the jury were directed, on the key issue of dishonesty, on a basis more favourable to the Appellant than if he was tried today'.[53]

Academic opinion has not been particularly positive over the departure from the two-limb test set out in *Ghosh*. However, Adam Jackson does offer a positive take on *Ivey*, commenting that it 'appears to be a sensible rationalisation of the test for dishonesty, a harmonisation of the approach taken to dishonesty by the criminal and civil courts and reflects the approach taken in other areas of the criminal law, it would appear that the direction expounded in the present case should now be preferred'.[54]

Graham Virgo was clear that, '[i]n *Ivey*, the Supreme Court considered that directions based on *Ghosh* should no longer be given in criminal trials . . . Although this analysis of dishonesty was clearly obiter the Supreme Court considered it was binding . . . In the criminal law, strictly the Court of Appeal will still need to determine whether *Ghosh* has been overruled . . .'[55] Virgo has observed that the Supreme Court's approach to dishonesty will have a negative impact on the offence of theft, as exemplified by the decision in *Hinks*.[56] Virgo considered that in light of the House of Lords' decision in *Hinks*, the subjective limb had provided a safeguard and as '[t]hat safeguard has now gone . . . Theft is now a crime which requires neither proof of harm nor subjective fault. Together with *Hinks*, *Ivey* has resulted in an unacceptable expansion of the criminal jurisdiction, one which is inconsistent with the civil jurisdiction and so constitutes an unprincipled divergence between criminal and civil law'.[57]

The argument advanced by Virgo is one that I agree with for the following reasons. The first is that the decision in *Hinks* was essentially an exercise in capturing conduct that was deemed criminal, even if on the face of the statutory provisions of the Theft Act 1968, it was clearly not, as according to Lord Hobhouse[58] (in his dissent) and Professor JC Smith[59] (in his academic criticism of the Court of Appeal's decision in *Hinks*[60]) there had been no appropriation. The hollowing out of the meaning of appropriation by Lord Steyn in his majority judgment did result in Karen Hinks being guilty of theft, as her conduct was 'dishonest'; as His Lordship reasoned: '[i]f the law is restated by adopting a narrower definition of appropriation, the outcome is likely to place beyond the reach of the criminal law dishonest persons who should be found guilty of theft. The suggested revisions would unwarrantably restrict the scope of the law of theft and complicate the fair and effective prosecution of theft.'[61] I have previously criticised Lord Steyn's approach, preferring the interpretation of Lord Hobhouse in his dissenting opinion.[62]

Lord Hobhouse had warned about the dangers of reducing theft to a dishonesty offence and these, as I have previously argued, were valid concerns.[63] It is arguable that *Hinks* might be regarded as an instance of judicial repugnance that an individual goes free when their conduct ought to be punished. JC Smith had observed that: '[i]f it unsatisfactory that the rogue escapes un-penalised, that is a reproach to the civil law, not the criminal law.'[64] Parallels could perhaps be drawn with Lord Hughes' criticism of the subjective limb in *Ghosh*, which provided a defence for individuals who ought to be punished.[65] One can have some sympathy with a concern that the subjective limb allows someone to argue that they did not know that their conduct would be regarded as dishonest, when on the face of it we might be of the opinion they *must* have known that it was. However, the safeguard contained within the subjective limb under *Ghosh* does still permit the tribunal of fact to reject the defendant's argument, without having to give a reasoned verdict for doing so.

Virgo is rightly concerned with the consequences of the Supreme Court's decision to reject the *Ghosh* test. It is clear that the law does not operate in isolation and that in reformulating the test for dishonesty, the Supreme Court has affected the scope of liability in other areas of the law. This is a concern that is perfectly valid, but it is dependent on how one views the majority's decision in *Hinks*. The second reason is that whilst *Hinks* could be criticised for making the offence of theft too dependent on dishonesty, I would agree with Virgo that the abandonment of the subjective limb is unsatisfactory, as in my opinion this compounds the impact of the House of Lords' decision in *Hinks*.

Karl Laird was unsurprised that the Supreme Court rejected *Ghosh*, but was of the view that the court should have waited for a more appropriate opportunity, as 'it would have been preferable for the Supreme Court to have waited until the validity of *Ghosh* in the criminal law was raised directly in an appeal. In this instance, patience would most definitely have been a virtue'.[66] The problem is that the rejection was in *obiter* and not *ratio*, which created uncertainty for trial judges seeking to determine which test to now apply. It was left to Sir Brian Leveson P in *Patterson* 'to bring clarity by stating that it was difficult to envisage the Court of Appeal preferring *Ghosh* to *Ivey*. This statement was made with the obvious intention of sending a message to judges that *Ivey* should be treated as binding'.[67] Laird continued in his criticism of the Supreme Court's approach: 'in expecting its obiter comments on *Ghosh* to be treated as authoritative and binding, the Supreme Court has distorted principles that are fundamental to the common law . . . The Divisional Court in *Patterson* did its best to deal with the havoc that *Ivey* had the potential to wreak'.[68]

Equally critical in their comment on *Ivey*, Matthew Dyson and Paul Jarvis, shared some of the concerns expressed by Virgo, namely that the consequences of rejecting the *Ghosh* test had not been considered: 'Leaving aside issues the UKSC did not consider in promoting the reform it did, the decision in *Ivey* leaves a number of questions unanswered, and already confusion is creeping into the case law'.[69] Furthermore, another criticism, one which is particular relevant to dishonesty for the purposes of the Fraud Act 2006, is that:

> [I]t could be said that when Parliament voted to enact the Fraud Bill it intended both that dishonesty should be an element of the new offences . . . and that the test for dishonesty should be the two-stage *Ghosh* test. If Parliament had wished to depart from *Ghosh* then it had the perfect opportunity to do so . . . [and] where Parliament has approved of a test devised by the courts and it has introduced legislation with that test in

mind then there is a very strong argument for saying that only Parliament should be able to alter that test and the UKSC overstepped the mark when it did so.[70]

Taken together with Laird's criticism above, it could be argued that the Supreme Court could be criticised as embarking on an ill-advised reform of the law, one which is an example of a reliance on the lower courts to address the legal and precedential issues which arise from the use of *obiter* to criticise the use of the *Ghosh* test beyond its application in civil law.

1.4.3 Fraud by failing to disclose information

Section 1(2)(b) of the Fraud Act 2006 provides that fraud can be committed by failing to disclose information. The elements of the offence are outlined in section 3 of the Fraud Act 2006, which states that the defendant is guilty of theft where he '(a) dishonestly fails to disclose to another person information which he is under a legal duty to disclose, and (b) intends, by failing to disclose the information – (i) to make a gain for himself or another, or (ii) to cause loss to another or to expose another to a risk of loss'. This substantive offence once again relies heavily on the element of dishonesty. There is also the issue as to just how remote any gain or loss can be.

1.4.4 Fraud by abuse of position

Section 1(2)(c) of the Fraud Act 2006 provides that fraud can be committed by abuse of position.[71] The elements of the offence are outlined in section 4, which states that:

(1) A person is in breach of this section if he –

    (a) occupies a position in which he is expected to safeguard, or not to act against, the financial interests of another person,

    (b) dishonestly abuses that position, and

    (c) intends, by means of the abuse of that position –

        (i) to make a gain for himself or another, or

        (ii) to cause loss to another, or to expose another to a risk of loss.

(2) A person may be regarded as having abused his position even though his conduct consisted of an omission rather than an act.

According to the authors of *Blackstone's Guide to the Fraud Act 2006*, '[i]t is likely that any relationship recognised by the civil law as importing fiduciary duties will fall within the definition of the section'.[72] The authors observed that whilst civil law legal relationships will be covered, there is the potential for non-legal relationships (that under civil law import no fiduciary duties) to be also covered by section 4.[73] It was the opinion of Mike O'Brien, the then Solicitor

General, that an abuse of position in a family environment may result in an offence under section 1(2)(c).[74] Section 4 covers those who owe fiduciary duties such as solicitors, trustees and company directors. Therefore it is possible to bring both civil and criminal cases (by way of a private prosecution) against an individual who has breached their fiduciary duties, whether under the common law, the Companies Act 2006 or the Fraud Act 2006. This demonstrates the breadth of the criminal offence of fraud.

1.5 Conclusion

Fraud as an ordinary word can denote an entire spectrum of behaviour as wrong and deserving of sanction. The deception offences had construed fraud as requiring deception, and each offence was narrowly drafted. The question remains as to what extent the reforms under the Fraud Act 2006 have been effective. The deception offences were criticised as overly complex, too narrow and unsuitable to meet the demands of technology. Mike O'Brien, the then Solicitor General, informed the House of Commons that the Fraud Act 2006 'should improve the prosecution process by reducing the chance of offences being wrongly charged, and provide greater flexibility to keep pace with the increasing use of technology in crimes of fraud'.[75] The Fraud Act 2006 creates such an offence. Finally it is worth considering Ormerod's observation that for all the practical advantages of the Fraud Act 2006, it is 'certainly questionable whether the Act has secured these practical advantages at the cost of under-mining important principles'.[76] The principles that are undermined are legal certainty under Article 7 of the European Convention on Human Rights, and the use of the 'ill-defined concept of dishonesty'.[77] Ultimately the key question is whether Parliament, when enacting legislation, favours prosecutorial efficiency over legal certainty. To conclude, the introduction of a substantive offence of fraud was needed, and with the benefit of hindsight it is still possible to conclude that on balance the Fraud Act 2006 should be welcomed as a means to prosecute fraud.

Notes

1   Senior Lecturer in Law, School of Law, University of Worcester.
2   Sections 15, 15A, 16 and 20(2) of the Theft Act 1968.
3   Sections 1 and 2(1)(a)–(c) of the Theft Act 1978.
4   Law Commission, *Legislating the Criminal Code: Fraud and Deception*, Consultation Paper 155 (1999).
5   Law Commission, *Fraud, Report 276* (2002).
6   V Tadros, 'Crimes and Security' (2008) 71 MLR 940, 952.
7   D Ormerod, 'The Fraud Act 2006 – criminalizing lying?' (2007) Crim LR 193, 194.
8   E Griew, 'The Theft Acts 1968 and 1978' (Butterworth 1982) 141.
9   Law Commission, *Fraud* (n 5) [1.6(2)].
10   *DPP v Ray* [1974] AC 370.
11   Law Commission, *Fraud* (n 5) [3.34].
12   ibid [3.35].

13 Tadros, 'Crimes and Security' (n 6) 952.
14 Ormerod, 'The Fraud Act 2006' (n 7) 218–219.
15 D Kirk, 'Fraud trials: a brave new world' (2005) 69(6) J Crim L 508, 515–517.
16 C Withey, 'The Fraud Act 2006 – some early observation and comparisons with the former law' (2007) 71(3) J Crim L 220, 236.
17 ibid [237].
18 [2009] EWCA Civ 1363; [2009] 2 CLC 991.
19 ibid [15].
20 ibid [16].
21 Letter from Lord Hardwicke to Lord Kames, 30 June 1759. Quoted by Longmore LJ in *Cavell USA Inc v Seaton Insurance Co* (n 18).
22 *Reddaway v Banham* [1886] AC 199, 221.
23 The definition of property under the Fraud Act 2006 covers money, things in action and other intangible property.
24 Section 4(1) of the Theft Act 1968.
25 [2005] EWCA Crim LR 505.
26 D Ormerod and K Laird, *Smith and Hogan: Criminal Law*, 14th edn (Oxford University Press: Oxford, 2015) 998 fn 67.
27 [2012] EWCA Crim 2392, [29].
28 See Tadros, 'Crimes and Security' (n 6) 953.
29 ibid.
30 J Horder, 'Harmless Wrongdoing and Anticipatory Perspective in Criminalisation' in GR Sullivan and I Dennis (eds), *Seeking Security: Pre-Empting the Commission of Criminal Harms* (Hart Publishing, 2012) 98–99.
31 Tadros, 'Crimes and Security' (n 6) 952.
32 Horder, 'Harmless Wrongdoing and Anticipatory Perspective in Criminalisation' (n 30) 97–98.
33 I Dennis, 'Editorial: Fraud Act 2006' (2007) Crim LR 1, 2.
34 Dyson and Jarvis noted that '. . . dishonesty is not a creature of the common law but the definition of dishonesty is. Parliament has never sought to define what dishonesty means but it has reflected on the meaning given to dishonesty by the courts'. M Dyson and P Jarvis, 'Poison Ivey or herbal tea leaf?' (2018) LQR 198, 200.
35 *Ghosh* [1982] QB 1053; [1982] 3 WLR 110. See 1057 (Lord Lane).
36 ibid [1064] (Lord Lane).
37 [2015] EWCA Crim 1944; [2018] 1 Cr App R 10.
38 ibid [29] (Lord Thomas LJ, Sir Brian Leveson and Gloster LJ).
39 [2017] UKSC 67; [2017] 3 WLR 1212.
40 ibid [56].
41 ibid [58].
42 ibid [59].
43 ibid [61].
44 [1995] 2 AC 378; [1995] 3 WLR 64.
45 [2005] UKPC 37; [2006] 1 WLR 1476.
46 ibid [75].
47 [2018] EWCA Civ 366.
48 ibid [93].
49 ibid [94].
50 [2017] EWHC 2820 (Admin).
51 ibid [16].
52 [2018] EWCA Crim 420.
53 ibid [23].
54 A Jackson, 'Goodbye to Ghosh: the UK Supreme Court clarifies the proper test for dishonesty to be applied in criminal proceedings' (2017) 81(6) J Crim L 448, 450.

55 G Virgo, 'Cheating and dishonesty' (2018) 77(1) CLJ 18, 20.
56 *Hinks* [2001] 2 AC 241 and Virgo 'Cheating and dishonesty' (n 55) 21.
57 Virgo 'Cheating and dishonesty' (n 55) 21.
58 *Hinks* (n 56) 261.
59 JC Smith, 'Theft – Appropriation' (1998) Crim LR 904.
60 [2000] 1 Cr App R 1.
61 *Hinks* (n 56) 252.
62 C Monaghan, 'Restricting the meaning of "Appropriation" under the Theft Act 1968 – A cool, calm and rational approach to the issue of "stealing" a perfectly valid gift' in N Geach and C Monaghan, *Dissenting Judgments in the Law* (Wildy, Simmonds & Hill, 2012) 304–305.
63 ibid.
64 JC Smith, 'Theft – Appropriation' (1998) Crim LR 904, 905–906.
65 *Ivey* (n 39) [61]-[62] and [67] (Lord Hughes).
66 K Laird, 'Case Comment: Dishonesty: *Ivey v Genting Casinos UK Ltd (t/a Crockfords Club)* (2018) 5 Crim LR 395, 399.
67 ibid [398].
68 ibid [399].
69 Dyson and Jarvis, 'Poison Ivey or herbal leaf tea?' (n 34) 202.
70 ibid [201].
71 For commentary on fraud by abuse of position see J Collins, 'Fraud by abuse of position and unlicensed gangmasters' (2016) 79(2) MLR 354, and J Collins, 'Fraud by abuse of position: theorising section 4 of the Fraud Act 2006' (2011) 7 Crim LR 513.
72 S Farrell, N Yeo and G Ladenburg, *Blackstone's Guide to the Fraud Act 2006* (Oxford University Press, 2007) 33.
73 ibid.
74 Hansard, HC Standing Committee B, Solicitor General 20 June 2005, cols 20–21.
75 Hansard, HC, Solicitor General 12 June 2006, col 534.
76 Ormerod, 'The Fraud Act 2006' (n 7) 219.
77 ibid.

Bibliography

Barlow Clowes International Ltd (In Liquidation) v *Eurotrust International Ltd* [2005] UKPC 37; [2006] 1 WLR 1476

Cavell USA Inc v Seaton Insurance Co [2009] EWCA Civ 1363; [2009] 2 CLC 991

Collins J, 'Fraud by abuse of position and unlicensed gangmasters' (2016) 79(2) MLR 354

Collins J, 'Fraud by abuse of position: theorising section 4 of the Fraud Act 2006' (2011) 7 Crim LR 513

Companies Act 2006

Dennis I, 'Editorial: Fraud Act 2006' (2007) Crim LR 1

DPP v Patterson [2017] EWHC 2820 (Admin)

DPP v Ray [1974] AC 370

Dyson M and Jarvis P, 'Poison Ivey or herbal tea leaf?' (2018) LQR 198

European Convention on Human Rights

Farrell S, Yeo N and Ladenburg G, *Blackstone's Guide to the Fraud Act 2006* (Oxford University Press 2007)

Fraud Act 2006

Ghosh [1982] QB 1053; [1982] 3 WLR 110

Gilbert [2012] EWCA Crim 2392

Griew E, 'The Theft Acts 1968 and 1978' (Butterworth 1982)

Hayes (Tom Alexander) [2015] EWCA Crim 1944; [2018] 1 Cr App R 10

Hinks [2001] 2 AC 241

Horder J, 'Harmless Wrongdoing and Anticipatory Perspective in Criminalisation' in Sullivan GR and Dennis I (eds), *Seeking Security: Pre-Empting the Commission of Criminal Harms* (Hart Publishing 2012)

Ivey v Genting Casinos UK Ltd (t/a Crockfords Club) [2017] UKSC 67; [2017] 3 WLR 1212

Jackson A, 'Goodbye to Ghosh: the UK Supreme Court clarifies the proper test for dishonesty to be applied in criminal proceedings' (2017) 81(6) J Crim L 448

Kennedy (No. 2) [2005] EWCA Crim LR 505

Kirk D, 'Fraud trials: a brave new world' (2005) 69(6) J Crim L 508

Laird K, 'Case Comment: Dishonesty: *Ivey v Genting Casinos UK Ltd (t/a Crockfords Club)* (2018) 5 Crim LR 395

Law Commission, *Legislating the Criminal Code: Fraud and Deception, Consultation Paper 155* (1999)

Law Commission, *Fraud, Report 276* (2002)

Monaghan C, 'Restricting the meaning of "Appropriation" under the Theft Act 1968 – A cool, calm and rational approach to the issue of "stealing" a perfectly valid gift' in Geach N and Monaghan C, *Dissenting Judgments in the Law* (Wildy, Simmonds & Hill 2012)

Misrepresentation Act 1967

Pabon (Alex Julian) [2018] EWCA Crim 420

Ormerod D, 'The Fraud Act 2006 – criminalizing lying?' (2007) Crim LR 193

Ormerod D and Laird K, *Smith and Hogan: Criminal Law*, 14th edn (Oxford University Press: Oxford, 2015)

Reddaway v Banham [1886] AC 199

Royal Brunei Airlines Sdb Bhd v Tan [1995] 2 AC 378; [1995] 3 WLR 64

Smith JC, 'Theft – Appropriation' (1998) Crim LR 904

Tadros V, 'Crimes and Security' (2008) 71 MLR 940

Theft Act 1968

Theft Act 1978

Virgo G, 'Cheating and dishonesty' (2018) 77(1) CLJ 18

Wingate v Solicitors Regulation Authority [2018] EWCA Civ 366

Withey C, 'The Fraud Act 2006 – some early observation and comparisons with the former law' (2007) 71(3) J Crim L 220

2 The Fraud Act's 10th anniversary

Time to celebrate? Not quite!

Axel Palmer[1]

2.1 Introduction

> What is being done for all the people losing small but vital sums every day? Scamming is big, growing and doing enormous harm: equity release, pension release, investment frauds – the opportunities are endless. It's the Wild West out there and it is not enough to leave these people with only an Action Fraud crime number and no hope of seeing a police officer, never mind an investigation.[2]

The tenth anniversary of the implementation of the Fraud Act 2006 provides a perfect opportunity to consider the first changes to fraud legislation for a generation. In 2006, the Fraud Review gave high hopes that there would be 'a reduction in fraud and the harm it does to the economy and society, an improvement in the way victims are compensated, and improved confidence in the criminal justice system'.[3] However, Kirk's comments regarding the 'Wild West' indicate that challenges remain. What can be said is that fraud, which is far from a new phenomenon, is estimated to cost the United Kingdom ('UK') economy £193bn a year.[4]

2.2 UK fraud policy

Fraud is a global issue with the potential to do significant damage to economies, as seen with the collapse of multinational corporations: in the UK, such as Bank of Credit and Commerce International and Barings; and in the United States ('US'), Madoff and Stanford.[5] The 2008 Financial Crisis shed light on the risks involved in 'Casino' Banking, as typified by Kerviel, Adeboli and 'London Whale'.[6] However, large as these cases may be, the threat which has over-shadowed the global financial markets is mortgage fraud 'where the home loans continue to be an attractive target for fraudsters' and still estimated to cost the UK £1.3bn pa.[7] Fraud is difficult to quantify (and government gave up trying) but University of Portsmouth recently estimated it at £193bn pa.[8] Historically, UK governments have commissioned various reports in the arena of fraud, the two most important being the 1986 Roskill Report and 2006 Fraud Review.[9] Together, these reports set the framework for the current UK anti-fraud regime.

2.3 Fraud Review

The Fraud Advisory Panel consider that the Fraud Review 'was a brave move by Lord Goldsmith, the then Attorney General, with no obvious political pay-back'.[10] Lord Goldsmith's view was that 'fraud was one gaping area where our response – from police, investigating authorities and justice system – was inadequate'.[11] To put this into perspective, 'it was obvious that fraud was costing people a huge amount of money yet very difficult to deal with. Police forces found it much easier to deal with the stealing of milk bottles than with the defrauding of people out of very much larger amounts'.[12] At the time of the Review, only a few police forces had their own fraud teams, tackling fraud was not a priority for them and trials were inefficient and took too long.[13] Lord Goldsmith's objective was to see a 'raised awareness of fraud as a serious social problem – not a victimless crime'.[14]

The Fraud Review ('Review'), which was asked to 'recommend ways of reducing fraud and the harm it does to society', positions fraud as it 'may be second only to class A drug trafficking as a source of harm from crime'.[15] However, unlike drug crime, police forces are often reluctant to take reports of fraud and, even if they do, take little action as a result because fraud has not been seen as a national policing priority. This then set the first question to be considered: 'what is the scale of the problem?'.[16] The lack of ability to answer the question, because data was not available, led the report to conclude that a body should be created to devise a strategic response: the National Fraud Authority ('NFA').[17] The Review also recommended the creation of the National Fraud Reporting Centre ('NFRC') to provide a central point for receipt of reports of fraud, together with the National Fraud Intelligence Bureau ('NFIB') which would analyse and assess fraud. To complete the organisational changes, City of London Police ('COLP') would become the national lead force, acting as a centre of excellence for fraud investigations and undertaking the more complex investigations.

The second and third questions considered by the Review were to determine the appropriate role of government in dealing with fraud and, how resources could be spent to maximise value for money across the system.[18] The Review noted the range of departments and agencies involved and the range of penalties and remedies they may deploy in the three areas: criminal, civil and regulatory. There were two specific recommendations: to increase the sentencing options available in the Crown Court; and establishment of a specialised 'financial court'.[19] The increased sentencing powers included the ability to order compensation to all victims, not just those specified in a particular case and the ability to make specific orders relating to other advisors such as solicitors and accountants. The 'financial court' proposal recognised the difficulties of trying fraud cases and proposed deploying judges with experience of financial cases to longer, more complex, criminal trials: 'all matters could be resolved on the basis of a single unified set of evidence at one facts hearing with a variety of outcomes under criminal, civil and regulatory powers'.[20] The Review concluded that the maximum sentence for serious or repeated fraud should be increased from ten years to fourteen years, to match money laundering penalties.[21] Neither of these proposals was adopted.

However, the proposal which excited the most comment was 'Plea Bargaining',[22] a system for reduced sentences in return for a guilty plea and agreement to other sanctions. The rationale for this being the benefits to be gained by reducing the length of trials and shortening investigations:

> Any solution should provide an opportunity for the prosecution and defence to enter into negotiations at an earlier stage than is currently possible, preferably pre-charge, at the point where the prosecuting authority is in a position to show the essential core of a case against an individual or individuals.[23]

At that stage there was no formal system in the UK for 'plea bargaining'.[24] Although discussions do take place between prosecution and defence legal teams, there is no certainty unlike the US model: 'plea bargaining is as integral to the US legal system as fast-talking, sharp suited attorneys,'[25] and 'if you look at fraud alone, you will see some form of plea bargaining in approximately two-thirds to three-quarters of cases'.[26] As with the 1986 Roskill Report, implementation of the Fraud Review recommendations was slow, with the NFA and COLP measures being the only concrete achievements.

Against this backdrop, it is clear that fraud is a significant and costly matter for government to tackle, as the NFA reported:

> The threats created by fraudsters are serious and real. Serious and organised crime groups are behind much fraudulent activity across the world. Funds generated by fraud are being used to support and expand other serious criminal activity such as people and drug trafficking. Fraud has also featured in terrorist cases both in the UK and abroad.[27]

The UK's fraud policy can be divided into three distinct parts – criminalisation, financial and law enforcement agencies, and the reporting of suspected instances of fraud.[28] The 'three distinct parts' to tackling fraud highlights a particular issue: namely, that policies created individually are not fully integrated with each other. As with the Roskill Report ('Roskill'), fraud policy evolved haphazardly rather than being strategically planned.

An appropriate base for considering fraud is how it is defined. A succinct definition would be helpful: the Fraud Act 2006 itself does not define 'fraud', merely stating that 'a person is guilty of fraud if he is in breach of any of the sections listed'.[29] Furthermore, there is no universal definition at common law.[30] Action Fraud states that:

Fraud is when trickery is used to gain a dishonest advantage, which is often financial, over another person. There are many words used to describe fraud: scam, con, swindle, extortion, sham, double-cross, hoax, cheat, ploy, ruse, hoodwink, confidence trick.[31]

The SFO previously defined fraud as 'abuse of position, or false representation, or prejudicing someone's rights for personal gain,'[32] but now does not provide any definition.

2.4 Criminalisation

In the financial crime arena dealing with fraud was neglected until Roskill recommended the establishment of the SFO,[33] and then, twenty years later, Parliament enacted the Fraud Act 2006.[34] The Fraud Act 2006 has simplified the law by providing a new offence of 'fraud' instead of a variety of ineffective deception offences under the Theft Acts.[35] In practice, the range of deception offences created 'a hazardous terrain for prosecutors' which, consequently, encouraged reliance on 'conspiracy to defraud'.[36] Under the Fraud Act 2006 a person is guilty of fraud by: false representation (section 1(2)(a)); failing to disclose information (section 1(2)(b)); and abuse of position (section 1(2)(c)).[37] Conviction on indictment carries a maximum sentence of ten years imprisonment or an unlimited fine or both.[38] The three ways fraud can be committed are: firstly, by false representation[39] where 'A representation is false if (a) it is untrue or misleading, and (b) the person making it knows that it is, or might be, untrue or misleading'.[40] This requires dishonesty, and intention 'to make a gain for himself or another, or to cause loss to another or expose another to a risk of loss'.[41] It is intention that is key: an actual gain or loss does not have to take place.

2.5 Dishonesty

The Fraud Act 2006 did not define dishonesty but *Ghosh*[42] set a two-stage test:

> The first question is whether a defendant's behaviour would be regarded as dishonest by the ordinary standards of reasonable and honest people. If answered positively, the second question is whether the defendant was aware that his conduct was dishonest and would be regarded as dishonest by reasonable and honest people.[43]

Although 'the *Ghosh* test has remained the prevailing authority on matters of dishonest in criminal proceedings since 1982 (. . .) it has not enjoyed the support of commentators'.[44] Thus, when the Supreme Court reviewed dishonesty in *Ivey v Genting Casinos*, they concluded that 'thirty years on, however, it can be seen that there are a number of serious problems about the second leg of the rule adopted in *Ghosh*'.[45] As a consequence, 'it has the unintended effect that the more warped the defendant's standards of honesty are, the less likely it is that he will be convicted of dishonest behaviour'.[46] As the authors of *Smith's Law of Theft* noted, 'the second limb allows the accused to escape liability where he has made a mistake of fact as to the contemporary standards of honesty', but questioned 'why should that be an excuse?'.[47] The Supreme Court in *Ivey v Genting Casinos*[48] recognised that:

> There have been relatively few appeals based upon *Ghosh* (. . .) because judges have dutifully given the two-leg direction where there has been any occasion for it. But the existence of the second leg has frequently led to trials being conducted on the basis that even if the defendant's actions, in his actual state of knowledge or belief about the relevant facts, would be characterised by most people as dishonest, the defendant himself thought that what he was doing was not wrong, and it was for that reason honest.[49]

The Fraud Act 2006, being some 24 years after *Ghosh*, could have defined dishonesty if it was thought necessary. Clearly, the courts have taken a view that a definition was unnecessary because 'dishonesty is a simple, if occasionally imprecise, English word'[50] and 'by no means a defined concept. On the contrary, like the elephant, it is characterised more by recognition when encountered than by definition. Dishonesty is not a matter of law, but a jury question of fact and standards'.[51] The Supreme Court said:

> Dishonesty is something which laymen can easily recognise when they see it. That is not to suggest that there is not room for debate at the fringes whether particular conduct is dishonest or not, but the perils of advance definition would no doubt have been greater than those associated with leaving the matter to the jury.[52]

Finally, there is the question of truthfulness:

> Truthfulness is indeed one characteristic of honesty, and untruthfulness is often a powerful indicator of dishonesty, but a dishonest person may sometimes be truthful about his dishonest opinions (. . .). For the same reasons which show that Mr Ivey's conduct was, contrary to his own opinion, cheating, the better view would be (. . .) that his conduct was, contrary to his own opinion, also dishonest.[53]

Although Hall and Smith note that *Ivey* strictly represents *obiter* rather than binding precedent, it has been followed in *LOCOG v Sinfield*.[54] Nevertheless, the issue of dishonesty is still subject to debate with Baroness Hale, the President of the Supreme Court, suggesting that Parliament should review the law.[55]

By representation, the Fraud Act 2006 'means any representation of fact or law including a representation of [any person's] state of mind'.[56] It can be express or implied and could be written, spoken or posted on a website. For example, dishonestly using a credit card, phishing on the internet or selling fake designer goods.[57] To, perhaps, 'future proof' legislation against technological developments, there is a provision to ensure that a fraud can be committed where a person makes a representation to a machine and a response can be produced without any need for human involvement.[58]

The second way fraud can be committed is 'fraud by failing to disclose information',[59] where a person 'dishonestly fails to disclose to another person information which he is under a legal duty to disclose'.[60] Again, there has to be an intention to cause gain or loss, for example: the failure of a solicitor to share vital information with a client or non-disclosure of a medical condition when entering into a life insurance contract.[61]

The third way to commit fraud is 'fraud by abuse of position',[62] again requiring dishonesty and with intent. This recognises situations where a person 'occupies a position where he is expected to safeguard, or not act against, the financial interests of another person'[63] and covers situations where his 'conduct consisted of an omission rather than an act'.[64] This would apply in circumstances of: employee and employer; director and company; professional and client; agent and principal.[65] Examples would include: someone acting for personal gain against the client's interests; a software company employee cloning the company's products; someone employed to care for an elderly person having access to bank accounts and taking funds for their own use; and includes omissions such as not taking up a favourable contract in order to allow a rival company to do so.[66]

The Fraud Act 2006 has other provisions (sections 6–9) which replace the quaint crimes of 'going equipped for stealing' and 'when not at his abode'[67] with 'possession etc. of articles for use in frauds',[68] which is a very far reaching provision. The Act states that 'A person is guilty of an offence if he has in his possession or under his control any article for use in the course of or in connection with any fraud'[69] and 'includes any program or data held in electronic form'.[70] This provision brings computers and software programs into scope. The Fraud Act 2006 section 7 states that 'making or supplying articles for use in frauds, knowing that it is designed or adapted for use in a fraud',[71] such as fake explosives detectors.[72]

Conspiracy to defraud, which the Law Commission wanted to abolish,[73] was retained because of serious practical concerns about the ability to prosecute multiple offences in the largest and most serious cases of fraud.

The offences under the Fraud Act 2006 are seen as being wide enough to meet current and future challenges, by being designed as 'modern and flexible statutory offences of fraud'.[74] However, the effectiveness of legislation is in the hands of prosecution agencies which deploy them, principally the SFO.[75]

2.6 Regulatory and law enforcement agencies

The second element of the UK's policy towards fraud is that of the regulatory and law enforcement agencies. Fraud detection and prosecution in the UK had been managed by a plethora of bodies with limited success. In 1986, Roskill recommended a 'fraud commission' for studying and advising on conduct of fraud cases.[76] Whilst Roskill's initial achievement was the creation of the SFO,[77] following the Fraud Review, the NFA, Action Fraud and NFIB were established.

The NFA had the role of co-ordinating the many parties involved in the fight against fraud. However, in 2014, the NFA was incorporated into the NCA.[78] Two constant themes emerged: firstly, the number of parties involved; and, secondly, the overall lack of police commitment. Levi observed 'the only force in which fraud was a core [policy] objective was City of London',[79] whereas in other forces, 'fraud is invariably *not* seen as core policing priority'.[80] Sarker's view was 'for too long tackling fraud has been a Cinderella issue: under reported and under resourced'.[81] Given the pervasive nature of fraud, the breadth of possible crimes should not be a surprise but what does attract attention is the sheer number of agencies deployed and tasked with investigation and prosecution. The principal agencies are:[82] 43 police forces,[83] SFO, FCA,[84] Competition and Markets Authority, Crown Prosecution Service, and NCA. This multiplicity of agencies with their various historic backgrounds, cultures and rivalries militated in favour of an "holistic" approach, focusing efforts and resources where they are likely to be most effective rather than the most attention grabbing'.[85] There was a clear intention to see that work was 'co-ordinated, duplication eliminated and gaps addressed'.[86] These issues still remain and in 2017, the government announced a new 'National Economic Crime Centre' (within NCA) overseen by a new 'Economic Crime Strategic Board', which indicates that the 2006 vision for a strategic board was correct.[87]

2.7 Serious Fraud Office

The primary anti-fraud agency is the SFO,[88] which was established by Criminal Justice Act 1987. It has the largest budget of the various agencies at £35.7m together with 'blockbuster' funding, has 400 staff and 60 active cases.[89] It 'is a specialist prosecuting authority tackling the top level of serious or complex fraud, bribery and corruption'.[90]

The SFO takes on a small number of large economic crime cases, taking into consideration whether the apparent criminality undermines UK commercial or financial interests in general and in the City of London in particular;[91] levels of actual or potential economic loss or harm is significant; significant public interest; or a new species of fraud.[92]

The SFO is unusual in the UK in that it both investigates and prosecutes its own cases. This follows the Roskill model,[93] because these kinds of cases are complicated and lawyers and investigators need to work together from the beginning.[94]

The SFO also pursue criminals for the financial benefit they have made from their crimes and assist overseas jurisdictions with their investigations into serious and complex fraud, bribery and corruption cases. Since 2017, the SFO has had the power to investigate and prosecute corporate failure to prevent the facilitation of overseas tax evasion.[95]

The SFO has investigated and prosecuted a wide range of frauds: selling bogus investments; 'Ponzi'; hedge fund; financial markets; LIBOR, foreign exchange, banking and mortgage; public sector; together with bribery and corruption. These areas highlight reputational risks for a high profile organisation very much in the public eye such as the BAE Systems, Maxwell and Levitt cases.[96] Historically, the SFO had a tarnished reputation because of failure to obtain expected convictions.[97] However, in recent years, it has successfully prosecuted a steady stream of cases, including high-profile LIBOR and others emanating from the 2008 financial crisis. Furthermore, the advent of Deferred Prosecution Agreements[98] have given fresh impetus to the SFO and its pursuit of bribery, as with *Rolls-Royce*.[99]

At a time when its sister agency the Financial Conduct Authority ('FCA') is achieving significant financial settlements, the SFO faced reduced resources, with a 40 per cent budget reduction from £50m to £30m between 2008/9 and 2014/15, and yet facing increased workload because of the Bribery Act 2010.[100]

2.8 Financial Conduct Authority

The second prominent agency is the FCA, established by the Financial Services and Markets Act 2000 and funded by those it regulates.[101] The FCA, which regulates 56,000 firms,[102] was created as a single agency responsible for authorising, regulating and policing the UK financial services sector. It has a single strategic objective to ensure that the relevant markets function well. Its operational objectives are to: protect consumers; promote competition; and protect and enhance the integrity of the UK financial system.[103] The FCA prosecutes: insider dealing on the financial markets; providing false or misleading market information to investors; boiler room frauds and instances of money laundering.[104] The FCA manage its regulatory responsibilities through a framework of regulations in the FCA Handbook.

The FCA 'have an extensive range of disciplinary, criminal and civil powers to take action against regulated and non-regulated firms and individuals who fail to meet the standards required'.[105] The FCA has powers to impose fines on authorised firms and persons breaching the regulations,[106] the fines amounted to £229m in 2017, £22m in 2016, £905m in 2015, and £1.47bn in 2014.[107] The FCA also requires that the firms which it regulates appoint a Money Laundering Reporting Officer,[108] which could, but is not required to do so, encompass fraud reporting. The general activities of the FCA are outside the scope of this chapter but they do have some prosecution powers.[109]

2.9 Crown Prosecution Service

The Crown Prosecution Service is the tertiary major fraud force, but its remit is purely prosecution. It prosecutes a variety of frauds: tax, benefits, money laundering, internet banking, electoral, bribery and by abuse of position. It has a specialist fraud division which handles more serious, complex or difficult cases which are not dealt with by SFO.[110] Investigation is handled by COLP and local police forces. The effect of this is that whilst the COLP have specialist resources to undertake the investigative work and financial budget to pay for it, for local Police forces to undertake the research themselves would possibly entail employing private sector forensic accountancy or computer analysis. As with all public sector organisations, police financial resources are under pressure, leading to the inevitable conclusion that this type of costly investigation would be of low priority.

2.10 Fraud reporting

The City of London Police hosts 'Action Fraud' and its sister agency NFIB.[111] Action Fraud is the UK's national reporting centre for fraud and cybercrime 'where you should report fraud if you have been scammed, defrauded or experienced cybercrime in England, Wales and Northern Ireland'.[112] Notwithstanding the name, the role of Action Fraud is rather limited:

> After a report has been made to Action Fraud, it will be sent for assessment by NFIB. The NFIB's systems assess reports of fraud and cybercrime from across the UK, helping to build a national picture of where fraud and cybercrime is taking place and how. Experts review the data from these reports to decide whether there is enough information to send to a police force for investigation.[113]

As Kirk comments, 'such reports rarely result in any direct action being taken: no policeman will arrive at your door and take a statement'.[114] Action Fraud is, thus, a data collection centre which takes crime and information reports on behalf of the police and gives advice and fraud prevention guidance whilst emphasising that it does not have investigation powers.[115] Furthermore, there is no general statutory obligation in the UK to report fraud as such, unlike money laundering and terrorist financing.[116]

Suspicious Activity Reports ('SAR') are required to be sent to the NCA 'as soon as you 'know' or 'suspect' that a person is engaged in money laundering or dealing in criminal property'[117] especially if consent to make a payment is required. If a SAR is made before a suspicious transaction is completed, NCA then have seven days to determine whether to give consent or whether to impose a 31-day moratorium to facilitate further enquiries. The Criminal Finances Act 2017 extended the moratorium to a possible 186 days.[118] Penalties for completing a transaction or 'tipping off' are up to five years imprisonment and or a fine.[119] This creates practical difficulties where, for example, a bank is required to process a transaction which being subject to a SAR, the bank is neither able to process the transaction nor explain why, as was discussed in *K v National Westminster Bank*.[120]

There are two other aspects to fraud reporting: firstly, the police are required to record crime notified to them under Home Office rules;[121] and, secondly, the FCA imposes obligations to tell the FCA promptly anything relating to the firm of which the FCA would reasonably expect prompt notice'.[122]

It is clear that fraud reporting in the UK is limited to areas where there is a connection to money laundering or terrorism financing and/or where a party involved is FCA regulated. This uncoordinated regime then leads to possible areas of either overlap or a gap in reporting to the NCA and the FCA. Outside those reporting structures, there is no general reporting requirement. Action Fraud, therefore, obtains incomplete data which means that the anti-fraud agencies have inadequate information. Victims of fraud have to rely upon local police forces investigating fraud, if such cases are referred to them.

2.11 Conclusion

The annual UK fraud loss of £193bn[123] serves as a striking barometer of the effectiveness of its fraud policy, notwithstanding the quantum being imprecise (because victims of fraud are reluctant to report allegations and there is no general legal duty to do so), it neatly identifies that fraud is a serious matter for the government. However, with public perception that fraud is a 'victimless crime'[124] combined with the authorities' focus on terrorist financing, it is clear that government should redefine its approach and realign its resources to combat this insidious threat.

Although legislation makes the law of fraud abundantly clear, several key issues remain. Firstly, the quantum of fraud is unknown with any degree of accuracy. The government should make reporting of fraud mandatory – logically to the NCA, since it is the reporting centre for SARs.

The second key issue remains the number of different actors involved. Roskill proposed a plan to re-organise the anti-fraud institutions into a single cohesive force and the reasons for so doing remain powerful. The Coalition government (2010–2015), having proposed to do just that then retreated to a 'co-ordination' model.[125] Disappointingly, fraud by being part of the NCA Economic Crime Command, is destined to play a supporting role, rather than as a lead actor reporting to HM Treasury, which retains responsibility for money laundering and terrorism financing. This is regrettable. The role of the NCA, within the Home Office, is merely to co-ordinate, rather than deal with issues of bringing together the disparate agencies such as the SFO, FCA, COLP and CPS to create an Economic Crime Agency.

Ten years on from the Fraud Review, the Fraud Act 2006 is regarded as having made fraud prosecutions more efficient, together with providing a single point for reporting fraud and an intelligence function. The government concludes that 'it provides a clear statutory basis for fraud offences, targets complex fraud and introduces new offences specifically designed to assist in the prosecution of technology focused crime'.[126]

However, Lord Goldsmith lamented the loss of strategic direction, observing that: 'it would be a great shame if the only resources to tackle fraud are concentrated in the Serious Fraud Office. I am a great supporter of the SFO, but there is a lot more fraud that needs strategic thinking'.[127]

Funding the anti-fraud response remains problematic since 'government's response to the 2008 financial crisis has seen sharp cuts to budgets in almost every area of criminal justice and fraud fighting'.[128] It is clear that higher levels of funding is required, and not just on a 'blockbuster' basis. The government's 2017 Economic Crime Centre is a positive initiative but far short of a single Economic Crime Agency.

Notes

1 Dr Axel Palmer holds a PhD specialising in economic crime and is a Visiting Lecturer at the Department of Law, University of the West of England, Bristol, UK. He is a former Head of Debt Management and a Head of Litigation at a major UK bank. His research interests are in the field of economic crime, encompassing fraud, bribery and corruption.

2 Fraud Advisory Panel, 'Fraud Review – ten years on' (David Kirk, Chairman, Fraud Advisory Panel) <www.fraudadvisorypanel.org/wp-content/uploads/2016/06/The-Fraud-Review-Ten-Years-On-WEB.pdf> accessed 12 February 2018.

3 Attorney General's Office, *Fraud Review – Final report.* (Attorney General's Office 2006) 16.

4 University of Portsmouth, 'Annual Fraud Indicator 2016' 6, 15 <www.port.ac.uk/media/contacts-and-departments/icjs/ccfs/Annual-Fraud-Indicator-2016.pdf> accessed 12 February 2018.

5 DV Dooley and M Radke, 'Does severe punishment deter financial crimes' (2010) 4 Charleston L Rev 619. Net loss estimated to be $17.5bn. Reuters, 'UPDATE 1-Madoff, Stanford fraud victims dealt setbacks by U.S. top court' <www.reuters.com/article/us-usa-court-madoff-stanford/madoff-stanford-fraud-victims-dealt-setbacks-by-u-s-top-court-idUSKBN0F51SV20140630> accessed 12 March 2018.

6 G Gilligan, 'Jérôme Kerviel the "Rogue Trader" of Société Générale: Bad Luck, Bad Apple, Bad Tree or Bad Orchard?' (2011) 32(12) Co Law 355; *R v Kweku Adoboli*. Accessed 12 March 2018; and Financial Conduct Authority, 'JPMorgan Chase Bank N.A. fined £137,610,000 for serious failings relating to its Chief Investment Office's "London Whale" trades' <www.fca.org.uk/news/ jpmorgan-chase-bank-na-fined> accessed 18 February 2018.

7 Portsmouth (n 4) 15.

8 ibid 13.

9 Fraud Trials Committee Report. (HMSO 1986) and Fraud Review (n 3)

10 Fraud Advisory Panel, Fraud Review (n 2).

11 ibid.

12 ibid. (Lord Goldsmith)

13 Fraud Advisory Panel, Fraud Review (n 2).

14 ibid.

15 *Fraud Review* (n 3) 4.

16 ibid 4.

17 Originally 'National Fraud Strategic Authority'.

18 *Fraud Review* (n 3) 4.

19 ibid 13.

20 T Coolican, 'Time out for fraud' (2006) 156 NLJ 1460.

21 Proceeds of Crime Act 2002 – Part 7.

22 R Rothwell, 'New: Plea bargaining' (2006) LS Gaz 27 Jul, 6 (3); K Hanley. 'Plea Bargaining: Striking a bargain'. (2006) LS Gaz 14 Sep, 20; Coolican (n 20) 1460.

23 *Fraud Review* (n 3) 40.

24 There are provisions in Serious Organised Crime and Police Act 2005 (sections 71–75) for immunity from prosecution or reduced sentences for offenders assisting with investigations or prosecutions.

25 Hanley (n 22).

26 ibid (Stone).

27 National Fraud Authority, '2009 Annual Report & Accounts'. (Herdan). <www.gov. uk/government/uploads/system/uploads/attachment_data/file/248204/0808.pdf> accessed 12 February 2018.

28 N Ryder, *Financial Crime in the 21st Century* (Edward Elgar 2010) 123.

29 Fraud Act 2006 s.1

30 A Doig and Ml Levi, 'Inter-agency work and the UK public sector investigation of fraud, 1996–2006: joined-up rhetoric and disjointed reality' (2009) 19(3) *Policing and Society* 199, 203.

31 Action Fraud, 'What is Fraud?' <www.actionfraud.police.uk/what-is-fraud> accessed 12 February 2018.

32 AA Palmer, *Countering Economic Crime: A Comparative Analysis* (Routledge 2017) 9.

33 Section 1 of the Criminal Justice Act 1987.

34 The Financial Conduct Authority is in a different category because it is a regulator of the financial markets, rather than primarily a prosecutor. However, it has raised its profile 'bringing criminal proceedings for conspiracy', thus developing its role 'as a specialist criminal prosecutor'. R Peat, I Mason, S Bazley. 'The FCA as a criminal prosecutor' (2010) 31(4) Comp Law 119, and Section 6A of the Serious Organised Crime and Police Act 2005.

35 D Ormerod, 'The Fraud Act 2006 – Criminalised Lying?' (2007) Crim L R 193. Theft Act 1968: section 15, Obtaining property; section15A, Obtaining a money transfer; section16, Obtaining a pecuniary advantage; section 20(2), Procuring the execution of a valuable security. Theft Act 1978: section 1, Obtaining services; section 2(1)(a), securing the remission of a liability; section 2(1)(b), Inducing a creditor to wait or forego payment; section 2(1)(c), Obtaining an exemption from or abatement of liability. Fraud Act 2006 s 1.

36 Ormerod (n 35).

37 Section 1(2) of the Fraud Act 2006.

38 Section 1(3)(b) of the Fraud Act 2006.

39 Section 2 of the Fraud Act 2006.

40 Section 2(2) of the Fraud Act 2006.

41 Section 2(1)(b) i & ii of the Fraud Act 2006.

42 *Ghosh* [1982] QB 1053.

43 Fraud Act 2006 – explanatory notes <www.opsi.gov.uk/acts/acts2006/en/ ukpgaen_20060035_en_1.htm> accessed 12 February 2018.

44 M Hall and T Smith, 'The disappearing Ghosh test' (2017) 181 *Criminal Law and Justice Weekly* 752, 753.

45 *Ivey v Genting Casinos* (UK) *Ltd t/a Crockfords* [2017] UKSC 67, 57 (Lord Hughes).

46 *Ivey v Genting Casinos* (n 45) 57.

47 D Ormerod and DH Williams, *Smith's Law of Theft* (OUP 2007) 2.296.

48 *Ivey v Genting Casinos* (n 45) 57.

49 ibid 61.

50 ibid 63. The issue of 'fundamental dishonesty' in personal injury claims is considered in *LOCOG v Sinfield* [2018] EWHC 51 (QB).

51 *Ivey v Genting Casinos* (n 45) 48.
52 ibid 53.
53 ibid 75.
54 Hall and Smith (n 44); *LOCOG v Sinfield* (n 50).
55 Law Society Gazette, 'Hale says test of dishonesty may be question for parliament' <www.lawgazette.co.uk/law/hale-says-test-of-dishonesty-may-be-question-for-parliament/5065120.article#.WqBSJWzmNgc.twitter> accessed 12 March 2018.
56 Section 2(3) of the Fraud Act 2006.
57 Action Fraud, 'A-Z of Fraud' <www.actionfraud.police.uk/a-z_of_fraud> accessed 12 February 2018.
58 Section 2(5) of the Fraud Act 2006.
59 Section 3 of the Fraud Act 2006. See, for example, Serious Fraud Office, 'Three convicted in JJB Trial' <www.sfo.gov.uk/2014/11/20/three-convicted-jjb-trial/> accessed 12 February 2018.
60 Section 3(a) of the Fraud Act 2006.
61 Fraud Act 2006 – explanatory notes (n 43) 3(19).
62 Section 4 of the Fraud Act 2006. See, for example, Serious Fraud Office, 'SFO charges David Ames of Harlequin Group' <www.sfo.gov.uk/2017/02/17/sfo-charges-david-ames-harlequin-group/> accessed 12 February 2018.
63 Section 4(1)(a) of the Fraud Act 2006.
64 Section 4(2) of the Fraud Act 2006.
65 The Law Commission, Fraud Cm 5562.
66 Action Fraud, 'A–Z' (n 57).
67 Section 25 of the Theft Act 1968.
68 Section 6 of the Fraud Act 2006.
69 Section 6(1) of the Fraud Act 2006.
70 Section 8 of the Fraud Act 2006.
71 Section 7 of the Fraud Act 2006.
72 *R v McCormick* <www.judiciary.gov.uk/wp-con tent/uploads/JCO/Documents/Judgments/r-v-mccormack-sentencing-rema rks-20130502.pdf> accessed 12 February 2018.
73 Fraud Act 2006 – explanatory notes (n 43) Note 6.
74 J Pickworth, 'The Fraud Act 2006: a death knell for conspiracy to defraud – the "prosecutor's darling"?'. Euro. News/ 2009, 64 (Aug), 1.
75 Ryder, *Financial Crime in the 21st Century* (n 28) 128.
76 M Levi, 'Reforming the Criminal Fraud Trial: An Overview of the Roskill Proposals' (1986) 13 JL & Soc'y 117.
77 Section 1(1) of the Criminal Justice Act 1987.
78 National Crime Agency (NCA), National Fraud Authority <www.gov.uk/government/organisations/national-fraud-authority> accessed 12 February 2018.
79 M Levi. 'The Roskill fraud commission revisited: an assessment'. (2003) 11(1) JFC 38.
80 M Levi, 'Fraud on trial: what is to be done?' (2000) 21(2) Comp. Law 38 (Emphasis added).
81 R L Sarker 'Fighting Fraud: a missed opportunity' (2007) 14(4) JFC 369.
82 Fraud Advisory Panel 'Roskill revisited: is there a case for a unified prosecution office?' <www.fraudadvisorypanel.org/wp-content/uploads/2015/04/Roskill-Revisited-Final-24-Mar10.pdf> accessed 12 February 2018.
83 College of Policing, 'Police forces' <www.police.uk/forces.htm> accessed 12 February 2018.
84 Ryder, *Financial Crime in the 21st Century* (n 28) 246.
85 *Fraud Review* (n 3) 6.
86 ibid.

87 Home Office, 'Home Secretary announces new national economic crime centre to tackle high level fraud and money laundering' <www.gov.uk/government/news/home-secretary-announces-new-national-economic-crime-centre-to-tackle-high-level-fraud-and-money-laundering> accessed 12 February 2018.

88 This covers England, Wales and Northern Ireland only. See Serious Fraud Office, 'About Us. What we do' <www.sfo.gov.uk/about-us/> accessed 12 February 2018.

89 This includes investigators, lawyers, forensic accountants, analysts, digital forensics experts. The SFO has a core budget, supplemented by additional funding agreed with the Treasury. This includes "blockbuster" funding to take on very big cases where the annual expenditure is expected to exceed an agreed percentage of core budget. ibid.

90 ibid.

91 ibid.

92 ibid.

93 Levi, 'Reforming the Criminal Fraud Trial (n 76).

94 ibid.

95 ibid.

96 *R (on the application of Corner House Research and another) v Director of Serious Fraud Office (BAE Systems plc, interested party)* [2008] All ER 927; *Bishopsgate Investment Management Ltd v. Maxwell (No.1)* [1993] BCC 120; *Re Levitt* [1992] Ch. 457.

97 J de Grazia, 'Report of the Serious Fraud Office' http://library.college.police.uk/docs/JdeGrazia-Final-Review-of-SFO.pdf accessed 12 February 2018.

98 Crime and Courts Act 2013.

99 Serious Fraud Office, 'SFO completes £497.25m Deferred Prosecution Agreement with Rolls-Royce PLC' <www.sfo.gov.uk/2017/01/17/sfo-completes-497–25m-defer red-prosecution-agreement-rolls-royce-plc/> accessed 12 February 2018.

100 Financial Times, 'Fraud watchdog weakened by budget cuts' 27 March 2011. <https://www.ft.com/content/8221aba2–58b5–11e0–9b8a-00144feab49a> accessed 12 February 2018. Serious Fraud Office, 'About Us' (n 88).

101 Financial Conduct Authority, 'About the FCA' <www.fca.org.uk/about/the-fca> accessed 12 March 2018.

102 ibid.

103 ibid.

104 Financial Conduct Authority, 'Enforcement Information Guide' <www.fca.org.uk/publication/corporate/enforcement-information-guide.pdf> accessed 12 March 2018.

105 ibid.

106 Ryder, *Financial Crime in the 21st Century* (n 28) 128.

107 Financial Conduct Authority, 'Enforcement' <www.fca.org.uk/about/enforcement> accessed 12 March 2018.

108 Financial Conduct Authority, Handbook. SYSC 6.3. <www.handbook.fca.org.uk/handbook/SYSC/6/3.html> accessed 12 March 2018.

109 For a discussion of Financial Conduct Authority enforcement powers see, for example: K Harrison and N Ryder, *The Law Relating to Financial Crime in the United Kingdom* (Routledge 2017).

110 Crown Prosecution Service, 'About CPS' <www.cps.gov.uk/specialist-fraud-division> accessed 12 February 2018.

111 City of London Police, 'Action Fraud – About Us' <www.actionfraud.police.uk/about-us/who-we-are> accessed 12 February 2018.

112 City of London Police, Action Fraud (n 111) (note: not Scotland).

113 ibid.

114 Palmer (n 32) viii (David Kirk).

115 City of London Police, Action Fraud (n 111).

116 For a discussion of money laundering and terrorism financing see: Harrison and Ryder (n 109).
117 Suspicious Activity Reports, introduced by Drug Trafficking Offences Act 1986. National Crime Agency, 'Making a NCA Regulated Sector Suspicious Activity Report (SAR)' <www.ukciu.gov.uk/(iht3y0yn5exjyc552fnwwy45)/Information/info.aspx?InfoSection=Submission> accessed 12 February 2018. National Crime Agency, 'Introduction to Suspicious Activity Reports' <www.nationalcrimeagency.gov.uk/publications/513-introduction-to-suspicious-activity-reports-sars/file> accessed 12 February 2018.
118 Section 336A of the Proceeds of Crime Act 2002.
119 Section 328 of the Proceeds of Crime Act 2002. *Squirrell Ltd v National Westminster Bank Plc* [2006] 1 W.L.R. 637.
120 *K Limited v National Westminster Bank Plc* [2007] 1 WLR 311.
121 Home Office, 'Counting Rules For Recorded Crime' <www.gov.uk/government/publications/counting-rules-for-recorded-crime> accessed 12 February 2018.
122 Prin 2.1.11 Financial Conduct Authority, 'Handbook. The Principles'. <www.handbook.fca.org.uk/handbook/PRIN/2/1.html> accessed 12 February 2018. The Supervision requirements (SUP 15.3.17) deal with significant events. Financial Conduct Authority, 'Handbook. Supervision'. <www.handbook.fca.org.uk/handbook/SUP/15/3.html> accessed 12 February 2018.
123 Portsmouth (n 3) 15.
124 C Nicholls & others, *Corruption and Misuse of Public Office* (OUP 2006) Ix. (Lord Phillips).
125 National Crime Agency, 'Economic Crime Command' <www.nationalcrimeagency.gov.uk/about-us/what-we-do/economic-crime> accessed 12 February 2018.
126 Ministry of Justice, 'Post-legislative assessment of the Fraud Act 2006. Memorandum to the Justice Select Committee' (Cm 8372) 10.
127 Fraud Advisory Panel, Fraud Review (n 2) 4.
128 ibid 7.

Bibliography

Action Fraud, 'A–Z of Fraud' <www.actionfraud.police.uk/a-z_of_fraud> accessed 12 February 2018.
Action Fraud, 'What is Fraud?' <www.actionfraud.police.uk/what-is-fraud> accessed 12 February 2018.
Attorney General's Office, *Fraud Review – Final report*. (Attorney General's Office 2006).
Bishopsgate Investment Management Ltd v. Maxwell (No. 1) [1993] BCC 120.
City of London Police, 'Action Fraud – About Us' <www.actionfraud.police.uk/about-us/who-we-are> accessed 12 February 2018.
College of Policing, 'Police forces' <www.police.uk/forces.htm> accessed 12 February 2018.
Coolican T, 'Time out for fraud' (2006) 156 NLJ 1460.
Criminal Justice Act 1987.
Crime and Courts Act 2013.
Crown Prosecution Service, 'About CPS' <www.cps.gov.uk/specialist-fraud-division> accessed 12 February 2018.
Doig A and Levi M, 'Inter-agency work and the UK public sector investigation of fraud, 1996–2006: joined-up rhetoric and disjointed reality' (2009) 19(3) Policing and Society 199.

Dooley DV and Radke M, 'Does severe punishment deter financial crimes' (2010) 4 Charleston L Rev 619.

Drug Trafficking Offences Act 1986.

Financial Conduct Authority, 'About the FCA' <www.fca.org.uk/about/the-fca> accessed 12 March 2018.

Financial Conduct Authority, 'Enforcement' <www.fca.org.uk/about/enforcement> accessed 12 March 2018.

Financial Conduct Authority, 'Enforcement Information Guide'.<www.fca.org.uk/publication/corporate/enforcement-information-guide.pdf> accessed 12 March 2018.

Financial Conduct Authority, Handbook. <www.handbook.fca.org.uk/handbook/SYSC/6/3.html> accessed 12 March 2018.

Financial Conduct Authority, 'JPMorgan Chase Bank N.A. fined £137,610,000 for serious failings relating to its Chief Investment Office's "London Whale" trades' <www.fca.org.uk/news/ jpmorgan-chase-bank-na-fined> accessed 18 February 2018.

Financial Times, 'Fraud watchdog weakened by budget cuts' 27 March 2011. <www.ft.com/content/8221aba2–58b5–11e0–9b8a-00144feab49a> accessed 12 February 2018.

Fraud Act 2006.

Fraud Act 2006 – explanatory notes <www.opsi.gov.uk/acts/acts2006/en/ukpgaen_20060035_en_1.htm> accessed 12 February 2018.

Fraud Advisory Panel 'Roskill revisited: is there a case for a unified prosecution office?' <www.fraudadvisorypanel.org/wp-content/uploads/2015/04/Roskill-Revisited-Final-24-Mar10.pdf> accessed 12 February 2018.

Fraud Advisory Panel, 'Fraud Review – ten years on' <www.fraudadvisorypanel.org/wp-content/uploads/2016/06/The-Fraud-Review-Ten-Years-On-WEB.pdf> accessed 12 February 2018.

Fraud Trials Committee Report. (HMSO 1986).

Ghosh [1982] QB 1053.

Gilligan G, 'Jérôme Kerviel the "Rogue Trader" of Société Générale: Bad Luck, Bad Apple, Bad Tree or Bad Orchard?' (2011) 32(12) Co Law 355.

de Grazia J, 'Report of the Serious Fraud Office' <http://library.college.police.uk/docs/JdeGrazia-Final-Review-of-SFO.pdf> accessed 12 February 2018.

Hall M and Smith T, 'The disappearing Ghosh test' (2017) 181 *Criminal Law and Justice Weekly* 752.

Hanley K, 'Plea Bargaining: Striking a bargain'. (2006) LS Gaz 14 Sep, 20.

Harrison K and Ryder N, *The Law Relating to Financial Crime in the United Kingdom* (Routledge 2017).

Home Office, 'Counting Rules For Recorded Crime' <www.gov.uk/government/publications/counting-rules-for-recorded-crime> accessed 12 February 2018.

Home Office, 'Home Secretary announces new national economic crime centre to tackle high level fraud and money laundering' <www.gov.uk/government/news/home-secretary-announces-new-national-economic-crime-centre-to-tackle-high-level-fraud-and-money-laundering> accessed 12 February 2018.

Ivey v Genting Casinos (UK) Ltd t/a Crockfords [2017] UKSC 67.

K Limited v National Westminster Bank Plc [2007] 1 WLR 311.

Law Society Gazette, 'Hale says test of dishonesty may be question for parliament' <www.lawgazette.co.uk/law/hale-says-test-of-dishonesty-may-be-question-for-parliament/5065120.article#.WqBSJWzmNgc.twitter> accessed 12 March 2018.

Levi M, 'Fraud on trial: what is to be done?' (2000) 21(2) Comp. Law 38.

Levi M, 'Reforming the Criminal Fraud Trial: An Overview of the Roskill Proposals' (1986) 13 JL & Soc'y 117.

Levi M, 'The Roskill fraud commission revisited: an assessment'. (2003) 11(1) JFC 38

Re Levitt [1992] Ch. 457.

LOCOG v Sinfield [2018] EWHC 51 (QB).

Ministry of Justice, 'Post-legislative assessment of the Fraud Act 2006. Memorandum to the Justice Select Committee' (Cm 8372).

National Crime Agency, 'Economic Crime Command' <www.nationalcrimeagency. gov.uk/about-us/what-we-do/economic-crime> accessed 12 February 2018.

National Crime Agency, 'Introduction to Suspicious Activity Reports' <www.nationalcrime agency.gov.uk/publications/513-introduction-to-suspicious-activity-reports-sars/file> accessed 12 February 2018.

National Crime Agency, 'Making a NCA Regulated Sector Suspicious Activity Report (SAR)' <www.ukciu.gov.uk/(iht3y0yn5exjyc552fnwwy45)/Information/info.aspx?Info Section=Submission> accessed 12 February 2018.

National Fraud Authority <www.gov.uk/government/organisations/national-fraud-authority> accessed 12 February 2018.

National Fraud Authority, '2009 Annual Report & Accounts'. <www.gov.uk/government/uploads/system/uploads/attachment_data/file/248204/0808.pdf> accessed 12 February 2018.

Nicholls C & others, *Corruption and Misuse of Public Office* (OUP 2006).

Ormerod D, 'The Fraud Act 2006 – Criminalised Lying?' (2007) Crim L R 193.

Ormerod D and Williams DH, *Smith's Law of Theft* (OUP 2007).

Palmer AA, *Countering Economic Crime: A Comparative Analysis* (Routledge 2017).

Peat R, Mason I, Bazley S, 'The FCA as a criminal prosecutor' (2010) 31(4) Comp. Law 119.

Pickworth J, 'The Fraud Act 2006: a death knell for conspiracy to defraud – the "prosecutor's darling"?'. Euro. News/ 2009, 64 (Aug), 1.

Proceeds of Crime Act 2002

R v Kweku Adoboli. www.judiciary.gov.uk/judgments/kweku-adoboli-sentencin g-remarks-20112012/ accessed 12 March 2018.

R (on the application of Corner House Research and another) v Director of Serious Fraud Office (BAE Systems plc, interested party) [2008] All ER 927.

R v McCormick <www.judiciary.gov.uk/wp-content/uploads/JCO/Documents/Judgments/r-v-mccormack-sentencing-remarks-20130502.pdf> accessed 12 February 2018.

Reuters, 'UPDATE 1-Madoff, Stanford fraud victims dealt setbacks by U.S. top court' <www.reuters.com/article/us-usa-court-madoff-stanford/madoff-stanford-fraud-victims-dealt-setbacks-by-u-s-top-court-idUSKBN0F51SV20140630> accessed 12 March 2018.

Rothwell R, 'New: Plea bargaining' (2006) LS Gaz 27 Jul, 6 (3).

Ryder N, *Financial Crime in the 21st Century* (Edward Elgar 2010).

Sarker RL, 'Fighting Fraud: a missed opportunity' (2007) 14(4) JFC 369.

Serious Fraud Office, 'About Us. What we do' <www.sfo.gov.uk/about-us/> accessed 12 February 2018.

Serious Fraud Office, 'SFO completes £497.25m Deferred Prosecution Agreement with Rolls-Royce PLC' <www.sfo.gov.uk/2017/01/17/sfo-completes-497–25m-defer red-prosecution-agreement-rolls-royce-plc/> accessed 12 February 2018.

Serious Fraud Office, 'SFO charges David Ames of Harlequin Group' <www.sfo.gov.uk/2017/02/17/sfo-charges-david-ames-harlequin-group/> accessed 12 February 2018.

Serious Fraud Office, 'Three convicted in JJB Trial' <www.sfo.gov.uk/2014/11/20/three-convicted-jjb-trial/> accessed 12 February 2018.

Serious Organised Crime and Police Act 2005.

Squirrell Ltd v National Westminster Bank Plc [2006] 1 W.L.R. 637.

Theft Act 1968.

Theft Act 1978.

The Law Commission, 'Fraud' Cm 5562.

University of Portsmouth, 'Annual Fraud Indicator 2016' <www.port.ac.uk/media/contacts-and-departments/icjs/ccfs/Annual-Fraud-Indicator-2016.pdf> accessed 12 February 2018.

3 An empirical review of the use of the Fraud Act 2006 and other criminal offences within the school application system

Chris Monaghan[1]

3.1 Introduction

This chapter builds upon my previous research on fraud and school application forms.[2] It does this through an empirical study of how prevalent the issue of parents submitting deliberately misleading or fraudulent information to local authorities is. Although the Office of the Schools Adjudicator does publish statistics on this and local authorities are obliged to submit such information to it,[3] the Freedom of Information requests upon which this chapter is based present a more detailed picture of how local authorities view and respond to this issue. I sent Freedom of Information requests to a cross-section of local authorities in England, as well as to the Office of the Schools Adjudicator and the Department for Education.

The concern that a minority of parents are 'cheating' the school application system is one that is often reported in the press.[4] It has been addressed by the Office of the Schools Adjudicator, firstly through a report at the request of the then Secretary of State for Children, Schools and Families, Ed Balls MP,[5] and secondly, in its annual report for 2015–16.[6] According to the current Chief Adjudicator, Shan Scott, '[s]eventy-five local authorities report concerns about fraudulent applications. Eighty-one local authorities reported that they withdrew some offers of places but the overall number of places withdrawn was very low at 267 given that well over a million applications for school places are processed each year'.[7] The number of places withdrawn may be 'very low' compared to the number of total applications processed, however, it does represent 267 instances of parents potentially including deliberately misleading or false information on their child's school application form.

As the numbers are relatively insignificant compared to the number of overall applications, the Department for Education has not been required to respond either by increasing the powers of local authorities or creating (via primary legislation) a bespoke criminal offence to capture this type of conduct, or by imposing a fine.[8] Nonetheless, despite the apparent relative numerical insignificance of these applications, it will be argued that the issue presents an opportunity to consider how the state (whether at a local level, or at central level) responds to this type of behaviour. My findings show that there is inconsistency in the approach adopted by different local authorities. While most local authorities do warn parents about the consequences to their child's school place if they provide deliberately misleading or false information (namely that the place would be withdrawn), two local authorities mistakenly took the view that this conduct amounted to an offence under the Perjury Act 1911, and a minority did not record information relating to the instances of such applications. The research showed that local authorities adopted a range of methods to check the validity of addresses, and where such applications were detected the school place would generally be withdrawn. It is submitted that this is an issue which is deserving of joined-up thinking between local authorities, the Office of the Schools Adjudicator and the Department for Education in order to provide a forum for those responsible for administrating the system to share best practice, raise concerns and suggest new approaches to deterring such conduct and educating parents about the consequences of submitting such applications.

3.2 Is the inclusion of deliberately misleading or false information on a school application a criminal offence?

My previous research has considered two instances of local authorities, Harrow Council and Havering Council, using the criminal law in instances where there were allegations that a parent had deliberately included an incorrect address on a school application form. In 2009, Harrow Council prosecuted Mrs Patel under the Fraud Act 2006. Harrow Council took the decision to abandon the prosecution before the case reached the Crown Court for trial. Previously, I have argued in the *Journal of Criminal Law* that the Fraud Act 2006 does not cover such conduct, as the provision of a deliberately misleading or fraudulent application did not fall within the scope of fraud by false representation under section 1(2)(a). Although the Fraud Act 2006 *might* appear to catch this type of conduct, fraud by false representation requires an *intention to gain or to cause loss*, which relates to *property* and clearly a school place is not to be regarded as property for the purposes of section 5. There might be an argument that the Fraud Act 2006 could capture certain types of conduct where parents were made aware that the local authority would suffer a financial loss if it were forced to fund additional school places, and they applied in the knowledge that by including an incorrect address they would be causing this loss. However, my view is that the criminal law should not be used to criminalise parents.[9]

In 2014, Havering Council successfully prosecuted Mrs Pacheco under section 4 of the Forgery and Counterfeiting Act 1981.[10] Mrs Pacheco had submitted a forged tenancy agreement, to verify the address contained within the school application form. This amounted to an offence under the Forgery and Counterfeiting Act 1981. If local authorities did wish to use the current law to prosecute (a view that I do not support), then they would be advised to include a requirement that parents submit supporting documentation when making an application. This could be accompanied by a warning in the declaration section of the form stating that the provision of a forged document would amount to a criminal offence and that the local authority could prosecute. However, it is important to distinguish between the inclusion of a false address and the use of a forged document to prove the validity of the false statement, as whilst the former is not a criminal offence, the latter is an offence under the Forgery and Counterfeiting Act 1981.

I have argued in the *Criminal Law Review* that parents who provided deliberately misleading or fraudulent information should not fall within the ambit of the criminal law.[11] In response to the media coverage surrounding the prosecution of Mrs Patel, the then Secretary of State for Education and Families, Mr Ed Balls MP, stated that the government did not regard the provision of a fraudulent address as a criminal matter.[12] I have argued that the appropriate response by local authorities should be to use the sanctions under the School Admissions Code[13] in a systematic manner to ensure that these are viewed as a real deterrent. Finally, if misleading and fraudulent applications are perceived to be a significant problem, then a response may be to consider whether the law could be changed to permit local authorities to recover the cost of providing a school place from parents, where a child has obtained its place as a result of a fraudulent application. I have proposed this in an earlier article and this would create a significant deterrent without treating such conduct as criminal.[14] This would ensure that a child is not punished as a result of their parent's decision to include an incorrect address, as at present the only sanction is to either revoke an offer, or to withdraw a place once a child has started at school.

3.3 Evaluating whether there is in fact a problem

This section considers the results of the Freedom of Information requests that were sent to a cross-section of local authorities in England, the Department for Education and the Office of the Schools Adjudicator. The coverage of the local authority responses represent approximately half of those received. The purpose of the Freedom of Information requests were to ascertain the extent of the problem and how local authorities viewed the issue of deliberately misleading or fraudulent applications. The pre-existing evidence does suggest that this is a problem, albeit a minor one in terms of the numbers involved. The Office of the Schools Adjudicator's annual report for September 2015 to August 2016 contained ten references to 'fraudulent applications', and stated that '[a]lmost a half of authorities reported concerns, and just over a half had withdrawn offers as a result of their investigations'.[15] In 2016, some 267 offers of places were withdrawn, in 2015 it was 284, and in 2014 it was 186.[16] By way of comparison the Office of the Schools Adjudicator's annual report for September 2016 to August 2017 does not refer to fraudulent school application forms.[17] However, the actual numbers may not reflect the impact that this conduct might have on the overall public confidence in the school admissions system, especially where there is high demand for particular schools.

The Freedom of Information requests reveal an interesting picture of how local authorities safeguard, identify and respond to the provision of deliberately misleading or fraudulent information. In order to provide an overview of different local authorities, I have used a sample of the overall responses that demonstrate the similarities and differences that exist across England.

3.3.1 Birmingham City Council

Birmingham City Council had 30,410 applications in 2015 and 30,916 applications in 2016. During the period in question 19 applications were investigated and were found to contain an incorrect address. In each case the place was withdrawn as the application was regarded as fraudulent. This amounted to 0.03 per cent of all applications. Birmingham City Council was not aware of any forged supporting documentation being used. The investigation process is triggered as follows:

> [W]hen applications are being processed, if an address is put forward that is different to that held by the local authority or the school, then proof of that address will be requested from the applicant. If the family fail to provide proof, then checks are made on council tax, housing and benefit records . . .[18]

Birmingham City Council confirmed that it 'would not refer cases to the Legal Team for action' but might 'seek advice and support'.[19] The council confirmed that it would not prosecute and would instead revoke a place using its powers under the School Admissions Code. In total, fourteen places were withdrawn prior to a child starting school, and five once a child had started at a school. This resulted in six appeals, albeit all were unsuccessful. Birmingham City Council warns applicants on its website that it might undertake home visits or seek proof of address and the declaration on the application form highlights the sanction of having a place withdrawn. However, Birmingham City Council does not warn parents that such an application could amount to a criminal offence. Birmingham City Council does have an internal procedure on how to respond to a fraudulent application. The procedure is comprehensive and contains guidance on different methods to verify an address, such as contacting the child's current nursery to confirm the address, and in what circumstances a place would be revoked once a child has started at the school.

3.3.2 Cambridgeshire County Council

Between November 2014 to November 2016 only sixteen applications had been investigated, or flagged up, as being incorrect regarding the child's home address. These were twelve in the academic year 2016/17, and four in 2015/16. None of these applications had provided an incorrect address in 2016/17 and Cambridgeshire County Council declined to provide numbers for 2015/16 as 'we are withholding this information under Section 40(2) of the Freedom of Information Act 2000 due to low numbers which could lead to the identification of individual people'.[20] The total number of applications was approximately 19,500 a year and therefore Cambridgeshire County Council regarded the number of applications providing the incorrect address as '[n]egligible'.[21] The council reported no cases of forged documentation and declined to provide information as to how many applications have been regarded as fraudulent pursuant to section 40(2) of the Freedom of Information Act 2000. Cambridgeshire County Council's policy is not to prosecute where there has been a fraudulent school application form. In response to the question of how many instances the sanctions in the School Admission Code have been used in this context the council did not reply, pursuant to section 40(2) of the Freedom of Information Act 2000.

In response to the question of whether a place has been withdrawn after the child had started school, the council confirmed that '[w]e do not withdraw a child's school place once they have started at that school'.[22] The council confirmed that it did not have an official policy regarding how it dealt with fraudulent or misleading school application forms. However, it stated that 'if a fraudulent address is identified, we will investigate until we are satisfied that there is no fraud. If there is fraud, the place is taken away as long as the child has not started at the school'.[23]

3.3.3 Central Bedfordshire Council

Between November 2014 to December 2016 Central Bedfordshire Council was responsible for 129 schools and received approximately 11,000 applications per year. During this time sixteen applications were investigated of which eight were found to have provided an incorrect address. This amounted to less than one per cent of all applications. There were no instances of forged supporting documentation. However, the applications that had provided an incorrect address resulted in the provision of extra school places and an extra financial cost for the council, namely '[t]ime and resources of School Admissions and Corporate Fraud Teams'.[24] No application was referred to the council's legal department as instead a referral was made to its Corporate Fraud Team. In total, five places were withdrawn before the child started school and one after a child had started school. None of the withdrawals resulted in an appeal. The council warns parents about the consequences of fraudulent applications on its website and school application form. The council does not regard this type of conduct as amounting to a criminal offence. The council confirmed that although there was not an official policy, there was a process that it followed where addresses of oversubscribed schools are verified using the council's records and this may lead to applications being referred to the Corporate Fraud Team to investigate.

3.3.4 Department for Education

The Department for Education confirmed that between November 2015 to November 2017 there had been only 'one instance of communication between a member of the Office of the Schools Adjudicator's secretariat (OSA) and department officials with regards to fraudulent applications' and that '[t]his was in relation to a press query the department received from ITV Central, on 19 October 2017, regarding school admissions and investigations on fraudulents (sic) applications. The journalist had queried figures for secondary school applications for the 2017–18 and 2016–17 school years, and requested confirmation regarding the method of data collection'.[25] The Department for Education also confirmed that it did not carry out any review concerning misleading school applications that are fraudulent, forged or deliberately misleading.[26]

3.3.5 Devon County Council

Between November 2014 to November 2016 Devon County Council was responsible for 354 schools. Due to a concern that the disclosure of a precise number could identify individuals, the council could not confirm the total number of investigations, but stated that 'a very small number of applications have been investigated'.[27] The council could confirm that there was no evidence of forged documentation being provided. In terms of the impact of such fraudulent applications, the council confirmed that this resulted in extra financial cost, but '[o]nly in staff resources to investigate and discuss with relevant schools'.[28] The council confirmed that places had been withdrawn, but only before a child had started school. The council does warn parents about the consequences of having a place withdrawn on its website and the application form, but does not say that it could amount to a criminal offence, as '[w]e say it will be taken seriously but do not threaten prosecution'.[29] The council stated that '[i]t is unlikely that Devon County Council would ever take a case to prosecution, we consider withdrawing the offer is sufficient'.[30]

3.3.6 Gloucestershire County Council

In the September 2014 entry there was one instance of fraud relating to a sibling connection. This resulted in the place being withdrawn. In the September 2015 entry two fraudulent addresses were used and in both instances the places were withdrawn. Finally, in the September 2016 entry there were three fraudulent addresses and all three places were withdrawn. In no instances were forged supporting documents used. All places were withdrawn before the child started at the school. In no instances were the sanctions under the School Admissions Code used or was the advice of the council's legal department sought. The council were aware of two appeals against the withdrawal of the place, although it is not aware of the outcome. The application form warns parents that providing fraudulent or misleading information could amount to a criminal offence under the Perjury Act 1911.[31]

3.3.7 Hampshire County Council

Hampshire County Council is responsible for 387 schools and it receives approximately 42,000 main round and in-year applications a year. During the period of September 2015 to September 2016 the council investigated some 24 applications, which were brought to its attention by either schools or parents. The council confirmed that of those applications that were investigated '11 applicants had applied using an incorrect address' and this amounted to 'approx. 0.02% of the admissions round applicants each year and therefore is not deemed to be problem within the Local Authority'.[32] The council confirmed that there were no instances of forged supporting documentation and it did not regard any of the eleven applications to have been fraudulent. The council did not refer any of the applications to its own legal department, the police or a prosecuting authority. In all eleven instances the place was withdrawn prior to the child starting school using the sanctions under the School Admissions Code. Only in one instance had there been an appeal, and this was unsuccessful. The council warns parents about the consequences of providing an incorrect address on the application form, with the declaration section stating 'I understand that any place offered may be withdrawn if I give false information, even if my child has started in the school'.[33] There is also a warning on the council's website.[34] Interestingly, in response to the question of whether the council had an official policy regarding fraudulent or misleading school application forms, the council replied, '[n]o, as there is no evidence that fraud is an issue with applications for school places in Hampshire. The department works very closely with its schools and address information is usually identified and followed up with the applicant very quickly'.[35]

3.3.8 Herefordshire Council

Herefordshire Council is responsible for 94 schools and received 3,650 admission round applications. The responses from the council related to the period from November 2014 to November 2016. The council checks all addresses 'against school census' and '[a]ny differences lead to a request to confirm new address as per the attached Information for Parents booklets'.[36] The council conformed that no applications contained an incorrect address. Parents are advised that their choice of preferred school might be refused where '[i]nformation provided by the parents (including information about addresses) is found to be fraudulent or intentionally misleading and such information may also be grounds for withdrawal of any place that has been allocated, even after the child has started at the school'.[37]

3.3.9 London Borough of Havering

As noted above the London Borough of Havering has been the only local authority to successfully bring a prosecution. For the period from November 2014 to November 2017 the council confirmed that it is responsible for

79 schools and the average cost of a school place is £4,253. During this period a number of applications were investigated in relation to the child's address. The council confirmed that, '[w]e do not record the number investigated, as part of the admissions process all addresses are checked and therefore many inaccuracies are picked up early on, sometimes these are genuine mistakes (for instance when a parent has moved since last using the admissions site)'.[38] In terms of the actual numbers of applications that contained an incorrect address, these were six in 2014, nine in 2015, four in 2016 and three in 2017. The council verifies all address against council tax records and housing benefit data. If the address cannot be verified electronically, then the parent must provide documents to verify the address. During this period 'no parent has provided documentation that has been determined as a forgery'.[39] The council confirmed that during this period no applications had been referred to its legal department nor has the advice of outside counsel been sought. For each of the applications that contained an incorrect address, the council withdrew the child's place prior to the child starting at the school. The council confirmed that it warns parents on its website[40] and school application form that the provision of fraudulent or misleading information on school application forms would amount to a criminal offence:

> By submitting the application form you agree to the following statement: 'I understand that if I give false or deliberately misleading information on this form or supporting information, then this application will no longer be valid and may be a criminal offence. This could result in the withdrawal of the school place offer and/or prosecution. I am aware that if I intentionally provided false or misleading information in this application, there may be a financial loss to Havering Council due to the expense of funding a school place for my child'.[41]

The warning does not confirm which offence this would be. However, it is arguable that if a parent made a fraudulent application having read the warning, then they would be aware that they would be causing financial loss to the council, and financial loss is property for the purposes of section 5 of the Fraud Act 2006. If the tribunal of fact were satisfied that the parent had been dishonest, then an offence under section 1(2)(a) of the Fraud Act 2006 would have been committed. The council confirmed that it did have an official policy relating to the use of fraudulent applications and invited members of the public to contact the council where they believed that another parent was using an address of convenience.[42]

3.3.10 *London Borough of Tower Hamlets*

For the period of November 2014 to November 2016 the London Borough of Tower Hamlets was responsible for 85 schools. During this period there were five instances of applications containing incorrect addresses which was less than 0.5 per cent of all applications received. There were no instances of forged supporting documentation being provided. All five places were withdrawn before the child started at the school and resulted in just one appeal, which was unsuccessful. The council warns parents on its website and on the application form that a place could be withdrawn.[43] It does not, however, regard this as amounting to a criminal offence. It has a policy regarding how it deals with such applications and this is outlined in the documentation for parents.

3.3.11 Manchester City Council

Manchester City Council is responsible for 176 schools and for places starting in September 2016 it received approximately 13,900 applications. The council was unable to confirm how many applications were investigated on suspicion of providing an incorrect address or were found to have had provided an incorrect address as this information is not recorded. None of the applications were regarded as fraudulent. The council confirmed that three places were withdrawn before a child started school and that there had been no appeals. The council warns parents that as:

> [I]n the past, some parents have given a false address, thinking this would give them a better chance of obtaining a place at certain schools. Please note that addresses are checked. If you give a false address, your child will lose their preferred school place.[44]

3.3.12 Milton Keynes Council

For the period relating to 2014–16 Milton Keynes Council investigated or flagged up 271 applications as being incorrect regarding the home address. Significantly, only one application was investigated or flagged in 2014, eight in 2015, and 262 in 2016. The reason for the increase in 2016 was due to a procedural change that required that all addresses were validated against council tax data. However, the actual numbers of applications that had provided an incorrect address were zero in 2014, three in 2015, and five in 2016. The increase in investigations for 2016 did not result in a corresponding increase in the number of findings that a parent had provided an incorrect address. In 2016, the five incorrect addresses amounted to just 0.07 per cent of all applications that the council received. The council confirmed that there were no instances of applications with forged supporting documents.

Interestingly, Milton Keynes Council's decision to change its processes for 2016 did result in 188 investigations relating to primary applications and 74 applications relating to secondary applications in 2016–17. In all instances the addresses were verified. In the case of the primary applications, only five admitted to having provided incorrect information, and in the case of the secondary applications, no applicant was found to have provided incorrect information. In 2014–15, just one primary application was regarded as fraudulent and the allocation was withdrawn, and in 2015–16 just three primary applications were regarded as fraudulent, which resulted in one application being withdrawn and subsequently resubmitted, one allocation being withdrawn, and in the final case the decision being devolved to the school to determine the outcome. In no instance did Milton Keynes Council either refer any application to its own legal department or instruct outside counsel. The approach taken by Milton Keynes Council is to treat the issue of misleading applications as giving rise to a possible sanction of revoking the allocation of a school place, as opposed to treating this as a possible criminal matter. The sanction of providing such information is outlined in the council's *Parent and Carer Guide*.[45]

3.3.13 Office of the Schools Adjudicator

The Office of the Schools Adjudicator confirmed that between November 2014–2016 there were '75 local authorities that reported an issue with fraudulent applications for school places for the period September 2015 to August 2016'.[46] The Office of the Schools Adjudicator also confirmed that the Department for Education had not been in contact about school applications that were either fraudulent, forged or deliberately misleading. Neither had the Office of the Schools Adjudicator reviewed the matter internally. However, the Office of the Schools Adjudicator confirmed that during this time it had been contacted by three individuals who were concerned about 'alleged fraudulent applications for school places'.[47] One parent had written to the Office of the Schools Adjudicator complaining that their local authority did not carry out a sufficient number of checks against the address given in an application. According to this parent this meant that fraudulent applications were not being identified and that places were not be allocated to those children living within the catchment area. They informed the Office of the Schools Adjudicator that those responsible within the local authority had told them that the issue was not regarded as an effective use of their time. Another individual had written that this has had a detrimental impact on public confidence in the system, as evidenced by conversation between parents at the school playground, in online chat forums and at social events. There was a perception that some parents were using a false address or a grandparent's address in order to obtain a place at a school that they would not have otherwise been entitled to apply for.

3.3.14 Royal Borough of Kensington and Chelsea

The Royal Borough of Kensington and Chelsea declined to provide information about the number of applications that could be regarded as misleading or fraudulent due to the time it would take to compile this information. The council does have a statement warning applicants about the consequences of 'any attempt to obtain a school place by fraud' and the measures in place to investigate the accuracy of addresses, such as 'unannounced address visits'.[48]

3.3.15 Suffolk County Council

Suffolk County Council is responsible for 166 primary schools and five secondary schools. For the period from November 2014 to November 2016 there were approximately 16,000 applications. The council confirmed that in 2015–2016 'there were no applications investigated or flagged up as being incorrect regarding the child's home address'.[49] However in 2016–2017 this had increased from zero to 148 applications. The reason for this increase was not outlined in the Freedom of Information response and so it would be useful to determine the cause for this increase. This increase may have been the result of the way that the council checks applications, and if it started to check all addresses against council tax data, then this could explain why there was such an increase. This could then demonstrate the need to ensure that all addresses are checked in order to detect all fraudulent applications. The consequence of this increase was that 'three school places were withdrawn before the child started school on the basis that the address the applicant gave was misleading or fraudulent'.[50] In all instances the places were withdrawn prior to the child starting at the school. Interestingly, the council confirmed that 'four cases were referred to our Legal Department, 0.02 per cent of the total number of applications received on-time for the 2016–2017 entry year'.[51] The council confirmed that whilst it does warn parents on its website, it does not include such a warning within the application form about the provision of fraudulent or misleading information.

3.3.16 Surrey County Council

Between the period November 2014 to November 2016 Surrey County Council's Admissions Team investigated 95 cases of potential 'addresses of convenience' from applicants applying for a school place. Of these, 21 cases turned out not to be where the child was living at the time. In each case the withdrawal occurred before the pupil started at the school and none of these cases resulted in prosecution. This was out of 89,974 applications during this period.[52] The council has a fifteen-page Address of Convenience Assessment Protocol which sets out how it will investigate and respond to fraudulent applications.[53] During this period Surrey County Council did not refer this issue to their legal department or the police, nor were any of the sanctions under the School Admissions Code used. The council's website warns parents that, '[w]e will investigate any applications where there is doubt about the address being given. Use of false information may lead us to withdraw an offer of a place, even after a child has started at a school'.[54]

3.3.17 Worcestershire County Council

Worcestershire County Council is responsible as the admissions authority for 134 schools. It receives 'approx. 15,000 applications per year (includes schools outside the county of Worcestershire)'.[55] However, between November 2014 to November 2016 only three applications were investigated and all of these were found to have provided an incorrect address. This amounted to just 0.0002 per cent of all applications received. In no instances had forged supporting documents been provided. The council withdrew all three places prior to the child starting school under section 2.12 of the School Admissions Code. The council confirmed that there were no referrals to its legal department and that no decisions were made to bring a prosecution as '[t]oo much officer time and financial cost – withdrawal of school offers felt to be sufficient punishment'.[56] Of particular interest is the warning given on the application form and the council's website which states that '[i]f you knowingly give false information in order to obtain a particular school place you could be guilty of an offence under the Perjury Act 1911'.[57] In response to the questions as to whether there is an official policy regarding how the council dealt with fraudulent or misleading school application forms, the council stated:

> No – each case is decided based upon its individual merits. It is very difficult to define whether a parent has "intentionally" misled the Local Authority, or whether circumstances have changed since an application was made. Each case is assessed based on the facts of the case.[58]

3.4 Analysis

The section above provided a sample of the responses received. A common theme from the responses was that most local authorities confirmed that there were cases of fraudulent school applications and in the majority of instances the School Admissions Code was used to withdraw the place prior to the child starting school (or in a number of instances after the child had started school). There were no reported instances of forged documentation being provided to support an application. On balance the total number of such applications was insignificant when compared to the total number of applications for each local authority. Only three local authorities warned parents that this could amount to a criminal offence, and in two cases the relevant offence cited was the Perjury Act 1911. However, it is clear that unless an Act of Parliament required someone making an application for a school place to declare that the information provided was correct, then the Perjury Act 1911 does not apply. This demonstrates the confusion that exists about the precise offence that would capture this type of conduct. Not a single response from any local authority made reference to the Fraud Act 2006 or the Forgery and Counterfeiting Act 1981, even though these were the two offences which had been used to bring prosecutions in the past. It was apparent that local authorities had different approaches in relation to confirming the address, and also at what point such an investigation would take place (i.e. if a school was oversubscribed). Some local authorities had very detailed policies and procedures to ensure that they safeguarded against such applications, and these varied from local authority to local authority. Most local authorities were able to confirm precise numbers, whilst a minority either did not record the information or relied on an exemption under the Freedom of Information Act 2000 to withhold such information.

The responses from these local authorities provided a snapshot of the school application system for each admissions authority and the efforts that different authorities have gone to in order to address the issue. The vast majority of local authorities included a warning in the declaration section of the application form outlining the consequences of providing an incorrect address. The sample of Freedom of Information requests upon which this analysis is based demonstrates that even if deliberate misleading fraudulent applications are not numerically significant, the issue is nevertheless taken seriously at a local authority level. Overall it is clear that there are inconsistencies in the approaches adopted by local authorities and arguably there is scope for collaboration between local authorities and the sharing of best practice. There is the opportunity to conduct further research that would analyse all of the Freedom of Information responses received and to identify examples of best practice, which then could be disseminated to local authorities.

The response from the Office of the Schools Adjudicator reflected the general picture that emerged from the local authority responses. Likewise, the Department for Education's response implied that at a governmental level this was not an issue that caused concern, and the only dialogue on this between the department and the Office of the Schools Adjudicator was in response to an enquiry by a journalist.

3.5 Conclusion

This chapter has built upon my previous research into whether the provision of deliberately misleading or fraudulent information should be criminalised and why at present it does not amount to an offence under section 1(2)(a) of the Fraud Act 2006.[59] It does this by analysing the responses from the Freedom of Information requests that were sent to local authorities, the Office of the Schools Adjudicator and the Department for Education in order to ascertain the extent of the problem, how different local authorities treat such conduct and how they respond where there is evidence that this has occurred. The responses from the Office of the Schools Adjudicator and the Department for Education further demonstrate the numerically insignificance of such applications according to statistics provided by local authorities and the fact that there has been no executive activity to review this issue. However, despite the relative numerical insignificance of such applications, it is clear that this is a matter taken seriously by local authorities, the existing sanctions are used to withdraw school places and a minority of local authorities do regard this conduct as amounting to a criminal offence.

Notes

1 Senior Lecturer in Law, School of Law, University of Worcester.
2 See C Monaghan, 'School application forms and the criminal law' (2015) Crim LR 270 and C Monaghan, 'To prosecute or not to prosecute? A reconsideration of the over-zealous prosecution of parents under the Fraud Act 2006' (2010) 74(3) J Crim L 259.
3 It should be noted that every local authority has published on its website its official report to the Schools Adjudicator which outlines the number of fraudulent applications and the action that each local authority is taking to prevent such applications. See Norfolk County Council, *Local Authority Report to the Schools Adjudicator from Norfolk County Council Local Authority*, 30 June 2016 <www.norfolk.gov.uk/-/media/ norfolk/downloads/education-learning/admissions/norfolk-county-council-report-to-the-school-adjudicator-2016.pdf> accessed 11 April 2018.
4 See J Shepherd, 'School admissions: Addressing concerns' *The Guardian*, 14 October 2008 <www.theguardian.com/education/2008/oct/14/schooladmissions-schools> accessed 11 April 2018.
5 Office of the Schools Adjudicator, *Report to the Secretary of State for Children, Schools and Families on Fraudulent or Misleading Applications for Admission to Schools, 1 October 2009* <http://dera.ioe.ac.uk/1167/1/fraud%200809.doc> accessed 11 April 2018.
6 Office of the Schools Adjudicator, *Annual Report September 2015 to August 2016*, November 2016 <www.gov.uk/government/uploads/system/uploads/attachment_ data/file/585915/OSA_Annual_Report_2016.pdf> accessed 11 April 2018.
7 ibid [9].
8 I previously have argued that a possible sanction (and deterrent) would be to make parents liable for paying the cost of the school place. This would require amending the Education Act 1996. See Monaghan, 'School application forms and the criminal law' (n 2).
9 Monaghan, 'School application forms and the criminal law' (n 2) 275–276.
10 I am grateful to Mr Giles Morrison, 15 New Bridge Street Chambers, who acted as counsel for Havering Council, for conforming the offence. Email from Giles Morrison to the author, 1 October 2014.
11 Monaghan, 'School application forms and the criminal law' (n 2).
12 J Shepherd, 'Ed Balls calls for crackdown on parents lying for school places', *The Guardian*, 3 July 2009 <www.theguardian.com/education/2009/jul/03/ed-balls-school-admissions> accessed 11 April 2018.
13 Department for Education, *School Admissions Code*, December 2014 <https:// assets.publishing.service.gov.uk/government/uploads/system/uploads/attachment_ data/file/389388/School_Admissions_Code_2014_-_19_Dec.pdf> accessed 11 April 2018. The relevant paragraphs are [2.12] and [2.13]. The Code contains guidance on how a local authority must proceed if it decides to withdraw an offer or a place. There are relevant considerations, which must be taken into account by the local authority.
14 Monaghan, 'School application forms and the criminal law' (n 2) 276–277.
15 Office of the Schools Adjudicator 2016 (n 6) [110].
16 ibid [110].
17 Office of the Schools Adjudicator, *Annual Report September 2016 to August 2017*, February 2018. <https://assets.publishing.service.gov.uk/government/uploads/ system/uploads/attachment_data/file/680003/2017_OSA_Annual_Report_- _Final_23_January_2018.pdf> accessed 11 April 2018.
18 Freedom of Information Response, Birmingham City Council, 19 January 2017.
19 ibid.
20 Freedom of Information Response, Cambridgeshire County Council, 20 January 2017.

21   ibid.
22   ibid.
23   ibid.
24   Freedom of Information Response, Central Bedfordshire Council, 13 January 2017.
25   Freedom of Information Response, Department for Education, 16 April 2018.
26   ibid.
27   Freedom of Information Response, Devon County Council, 17 January 2017.
28   ibid.
29   ibid.
30   ibid.
31   Freedom of Information Response, Gloucestershire County Council, 18 January 2017.
32   Freedom of Information Response, Hampshire County Council, 12 January 2017.
33   ibid.
34   Hampshire County Council, 'Address information' <www.hants.gov.uk/ed-ad-addresses> accessed 11 April 2018.
35   Hampshire (n 32).
36   Freedom of Information Response, Herefordshire County Council, 9 January 2017.
37   Herefordshire County Council, *Information for parents: Admission to primary school Commencing September 2017*, 11. An identical warning is found within the guidance document for parents whose children are applying to a secondary school.
38   Freedom of Information Response, London Borough of Havering, 11 April 2018.
39   ibid.
40   London Borough of Havering, *Apply for an infant, junior or primary school place for September 2018* <www.havering.gov.uk/info/20008/school_admissions/479/apply_for_an_infant_junior_or_primary_school_place_for_september_2018> accessed 11 April 2018.
41   London Borough of Havering, *School admissions terms and conditions* <www.havering.gov.uk/download/downloads/id/972/school_admissions_online_application_terms_and_conditions.pdf> accessed 11 April 2018.
42   London Borough of Havering, *Fraudulent applications/Address of convenience* <www.havering.gov.uk/info/20008/school_admissions/483/fraudulent_applications_address_of_convenience> accessed 11 April 2018 and London Borough of Havering, *Address of Convenience Assessment Protocol*, Version 1, Academic Year 2015/16. <www.havering.gov.uk/download/downloads/id/1007/address_of_convenience_assessment_protocol_document.pdf> accessed 11 April 2018.
43   Havering (n 38).
44   Freedom of Information Response, Manchester City Council, 18 January 2017.
45   Freedom of Information Response, Milton Keynes Council, 19 January 2017.
46   Freedom of Information Response, Office of the Schools Adjudicator, 31 January 2017.
47   ibid.
48   Freedom of Information Response, Royal Borough of Kensington and Chelsea, 18 January 2017.
49   Freedom of Information Response, Suffolk County Council, 11 January 2017.
50   ibid.
51   ibid.
52   Freedom of Information Response, Surrey County Council, 23 January 2017. This includes applications for academic years 2014, 2015, 2016 and applications for in year.
53   Surrey County Council, *Addresses of Convenience Assessment Protocol* <www.surreycc.gov.uk/__data/assets/pdf_file/0007/18673/Item-15v-Addresses-of-Convenience-Assessment-Protocol-V1.pdf> accessed 11 April 2018.
54   ibid.
55   Freedom of Information Response, Worcestershire County Council, 12 January 2017.
56   ibid.

57 Worcestershire County Council, Information for Parents Admissions & Transfers to Schools 2017/2018, 117.
58 ibid.
59 It is acknowledged that section 1(2)(a) of the Fraud Act 2006 could apply where the applicant has been made aware that they are causing a financial loss to the local authority and they still apply in the knowledge that they will be causing this loss. However, it is important to appreciate that the loss would only occur where the applicant would never have been entitled to apply for a school place within the area administered by the local authority. To capture such conduct there would need to be a clear warning in the declaration section of the application form and an explanation of how the applicant would cause a loss to the local authority, namely the cost of the school place. It important to appreciate that liability under section 1(2)(a) is limited in terms of the circumstances in which it would apply. For further discussion on this point see Monaghan 'School application forms and the criminal law' (n 2).

Bibliography

Department for Education, *School Admissions Code*, December 2014
Education Act 1996
Forgery and Counterfeiting Act 1981
Fraud Act 2006
Freedom of Information Act 2000
Hampshire County Council, 'Address information'
Herefordshire County Council, *Information for parents: Admission to primary school Commencing September 2017*
London Borough of Havering, *Fraudulent applications/Address of convenience*
London Borough of Havering, *Address of Convenience Assessment Protocol*, Version 1, Academic Year 2015/16
London Borough of Havering, *Apply for an infant, junior or primary school place for September 2018*
Monaghan C, 'To prosecute or not to prosecute? A reconsideration of the over-zealous prosecution of parents under the Fraud Act 2006' (2010) 74(3) J Crim L 259
Monaghan C, 'School application forms and the criminal law' (2015) Crim LR 270
Norfolk County Council, *Local Authority Report to the Schools Adjudicator from Norfolk County Council Local Authority*, 30 June 2016
Office of the Schools Adjudicator, *Report to the Secretary of State for Children, Schools and Families on Fraudulent or Misleading Applications for Admission to Schools*, 1 October 2009
Office of the Schools Adjudicator, *Annual Report September 2015 to August 2016*, November 2016
Office of the Schools Adjudicator, *Annual Report September 2016 to August 2017*, February 2018
Perjury Act 1911
Shepherd, J, 'School admissions: Addressing concerns' *The Guardian*, 14 October 2008
Shepherd J, '*Ed Balls calls for crackdown on parents lying for school places*', *The Guardian*, 3 July 2009
Surrey County Council, *Addresses of Convenience Assessment Protocol*
Worcestershire County Council, *Information for Parents Admissions & Transfers to Schools 2017/2018*

4 Food fraud and the Fraud Act 2006

Complementarity and limitations

Cecilia J. Flores Elizondo,[1] Nicholas Lord,[2] and Jon Spencer[3]

4.1 Introduction

Food fraud has not been sufficiently addressed as a policy (or scientific) construct despite anecdotal concerns about the extent and scope of the phenomenon. Currently, there is no statutory definition of food fraud, either at the level of the European Union (EU), or within the United Kingdom (UK), and guidance for regulatory enforcement continues to be ambiguous, despite now differentiating between food fraud and food crime.[4] Food fraud is not a new phenomenon;[5] however, the focus on food fraud only took off after the horsemeat scandal shocked both the UK and the EU in 2013. Despite undermining the trust of both consumers and industry, the number of food fraud prosecutions remains negligible with authorities mostly pursuing food-related offences for administrative breaches, such as traceability, and inappropriate record keeping as opposed to fraud.

The horsemeat scandal is a case in point. Prosecutions following the scandal were related to breaches to traceability obligations under the General Food Law Regulation (EC) 178/2002,[6] for which Peter Boddy was convicted and sentenced to a fine of £8000 for two counts for failing to comply with traceability requirements.[7] Only four years later, Andronicos Sideras, Ulrich Nielsen and Alex Ostler-Beech were convicted for conspiracy to defraud under the common law for mixing horsemeat with beef and labelling the mixture as beef.[8] More generally, the Food Standards Agency ('FSA'), the regulator responsible for food safety in England, Wales and Northern Ireland, has begun to publicise prosecution data, which shows that from 2015 to 2016 there were circa 13 prosecutions related to food standards breaches under sections 14 and 15 of the Food Safety Act 1990, the remaining ones were related to hygiene and other offences, but none of them concerned food fraud under the Fraud Act 2006.[9]

The limited number of food fraud prosecutions, together with decisions to prosecute under the General Food Law or the Food Safety Act 1990, as opposed to the Fraud Act 2006 or the common law, raises questions about the potential limits and complementarity between the provisions in the General Food Law, the Food Safety Act 1990, the Fraud Act 2006 and common law. A recent consultation on whether the National Food Crime Unit ('NFCU') should be given enforcement powers has made clear the will of key stakeholders to provide more enforcement authority to the NFCU, as well as stakeholders' perception that fraudsters would be deterred if the NFCU prosecuted 'high profile' food fraud cases;[10] although there is currently no valid data to support the latter assertion. However, food fraud prosecutions face substantial challenges. First, the General Food Law and the Food Safety Act 1990 are both framed as a response to safety concerns after the bovine spongiform encephalopathy ('BSE') crisis, resulting in the conceptualisation of food fraud both at the UK and EU levels as administrative violations, rather than as criminal, fraudulent behaviours. Second, this has left those responsible for prosecution predisposed to responding to fraud offences within food supply networks through a regulatory rather than criminal law framework with corresponding enforcement powers geared towards strict liability offences, rather than the pursuit of dishonesty as criminal behaviour. There is no statutory offence of food fraud and this might present gaps and uncertainties for the prosecution of dishonest acts or omissions that, whilst potentially criminal in nature, do not constitute a safety issue. In this regard, the Fraud Act 2006 provides a broader conceptualisation of fraud that is not limited to financial gains and may include a diversity of motivations and criminals such as a broader definition of 'gain' and 'loss',[11] as well as offences related to the possession of,[12] or the involvement in making, adapting or supplying, articles for use in frauds.[13] However, successful fraud prosecutions require a high level of evidence to prove beyond reasonable doubt the commission of a crime, which in turn creates notable obstacles to the authorities and leads to alternative means for concluding cases for pragmatic reasons.

This chapter addresses the question of whether reliance on the Fraud Act 2006 for food-related fraud offences provides a more suitable approach to prosecution, and sanctioning. Following the introduction, Section 4.2 explores the problems of the official conceptualisation of food fraud which restrict the motivations behind food frauds, preventing the identification of the offence of food fraud as distinct to regulatory breaches. Section 4.3 comprises three subsections exploring the limitations and complementarity between current food law and the Fraud Act 2006. Subsection 4.3.1 looks into the limitations of the General Food Law and the Food Safety Act 1990 to deal with food fraud, limitations arising from their regulatory focus on safety. In subsection 4.3.2, the chapter expounds on how the Fraud Act 2006 could fill-in the gaps in current food law. The complexity and fragmentation of law and regulatory enforcement are dealt with in subsection 4.3.3. Finally, Section 4.4 provides some concluding remarks. Rather than the dichotomy between General Food Law and the Fraud Act 2006, the chapter foregrounds the limitations, and therefore, complementarity of these statutory provisions. In so doing, we argue that the Fraud Act 2006 complements and better informs the understanding, investigation and prosecution of food fraud. The chapter contends that provisions for the successful prosecution of food fraud exist. Nevertheless, insofar as the concept of food fraud remains elusive and regulatory enforcement is fragmented, current provisions will fall short to successfully prosecute food fraud offences.

4.2 Food fraud: the limitations of current official conceptualisations

The EU emphasises that despite the absence of a harmonised definition of food fraud, the EU Commission and Member States can take actions against 'fraudulent practices' in the food supply chain.[14] As such, the EU commission has established that '[i]t is broadly accepted that food fraud covers cases where there is a violation of EU food law, which is committed intentionally to pursue an economic or financial gain through consumer deception'[15] (though we might add that other communities can be deceived also e.g. trading partners). At the UK level, the NFCU, established by the FSA in 2014 following the recommendations of the *Elliot Review into the Integrity and Assurance of Food Supply Networks*,[16] differentiates between food fraud and food crime. The NFCU states that whilst food fraud and food crime are usually used interchangeably, the conflation between the terms can affect our understanding of the 'range of threats we face to the safety and authenticity of UK food'.[17] The NFCU has defined food fraud as '[a] dishonest act or omission, relating to the production or supply of food, which is intended for personal gain or to cause loss to another party', whereas food crime has been conceptualised as '[d]ishonesty relating to the production or supply of food, that is either complex or likely to be seriously detrimental to consumers, businesses or the overall public interest'.[18] The Food Law Code of Practice,[19] which comprises statutory guidelines for local authorities, clarifies that food crime is not a legal term. Food crime, it states, is '*serious dishonesty* which has a *detrimental impact* on *the safety or the authenticity* of food, drink and animal feed,' adding that 'food crime can be thought of as serious food fraud'.[20] According to the Food Law Code of Practice, the difference between food crime and food fraud depends on the scale and complexity of acts or omissions, where the commission of food crime would be potentially cross-regional, national or international in nature, as well as representing a 'significant risk to public safety' or a 'substantial financial loss to consumers or businesses'.[21]

The NFCU has certainly taken steps to elucidate the difference between food fraud and food crime. Noticeably, the NFCU's definition of food fraud is more broadly construed on the elements of the offence of fraud as established in the Fraud Act 2006, where dishonesty, and the intention 'to make a gain for himself [sic] or another, or to cause loss to another or to expose another to a risk of loss'[22] are constituent of the offence of fraud, i.e. fraud by false representation,[23] by failing to disclose information[24] and by abuse of position.[25] However, the authorities pursuing investigations on potential food frauds would have to abide by the guidance on the Food Law Code of Practice, where the concept of food fraud remains elusive and the assessment of whether an act or omission is 'serious' enough to constitute a food crime depends on the safety implications and the financial loss that such acts or omissions cause to consumers or businesses. Elsewhere we have argued that the concept of food fraud is too prescriptive and therefore, it limits the scope of motivations and criminals that might be involved in food frauds,[26] an argument that applies *mutatis mutandis* to the concept of food crime. Hence, we have advocated for the conceptualisation of food fraud:

> [A]s relating to the abuse of an otherwise legitimate business transaction and an otherwise legitimate social/economic relationship in the food system in which one or more actors undertakes acts or omissions of deception or dishonesty to avoid legally prescribed procedures (processes) with the intent to gain personal or organisational advantage or cause loss/harm (outcome).[27]

This concept encompasses a diversity of actors and motivations that can be conducive to food frauds, for instance, frauds that are a one-off act to dispose of products resulting from a production error, acts taken on a more consistent basis to keep a business afloat when margins are tight, and acts to ensure social ties are maintained (e.g. with key trading partners) even if such actions represent a financial loss.[28] The limitations to prosecute food fraud may arise from the official concept provided in the Food Law Code of Practice to the extent that the authorities dealing with potential food frauds are unable to identify that food frauds are distinct to food law regulatory breaches, therefore dealing with food fraud as a subset of their safety and hygiene inspection powers. Enforcement authorities, for instance, might not prosecute conduct that under the Fraud Act 2006 would be conducive to an offence of fraud, where the evidence is insufficient to demonstrate the financial gains of the alleged offender or the financial loss caused to another, or where the food fraud is not detrimental to safety.

4.3 Food Law and the Fraud Act 2006: their limitations and complementarity

4.3.1 Dealing with food fraud under a regulatory framework

In the absence of a statutory definition of food fraud, the General Food Law and the Food Safety Act 1990 continue to be the main laws to investigate actions or omissions that could be constitutive of food frauds. The General Food Law, which is the basis for food law and regulation in the EU and its Member States, and the Food Safety Act 1990, were enacted as a response to the BSE crisis in the 1990s.[29] The General Food Law establishes under Article 1(1) and 1(2) respectively that it 'provides a basis for the assurance of a high level of protection of human health and consumers' interests' ... 'lay[ing] down the general principles governing food and feed in general and food and feed safety in particular, at the [European] Community and national level'. The objective to protect human health in the Food Safety Act 1990 is reflected in section 7 comprising the offence to render food 'injurious to health'[30] and section 8 regarding the sale of food without complying with food safety obligations.[31] Furthermore, the protection of consumers is covered under sections 14 and 15 of the Food Safety Act 1990. In this regard, section 14 concerns the sale of food that is not of 'the nature or substance or quality demanded',[32] whilst under section 15, a person commits an offence when (s)he falsely describes food,[33] or misleads as regards 'the nature or substance or quality of the food'.[34]

Arguably, selling food not of the quality or standard requested, falsely presenting food, or misleading as regards the quality or standard of food could be prosecuted as food fraud, if the elements of any of the three ways of committing the offence of fraud are proven – that is, intention, dishonesty and a gain, or causing loss to others or exposing others to risk of loss.[35] However, there seems to be a misconception that food fraud is captured under the General Food Law and the Food Safety Act 1990, particularly under sections 14 and 15 of the Food Safety Act 1990 protecting consumers' interests. Recent convictions for offences such as the substitution of beef for cheaper meats, the substitution for cheaper gins, and counterfeit alcohol were prosecuted under sections 14 and 15 of the Food Safety Act 1990. The penalties imposed for such offences were fines ranging from £2,500 to £10,000.[36] These convictions included Freeza Meats, a business operator involved in the horsemeat scandal, in which falsely describing burgers and selling burgers not of the quality requested was sanctioned with lenient fines.[37] Hence, offences that could be constitutive of food fraud are more likely to be presented as regulatory non-compliance such as not following proper due diligence as opposed to criminal acts.[38]

Indeed, Food Law[39] is ill-equipped to deal with food fraud prosecutions. The Food Safety Act 1990 comprises strict liability offences and was established to deal mainly with safety concerns. This is reflected on the sanctions which range from prohibition orders[40] and emergency control orders[41] for the most serious breaches involving 'risk of injury to health', to fines and imprisonment. Breaches of section 14 of the Food Safety Act 1990, for instance, could be punishable with a fine of maximum £20,000 and/or imprisonment for a maximum time of 2 years (on indictment).[42] Furthermore, Article 19 of the General Food Law imposes an obligation on business operators to recall products when there is reason to believe that such products might have a risk to health or do not comply with food safety requirements. Article 19 has led to diverse interpretations by Member States, for instance, Greece, the Netherlands and Portugal consider this provision to be applicable to respond to frauds such as the horsemeat fraud, whilst Ireland and Italy consider that a safety concern is required for a withdrawal to take place.[43] Van der Meulen argues that safety concerns entrenched on the General Food Law, along with the financial gain attributed to food frauds, does not seem conducive to a proper response to food fraud.[44] Certainly, food laws both at the EU and UK levels provide mechanisms to deal with hazards that are injurious to health and therefore present a safety concern – be they recalls, prohibition orders or emergency controls. However, the law is limited when dealing with food frauds despite the provisions in sections 14 and 15 of the Food Safety Act 1990. In addition to this, both the General Food Law and the Food Safety Act 1990 are foregrounded on the assumption that business operators are, and want to be compliant, an assumption that inhibits an understanding of a variety of motivations behind food frauds, as well as of the normalisation of behaviours in certain industries that lie between blurred lines of compliance and non-compliance.[45] The EU authorities' reliance on business operators to behave responsibly and according to the General Food Law was evidenced in the horsemeat scandal.[46] As the horsemeat scandal showed, business structures and complex supply chains enable the misuse and abuse of otherwise legitimate business structures for the commission of food fraud.[47] More significantly, following the horsemeat scandal, the policy discourse shifted towards a focus on *fraud* committed in food-related contexts but within a regulatory framework that does not provide a legal definition of 'food fraud'. This conflation has prevented an understanding that food frauds are not merely regulatory breaches. Rather, food frauds are food-related offences within the broader criminal offence of fraud, one which entails dishonesty and for which there is a statutory law, ie the Fraud Act 2006.

4.3.2 The Fraud Act 2006: filling a gap in food law

The General Food Law, and specifically the Food Safety Act 1990, provide a specialised regulatory framework for food inspections and/or investigations. However, the Fraud Act 2006 comprises a range of motivations and criminals that would enable the prosecution of, and a more *ad hoc* enforcement to, food fraud offences. The Fraud Act 2006 prescribes three ways of committing fraud: by false representation,[48] by failing to disclose information,[49] and by abuse of position.[50] In order to convict for fraud, three elements would have to be proven alongside the breach to food law, i.e. intention, dishonesty and the objective or purpose 'to make a gain for himself or another, or to cause loss to another or to expose another to a risk of loss'.[51] The Fraud Act 2006 further expounds on the meaning of 'gain' and 'loss' in the context of sections 2 to 4. Both 'gain' and 'loss' are related to money or other property (inclusive of real estate or personal property either tangible or intangible) that can be either temporal or permanent.[52] By 'gain' the Fraud Act 2006 comprises both keeping what one has and getting money or property that one does not have. Likewise, a 'loss' refers to 'not getting what one would get or by parting with what one has'.[53] In this regard, food fraud would not only entail a direct financial gain but might also include other indirect tangible benefits, such as generating future business contracts or connections, or less tangible benefits such as establishing or maintaining social ties. Previously, it was noticed that the NFCU's definitions for food fraud and food crime are more akin to the elements of fraud but are not legal statutory definitions. The Fraud Act 2006 would include, for example, acts or omissions in which a business operator commits a one-off fraud, even if this represents a loss for the company in order to maintain a contract with a supplier. The Fraud Act 2006 also comprises offences related to having possession or control of any article for use or in connection to the fraud,[54] or adapting, making or supplying articles used in the fraud.[55] Hence, individuals facilitating the commission of a fraud by adapting machinery or supplying foodstuffs (e.g. for diluting or mixing liquid foodstuffs) could also be prosecuted under the Fraud Act 2006. Moreover, the potential sanctions for a conviction of fraud range from 12 months imprisonment for a summary conviction and/or a fine, to a prison term of maximum 10 years and/or a fine. Convictions under the Fraud Act 2006 would enable the imposition of more stringent penalties that could act as a deterrent (general and specific) for the commission of food fraud, but only if potential or actual offenders perceive a high proportion of frauds are detected, or consider the likelihood of being caught to be high. However, the investigation, and potential prosecution, of food fraud under the Fraud Act 2006 would raise questions about the even-handedness of differentiating between offences that are categorised as regulatory breaches and those which constitute criminal acts, a distinction that could affect smaller businesses as opposed to big corporations.[56] Arguably, increasing training and resources could counter the problems of differential treatment as authorities would be better equipped to identify, and gather the necessary evidence, on food frauds. However, overcoming differential treatment is not straightforward when local authorities rely on businesses' private certification and auditing schemes,[57] and big corporations can get into partnerships with local authorities for advice through the Primary Authority System that protects businesses from enforcement actions from other authorities insofar as they follow the advice from their primary authority.[58] Thus, enforcement is not only a product of investigatory capacity and expertise, but can also be shaped by underlying political interests. However, in principle, the Fraud Act 2006 would generally complement the lack of a statutory provision for food fraud under current law and regulation.

Indeed, the Food Law Code of Practice establishes that food crime would normally be prosecuted under the Fraud Act 2006, or as conspiracy to defraud under the common law, except for rare situations in which food crime would be prosecuted under food regulation or other appropriate legislation.[59] Thus, in order to prosecute for food fraud, the authorities would have to assess whether 1) the acts or omissions are constitutive of food fraud, although there is no clear definition in the guidelines; 2) the food fraud is serious enough to be prosecuted as a food crime; and, 3) the Fraud Act 2006 is the relevant statutory law to prosecute an alleged food crime. The prosecution of food frauds, as one offence within the broader scope of food crimes, would depend on the determination of seriousness. The guidelines establish that the subjective test for seriousness is one where the detriment to the general public, a food business or the UK food industry should be taken into account, as well as the geographic scope, scale, political sensitivities and media coverage.[60] According to the NFCU, the determination of seriousness does not necessarily entail a high threshold in order to prosecute food crime. However, in practice there seems to be a gap as the number of prosecutions remain minimum despite concerns in the increase in food frauds.[61] Indeed, the decision to prosecute Andronicos Sideras, Ulrich Nielsen and Alex Ostler-Beech for food fraud offences related to the horsemeat scandal for conspiracy to defraud under the common law,[62] raises questions of whether, and if so why, the Fraud Act 2006 was not deemed appropriate for such prosecutions. The Attorney General's Guidelines to the Legal Profession establishes that those prosecuting ought to justify why statutory offences are inappropriate for the successful prosecution of a case, for instance when due to the diversity of offences and/or conspiracies, one single count could better reflect the nature of the criminal conduct.[63] The use of the common law offence of conspiracy to defraud would include, for example, offences where evidence for diverse types of criminality is needed, as well as those involving a number of jurisdictions, various types of victims or involving organised crime networks.[64]

However, decisions to prosecute under the common law as opposed to the Fraud Act 2006 might be more related to an assessment of the rates of success under the latter, instead of the inadequacy of the former. So, even though guidelines exist as regard the prosecution of food crimes, there are a diversity of factors that may prevent a prosecution for food fraud under the Fraud Act 2006. Limitations arise not only from squeezing a criminal offence into a regulatory framework, but also from the concept itself and the subjectivity of the guidelines, which remain elusive as regards those frauds that are not serious enough to be prosecuted as food crimes. These limitations inhibit the ability of the authorities to identify, investigate and potentially pursue a prosecution for fraud. The creation of the NFCU might fill-in this gap providing intelligence and guidance when possible. However, as the NFCU has described, food crimes tend to be complex. Thus, enforcement authorities might not recognise a food fraud as part of their statutory obligations, for which they have been given powers (e.g. entry or search) that are designed for strict liability offences. For local authorities, we might infer that the Food Safety Act 1990, specifically sections 14 and 15, suffices to pursue potential fraud investigations. Moreover, authorities have to decide whether to investigate a food fraud, or not, based on a diversity of reasons ranging from the limited resources they have to the lack of expertise in food fraud investigations.

4.3.3 Food fraud prosecutions: complexity and fragmentation

In the UK, food law and regulatory enforcement are complex and fragmented. The FSA focuses exclusively on safety in England, Wales and Northern Ireland

and the Department for Environment, Food and Rural Affairs ('DEFRA') is responsible for food composition and authenticity. However, DEFRA has delegated enforcement to the FSA, which in turn has delegated this to local authorities. The horsemeat scandal evidenced the fragmentation of regulatory enforcement, in which the need for coordination amongst diverse authorities, in addition to the inexperience of some authorities to deal with fraud investigations, was highlighted in the Elliot Review.[65] However, the NFCU, which was created to oversee food crime in the UK, lacks credible authority for the enforcement of laws and regulation. The NFCU depends on local authorities and police forces to conduct food fraud and food crime investigations. The convictions of Andronicos Sideras, Ulrich Nielsen and Alex Ostler-Beech for the conspiracy to defraud related to the horsemeat scandal are but one example. The FSA passed their investigating responsibility to the police force, City of London, when it 'became apparent the evidence was suggesting potential fraudulent criminal activity beyond that which the FSA or local authorities would be in a position to pursue'.[66] However, the investigation was funded by the FSA, costing more than £400,000 pounds.[67] The success of food fraud prosecutions therefore depends on capacity both in terms of resources and expertise from the local authorities and police forces to investigate food frauds. There may also be an element of cultural preferences within policing authorities as 'cops' are unlikely to view food fraud, particularly where it is complex and time-consuming to investigate, as being 'real' policing or a local priority. In any case, the stringent cuts faced by local authorities and police forces inform the decisions on whether to pursue an investigation on food fraud or food crime, which is only one of their priorities, one that has a 'relative low status' for police forces.[68]

The NFCU reliance on local authorities and the police to conduct investigations leaves a gap in regulatory enforcement, at a time when local authorities have limited resources to comply with their statutory obligations to inspect registered food establishments. The Annual Report on UK Local Authority Food Law Enforcement acknowledges, for example, that increasingly food standards authorities follow an intelligence-led approach to the inspection of low risk category establishments, in addition to reporting that 21 per cent of local authorities had more than 20 per cent of their registered establishments waiting for their first inspection.[69] Hence, the prospect of local authorities engaging in fraud investigations in addition to their statutory obligations seems limited. Furthermore, the powers granted to the authorities have been designed to investigate strict liability offences, limiting their capacity to gather the sufficient evidence of guilty knowledge to prosecute for fraud under the Fraud Act 2006.[70] In any case, the hierarchy of enforcement established in the FSA's prosecution policy limits the number of cases brought to court, only pursuing those that have a realistic prospect of conviction, and are in the 'public interest'.[71] One would assume that it would be in the public interest to prosecute food fraud as a means of increasing the consumers' trust both in the regulator and the food system. However, full enforcement of the law has long been recognised as idealistic, particularly given extensive police discretion,[72] in addition to the restrictions of limited resources leading to decisions only to prosecute the 'worst offenders' and instead pursue modes of governance at a distance, as we see in the regulation of large and complex markets such as financial services.[73] Hence, greater transparency in these underlying decision-making processes is necessary to justify such strategies.

The absence of investigative capacity of the NFCU has led to the underuse of valuable intelligence, in which intelligence packages developed by the NFCU have not been taken forward by the police.[74] In this regard, the reduced number of prosecutions for food fraud, and the restraint to pursue food fraud prosecutions, particularly under the Fraud Act 2006, seems to be related not only to the limitations arising from Food Law itself, but also from the dependence of the NFCU on the police and local authorities, even when the FSA is the one generally funding food fraud investigations and the NFCU provides intelligence and guidance. In these terms, there is an internal incompatibility in the NFCU's base within the FSA, as the former seeks to foreground the fraudulent, criminal nature of dishonesty within the food system, while the latter seeks to regulate violations of administrative offences. In any case, there are blurred lines between food-related offences, food frauds and food crimes, making their separation artificial. However, a recent review of the NFCU recommended that it operates as an Arm's Length Body of the FSA in order to facilitate the engagement of the food industry and other stakeholders in the sector, as well as to transfer knowledge and experience in food crime into the FSA's thinking on food policy and regulatory enforcement.[75] So, food fraud and food crime, whist being a subset of a broader offence of fraud, cannot be disconnected from their food roots as their prevention and enforcement relies on their complementarity.

4.4 Final remarks

In this chapter we argue that the Fraud Act 2006 can supplement current food law by filling-in the gaps produced by the absence of a statutory definition of food fraud, the incorporation of the criminal offence of food-related fraud within a regulatory framework, and the safety focus within the General Food Law and the Food Safety Act 1990. In this regard, the Fraud Act 2006 complements and better informs the understanding, investigation and prosecution of food fraud. Nevertheless, the chapter has identified a number of difficulties for the prosecution of food frauds that are not restricted to the limitations deriving from current food law. Firstly, there is a need to revise the conceptualisation of food fraud in order to encompass a variety of motivations and criminals that are excluded from official concepts that continue to emphasise safety concerns and financial gains or losses. Despite differentiating between food fraud and food crime, official conceptualisations, and interpretations thereof, still prescribe characteristics that do not facilitate the adequate investigation and prosecution of food frauds. Secondly, the assumption that business operators act responsibly, and are willing to act in accordance to the law, whilst valid, underestimates that legitimate business structures, complex supply chains and dysfunctional markets provide ready-made structures for the commission of food fraud.[76] Thirdly, the complexity and fragmentation of current food law, and particularly of regulatory enforcement, inhibit the adequate investigation and prosecution of food frauds. Since its inception, the NFCU has provided intelligence and guidance to local authorities as regard food fraud and food crime. However, the NFCU's dependence on local authorities and the police forces to take forward food fraud investigations puts to rest otherwise valuable intelligence. The NFCU's lack of investigative capacity as opposed to the Scottish Food Crime and Incidents Unit and other food agencies in the EU which do have them, places the NFCU at a disadvantage to pursue food fraud.

The number of food fraud and/or adulteration incidents reported from April 2016 to March 2017 is considerable.[77] During this period there were 91 cases related to adulteration and/or fraud.[78] The number of cases is restricted due to the narrow definition used by the NFCU by which incidents are not accounted as adulteration or fraud if there is limited evidence of the intention to deceive. So far, prosecution data for the same period is unavailable to determine the percentage of incidents that were successfully prosecuted for food fraud. However, numbers would most likely remain negligible. The problems in the prosecution of food fraud go beyond the existence of current regulatory offences under the General Food Law and the Food Safety Act 1990 (e.g. traceability) and the broader offence of fraud under the Fraud Act 2006. We contend that the provisions for the successful prosecution of food fraud exist. Despite their limitations and potential improvements, the General Food Law, the Food Safety Act 1990 and the Fraud Act 2006 complement each other. Nevertheless, insofar as steps are not taken to provide a clear and broader conceptualisation of food fraud, one which encompasses a variety of motivations and criminals, and regulatory enforcement remains fragmented, current provisions will most likely fall short for the successful prosecution of food fraud offences. Overall, a strategy to enforce food fraud will require a better understanding of the motivations behind, and the constitutive elements of, food fraud so that authorities are capable to identify, investigate and gather sufficient evidence to prosecute for food fraud. Only then, will sentences reflect the severity of the crimes.

Notes

1 Centre for Criminology and Criminal Justice, Williamson Building, University of Manchester, Oxford Road, Manchester, M13 9PL. Email: cecilia.floreselizondo @manchester.ac.uk.
2 Centre for Criminology and Criminal Justice, Williamson Building, University of Manchester, Oxford Road, Manchester, M13 9PL. Email: nicholas.lord@manchester. ac.uk Tel: 0161 275 5466.

3 Centre for Criminology and Criminal Justice, Williamson Building, University of Manchester, Oxford Road, Manchester, M13 9PL. Email: jonathan.w.spencer@manchester.ac.uk.

4 Food Law Code of Practice (England), 2017.

5 P Shears. 'Food Fraud – A Current Issue but an Old Problem' (2010) 112(2) *British Food Journal* 198–213.

6 Hereinafter General Food Law.

7 http://blog.cps.gov.uk/2015/03/peter-boddy-and-david-moss-sentenced-in-first-prosecution-related-to-the-horsemeat-scandal-of-januar.html, accessed 5 March 2018.

8 www.food.gov.uk/news-updates/news/2017/16397/two-men-jailed-over-horsemeat-fraud, accessed 5 March 2018.

9 FSA, Local Authority and Food Standards Agency Food Law Prosecution Outcomes 2015–2016. Available at https://data.food.gov.uk/catalog/datasets/b2166e02-d36e-4050–8d91–20b9f3c3e590, accessed 3 April 2018.

10 R Ainsworth. *Review of the National Food Crime Unit.* Food Standards Agency (2016).

11 Fraud Act 2006, s 5.

12 ibid s 6.

13 ibid s 7.

14 https://ec.europa.eu/food/safety/food-fraud_en, accessed 5 March 2018.

15 ibid.

16 Elliot Review into the Integrity and Assurance of Food Supply Networks – Final Report, A National Food Crime Prevention Strategy, July 2014.

17 www.food.gov.uk/enforcement/the-national-food-crime-unit/what-is-food-crime-and-food-fraud, accessed 5 March 2018.

18 ibid.

19 Food Law Code of Practice (n 4).

20 ibid (emphasis added).

21 ibid.

22 Fraud Act 2006 ss 2(1)(b)(i) and (ii); 3(b)(i) and (ii); and, 4(1)(c)(i) and (ii).

23 ibid s 2.

24 ibid s 3.

25 ibid s 4.

26 N Lord, CJ Flores Elizondo, & J Spencer. 'The Dynamics of Food Fraud: the interactions between criminal opportunity and market (dys)functionality in legitimate business' (2017) 17(5), *Criminology and Criminal Justice* 605–623.

27 ibid.

28 ibid.

29 For the history of Food Law, see C MacMaoláin . *Food Law European, Domestic and International Frameworks* (Hart Publishing 2015); J Phillips & M French. 'Adulteration and Food Law, 1899–1939' (1998) 9(3),*Twentieth Century British History* 350–369.

30 Food Safety Act 1990 s 7 (1) (a) adding any article or substance to food; s 7 (1) (b) using any article or substance as ingredients in the preparation of food; s 7 (1) (c) abstracting any constituent from food; and, s 7 (1) (d) subjecting the food to any other process or treatment.

31 ibid s 8(2) food which is unsafe within the meaning of Article 14 of Regulation (EC) No 178/2002.

32 ibid s 14 (1).

33 ibid s 15 (1) (a) and s 15 (2) (a).

34 ibid s 15 (1) (b) and s 15 (2) (b).

35 Fraud Act 2006 s 2 (fraud by false representation); s 3 (fraud by failing to disclose information); and, s 5 (fraud by abuse of position) .

36 FSA, Local Authority and Food Standards Agency Food Law Prosecution Outcomes 2015–2016 (n 9). Latest data is currently unavailable.

37 ibid. See: www.bbc.co.uk/news/uk-northern-ireland-33317601, accessed 3 April 2018.
38 N Lord, CJ Flores Elizondo, & J Spencer, 'The Dynamics of Food Fraud: the interactions between criminal opportunity and market (dys)functionality in legitimate business' (n 26) 611–612.
39 In this context, food law is an overarching term referring to both EU and domestic legislation regarding safety and standards, i.e. the General Food Law and the Food Safety Act 1990.
40 Food Safety Act 1990 s 11.
41 ibid s 13.
42 ibid s 35.
43 B van der Meulen, 'Is Current EU food safety law geared up for fighting food fraud?' (2015) 10 *Journal of Consumer Protection and Food Safety* 19–23.
44 ibid. For van der Meulen, food fraud should be dealt with financially.
45 N Lord, CJ Flores Elizondo, & J Spencer. 'The Dynamics of Food Fraud: the interactions between criminal opportunity and market (dys)functionality in legitimate business' (n 26) 605–623.
46 For a thorough description of the horsemeat fraud, see: C Barnard& N O'Connor. 'Runners and Riders: The Horsemeat Scandal, EU Law and Multi-Level Enforcement' (2017) 76(1) *Cambridge Law Journal* 116–144.
47 N Lord, CJ Flores Elizondo, & J Spencer. 'The Dynamics of Food Fraud: the interactions between criminal opportunity and market (dys)functionality in legitimate business' (n 26) 605–623.
48 Fraud Act 2006 s 1(2)(a).
49 ibid s 1(2)(b).
50 ibid s 1(2)(c).
51 ibid ss 2, 3 and 4. It is worth nothing that the Fraud Act 2006 is gender specific in relation to the commission of fraud.
52 ibid s 5.
53 ibid.
54 ibid s 6.
55 ibid s 7.
56 N Lord, CJ Flores Elizondo, & J Spencer. 'The Dynamics of Food Fraud: the interactions between criminal opportunity and market (dys)functionality in legitimate business'(n 26) 611–612.
57 www.food.gov.uk/sites/default/files/rof-paper-july2017.pdf, accessed 3 April 2018.
58 www.gov.uk/guidance/primary-authority-a-guide-for-businesses#primary-authority-advice, accessed 3 April 2018.
59 Food Law Code of Practice (n 4).
60 ibid.
61 See: ibid; NFCU, Food Crime Annual Strategic Assessment 2016.
62 www.theguardian.com/uk-news/2017/jul/31/two-men-jailed-in-uk-for-horsemeat-conspiracy, accessed 3 April 2018.
63 (29 November 2012) www.gov.uk/guidance/use-of-the-common-law-offence-of-conspiracy-to-defraud—6, accessed 5 March 2018.
64 ibid.
65 C Elliot. Elliot Review into the Integrity and Assurance of Food Supply Networks – Final Report (16).
66 www.food.gov.uk/news-updates/news/2017/16393/businessman-guilty-horsemeat-trial, accessed 5 March 2018.
67 R Ainsworth. Review of the National Food Crime Unit (n 10).
68 NFCU, Food Crime Annual Strategic Assessment 2016 (n 61).
 9 2017.

70 Food Safety Act 1990 s 32. For example, powers of entry to uphold provisions related to ensuring compliance with food standards, as well as powers of inspection, search and seizure when applicable.
71 https://www.food.gov.uk/about-us/data-and-policies/fsa-prosecution-policy, accessed 5 March 2018.
72 See: J Goldstein. 'Police Discretion Not to Invoke the Criminal Process: Low-Visibility Decisions in the Administration of Justice' (1960) *The Yale Law Journal* 69(4): 543–594.
73 A Jordanoska. 'The Dark Side of Finance: Policing Corruption through Regulatory Means'. in L Campbell and N Lord (eds.) *Corruption in Commercial Enterprise: Law, Theory and Practice*, Routledge (2018).
74 R Ainsworth. Review of the National Food Crime Unit (n 10).
75 ibid.
76 N Lord, CJ Flores Elizondo, & J Spencer. 'The Dynamics of Food Fraud: the interactions between criminal opportunity and market (dys)functionality in legitimate business' (n 26) 605–623; N Lord, J Spencer, J Albanese, & CJ Flores Elizondo. 'In pursuit of food system integrity: the situational prevention of food fraud enterprise' (2017) *European Journal on Criminal Policy and Research* pp?483–501.
77 FSA, Annual Report of Food Incidents 2017.
78 ibid.

Bibliography

Ainsworth R, *Review of the National Food Crime Unit*. Food Standards Agency (2016)
Attorney General's Guidelines to the Legal Profession (29 November 2012)
Barnard C & O'Connor N, 'Runners and Riders: The Horsemeat Scandal, EU Law and Multi-Level Enforcement' (2017) 76(1) *Cambridge Law Journal* 116–144
Elliot C, *Elliot Review into the Integrity and Assurance of Food Supply Networks – Final Report* (July 2014)
Food Law Code of Practice (England). (2017, March)
Food Safety Act 1990 (as amended)
Fraud Act 2006
FSA. *Local Authority & Food Standards Agency Food Law Prosecution Outcomes 2015–2016*
FSA. *Annual Report of Food Incidents 2017*
FSA. *Annual Report on UK Local Authority Food Law Enforcement* (2017)
General Food Law Regulation (EC) 178/2002
Goldstein J, 'Police Discretion Not to Invoke the Criminal Process: Low-Visibility Decisions in the Administration of Justice' (1960) 69 (4) *The Yale Law Journal* 543–594
Jordanoska A, 'The Dark Side of Finance: Policing Corruption through Regulatory Means' in Campbell L and Lord N (eds.) *Corruption in Commercial Enterprise: Law, Theory and Practice* (Routledge: 2018)
Lord N, Flores Elizondo CJ & Spencer J, 'The Dynamics of Food Fraud: the interactions between criminal opportunity and market (dys)functionality in legitimate business' (2017) 17 (5) *Criminology and Criminal Justice* 605–623
Lord N, Spencer J, Albanese J & Flores Elizondo CJ, 'In pursuit of food system integrity: the situational prevention of food fraud enterprise' (2017) 23 (4) *European Journal on Criminal Policy and Research* 483–501
MacMaoláin C, *Food Law European, Domestic and International Frameworks* (Hart Publishing 2015)
NFCU. *Food Crime Annual Strategic Assessment 2016*

Phillips J & French M, 'Adulteration and Food Law, 1899 -1939' (1998) 9(3), *Twentieth Century British History* 350–369

Shears P, 'Food Fraud – A Current Issue but an Old Problem' (2010) 112(2) *British Food Journal* 198–213

van der Meulen B, 'Is Current EU food safety law geared up for fighting food fraud?' (2015) 10 *Journal of Consumer Protection and Food Safety* 19–23

5 Fraud in the twenty-first century

Is the criminal law fit for purpose?

Caroline Collins[1] and Noel McGuirk[2]

5.1 Introduction

The freedom of the internet on a global scale allows criminals to access and create opportunities for crime and criminality. The primary aim of the discussion in this chapter is to analyse whether the UK counter-fraud framework of laws can be considered adequate in managing instances of online fraud. This will be done by analysing online fraud and the functioning of the UK's criminal law framework, and contrasting it with that in other jurisdictions including Canada, Australia and New Zealand.

It has been argued by some academics, such as Garland,[3] that a key trend in some jurisdictions, such as the UK and the US, is for successive Parliaments to utilise the criminal law as a political tool of social control to manage the occurrence of criminality. As a result, when new manifestations of crime emerge in society, one approach is to look towards Parliament as the basis to provide solutions capable of managing these new instances of criminality by adopting policies capable of preventing, detecting and punishing offenders.

The discussion in this chapter explores that while the UK Parliament has developed and enacted a raft of laws specifically aimed at addressing fraudulent activities, such as the Fraud Act 2006, the Theft Act 1968 and the Theft Act 1978, there is a particular weakness in the operation of the law in relation to online fraudulent offending. It is contended that this weakness is symptomatic of a broader problem in other jurisdictions where there is significant chatter about the need to develop the criminal law to allow for the criminalisation of fraudulent activities perpetrated in online environments. However, the concern in official circles has not resulted in the development and adoption of law capable of stemming the problem of fraud perpetrated in online environments. Specifically, the law remains out of step with those engaging in online fraud by failing to prevent, detect and deter those from engaging in fraudulent activities.

Over the course of the last few decades there have been considerable developments in digital technologies, which have transformed society. This transformation relates to the creation of seamless and instantaneous communication between individuals regardless of their physical location. It is now possible for individuals to conduct their private and public life through the use of digital technologies. For example, individuals can purchase goods and services, utilise electronic banking, social media communication, dating etc. In the business world, new opportunities more commonly known as e-commerce have arisen from the emergence of the digital era.

The economic implication of the emergence of the digital era is significant as in 2016 the e-commerce industry was worth £511 billion to the UK economy. This meant that the UK was the third largest e-commerce market in the world, behind China and the United States ('US').[4] In 2015–16, Cao *et al* estimated that around 51 per cent of all these sales was conducted on mobile computing devices, which demonstrates the high degree of connectivity between individuals in the digital era.[5]

A consequence of the emergence of the e-commerce industry is that private companies can collect, store and analyse personal information gleaned through individual private usage of online environments. For example, internet tracking software allows companies to collect and analyse immense collections of personal information, from internet searches and shopping patterns to highly sensitive personal information found within online social networking accounts such as Facebook, Google and Twitter. Recently, media reports indicate that around 50 million Facebook profiles were allegedly harvested for personal data by Cambridge Analytica in 2016.[6] Similarly, Curran's research has revealed the extent to which companies like Facebook and Google collect, store and analyse data about their customer's internet activities to make certain predictions about their customer's preferences.[7] In effect, the dawn of the digital era has resulted in personal information becoming a kind of currency where companies seek out this information as the basis to market opportunities to end customers.

The availability of this individual personal information through these new developments can be commercially significant. It allows companies to target sales, promote products and services to end consumers. As a result, this personal information can be considered of significant commercial value to be collected, sold and analysed by companies as the basis to develop their sales. A corollary of this shift from the physical to the virtual world has been the creation of new opportunities that criminals can exploit.[8] Specifically, this development creates new opportunity for crime and criminality by offenders developing a virtual 'on-line' presence to tap into this growing vast economic and social activity to identify, target and connect with victims without having to physically connect with them.[9]

5.2 The definition of fraud: the problem of a retrospective focus

In order to begin evaluating the approach taken in criminal law towards managing fraud perpetrated in online environments, it is necessary to begin by considering the definition of fraud in the current statutory framework. It is contended that part of the problem with the current definition found in the Fraud Act 2006 is attributable to the law adopting a retrospective focus in defining what constitutes fraud. Specifically, the definition of fraud is premised upon the weaknesses of the older formulations of deception-based offences. As a consequence, this approach is arguably out of step with the way criminals can currently use the internet to commit crimes not entirely covered by the statutory framework.

Fraud is a common word used extensively in colloquial and formal settings. In the context of the UK, the Fraud Act 2006 now defines fraud as a statutory offence by which a person is guilty of fraud if he or she has committed any of the following: (i) knowingly makes a false representation; (ii) fails to properly disclose information where required; and (iii) misuses a position of trust for personal benefit or causing losses to another party.[10] However, it is important to recognise that as a result of the many ways fraud can be perpetrated by defendants, there is a degree of overlap between the offences in the Fraud Act 2006 and other statutory offences. Specifically, some frauds may also be considered theft under section 1(1) of the Theft Act 1968, or making off without payment contrary to section 3(1) of the Theft Act 1978. Equally, there are other offences of misusing computer technology such as the Computer Misuse Act 1990, which contains a range of offences. Further, there are international laws that aim to manage the prevalence of fraud in online environments such as the Council of Europe Cybercrime Convention, seeking to align the work of police intelligence, and enforcement against offenders who use computers to engage in criminal acts.

However, the discussion in this chapter contends, that if the UK domestic statutory framework is to manage modern manifestations of fraud by identifying, preventing and prosecuting fraudulent acts, the construction of the offence needs a clear legal basis. Presently this is scattered across numerous statutes not designed to manage this type of offending.

Prior to the enactment of the Fraud Act 2006, the Theft Acts of 1968 and 1978 contained the predecessor to the offence of fraud, premised on deception offences. It is important to briefly consider these offences, as the current definition of fraud is attributable in part to the weaknesses inherent in the way that these statutes defined offences. These offences offered several ways in which a defendant could deceive a victim, and from that deception, commit an offence. There were three offences of note. The first, under the Theft Act of 1968, section 15, obtaining property by deception. The second, obtaining of a money transfer by deception, under section 15A. Finally, under the Theft Act 1978, section 1, obtaining services by deception. Although these deception-based offences had a variety of elements, two of the core elements across the offences created a particular weakness in dealing with this type offending. Firstly, the law required that the prosecution proved the existence of a causal link between the 'deception' and the 'obtaining'. Secondly, there had to be reliance by the victim due to the defendant's act, or deception.

A plethora of cases failed to secure convictions on these precise points, illustrating a historic mismatch between the statutory framework and its ability to manage offending in practice. Deception had to occur prior to obtaining, and be intrinsically linked to the obtaining. These requirements produced surprising results and some robust judicial interpretation of legal rules. In *R v Rashid*,[11] a steward on British Rail trains planned to sell his own sandwiches by passing them off as British Rail sandwiches. He was caught with supplies to make the sandwiches prior to boarding the train. Lord Bridge suggested that even if he had boarded the train and started to sell the sandwiches, it would not have been sufficient conduct to come within the requirements of a deception. In *DPP v Ray*[12] the defendant had ordered a meal with the expectation that his companion would pay for his meal. However, when it transpired that his companion was not willing to pay for for his meal, the defendant absconded so as to avoid payment. In this particular case, there was considerable disagreement amongst the judges as to the point at which the defendant had deceived the waiter about his capacity to pay the bill. It was either at the point of ordering the meal or at the point at which the defendant led the waiter to believe he was still going to pay after his companion left. Lord Reid in the minority suggested that dishonestly intention to avoid the payment was insufficient to equate a deception. There was a requirement for the defendant to have done something to effectively induce the waiter into the belief he was still going to pay after the point at which his companion left. However, the majority suggested that the defendant's conduct at the outset was sufficient to equate to a deception.

The overlap between theft and deception meant that some cases were sometimes charged incorrectly, blurring the lines for successful conviction. Examples include *Davies v Flackett*[13] where the defendant could not be convicted, as 'deception' could not be proven when a 'machine' was deceived. Similarly, in *R v Roziek*[14] the defendant was not convicted as the deception was against a company.

These cases illustrate the complex nature of the statutory framework. It ultimately failed to deal with different means adopted. The dawn of the internet age exposed the pressing need for reform. Computers became the new means by which defendants could commit fraud. Defendants and victims needed no physical contact. Therefore, one of the core strands that underpinned the development and enactment of the Fraud Act 2006 was to create broad offences to future proof the law and deal with new and emerging offending.[15] It is now pertinent to consider whether the Fraud Act 2006 has managed to deal with fraud conducted in online environments as a prevailing pressing social concern.

5.3 Modern manifestations of fraud in online environments: cybercrime in the digital age

In recent years, the term cybercrime has become associated with the use of modern emerging technologies to commit criminal acts, which principally involves the use of the internet.[16] It has also become acceptable to label other forms of digital crime and criminality including the use of 'networked technology as "cybercrime"'.[17] However, the ability of criminals to carry out 'hi-tech' crime is nothing new in the current information age. These forms of crime have long been the subject of investigation of police authorities across the globe.[18] The impact of the internet has been the ability of criminals to create 'virtual' profiles to engage in offences with greater anonymity with the capacity to reach into our private lives without us even knowing about it.

As a result, cybercrime has become a major concern for governments. The fast pace of the evolution and development of technology tends to outstrip the capacity of the criminal law to deal with criminal offending.[19] Gordon and Ford classify cybercrime in three ways including violent or potentially violent, non-violent and white collar.[20] The perpetration of fraud in online environments tends to be primarily non-violent as the victim often never comes into physical contact with the perpetrator of the crime as the internet is the conduit through which the criminal conducts their criminality. In essence, the internet provides the criminal with a high degree of anonymity where the victim will very unlikely ever find out even the location of the offender.

It has long been noted that the occurrence of cybercrime in the UK is on the rise with some academics such as Garlik estimating at least 3.6 million fraudulent acts being perpetrated online every year.[21] It is argued by Graboksy *et al* that 'a fundamental principle of criminology is that crime follows opportunity'.[22] As the internet has grown so too has the opportunity for individuals to engage in crime and criminality. Bryant argues that the internet and networked technologies allow criminal to engage in 'simplified, cost effective and repeatable means' to engage in large scale crime and criminality.[23] Fletcher argues that the internet provides the criminal with the ability to approach unsuspecting victims with the anonymity that decreases the risk of getting caught but also escalates the legitimacy of the criminal in the eye of the victim.[24] With an increasing proportion of young people going on-line and creating virtual profiles through social networking sites such as Facebook and Twitter the opportunity for cybercriminals to engage in criminality has broadened over the past decade. Increasingly, social networking sites will allow users to upload vast arrays of personal information including an individual's personal status, personal information, information about their friends, their pictures and videos, sensitive information about their family which allows a broad picture to be gleaned about individual social networkers from their virtual profile.

The common cybercrimes include 'fraud, identity theft and the theft of intellectual property rights'.[25] The techniques used by cybercriminals to engage in these types of crimes range from spamming emails to the use of digital viruses to the hacking of personal databases and social networks. The internet has facilitated the ability to engage in a vast array of new crimes from identity theft to impersonation. The perpetration of fraud in online environments is now manifested in a very broad range of activities that have increasing levels of sophistication. For example, criminals may impersonate legitimate business actors in an attempt to make a personal gain from their targeted victim. For example, criminals may seek to target victims by masquerading as their bank, seeking the victim to confirm their identity as the basis to gain sufficient personal information about their target victim to make financial gains. This manifestation of fraud is common where the criminal may gain sufficient information about the victim, so that they know their location, employment status, banking provider, and contact details. They may even find some information about their recent movements, depending on the level of personal information shared by that individual in online forums. Information may be freely gleaned from social media such as Google, Facebook or Twitter profiles, harvested by a preying criminal seeking an opportunity to open a line of communication. They may ask the target to confirm further personal information as an attempt to stop some alleged suspicious activity in their accounts. However, the criminal is simply seeking sufficient further information to make fraudulent financial gains by perhaps accessing their bank accounts or their debit or credit cards.

Other less sophisticated levels of fraud include the placement of covert equipment on automated banking machines, which simply scans a bank card when a legitimate customer uses the machine to withdraw money. The result is that the legitimate customer has given their details to the criminal by merely inserting their card into the machine.

In light of this discussion, it is contended that the digital era has given criminals new opportunities to engage in acts tantamount to fraud but are not technically capable of being prosecuted under the current Fraud Act 2006 as the perpetrators of these crimes are often located outside of the jurisdiction or their identify is anonymous. It is now appropriate to progress to examine the management of fraud in other jurisdictions as the basis to question how, if at all, fraud perpetrated online may be managed by the criminal law.

5.4 Other jurisdictional approaches to fraud

The discussion in this section examines the counter-fraud framework in Canada, Australia and New Zealand as a basis of comparison to the UK's approach in dealing with fraud perpetrated in online environments. The primary exploratory argument in this section is that a theme emerges from other common law jurisdictions. A range of laws exist that simply fails to coherently define fraud as a basis to capture modern manifestations of fraud perpetrated in online environments.

5.4.1 The Canadian model

The Canadian Criminal Code contains the offence of fraud by referral to the Revised Statutes of Canada, in Criminal Code 380(1) (R.S.C., 1985, c.C-46).[26] The Canadian Criminal Code sets out a widely framed, quasi-inchoate offence of fraud by various means. As is the case under the Fraud Act 2006, no actual gain or receiving of a service(s) is required. In its penalties, the Canadian Code has apparent linkage between subject matter and the monetary value of a fraud. A minimum imprisonment term may be imposed in certain conditions, section 380 (1.1). This may indicate the statutory framework is tilted towards preservation of the economy, as opposed to protection of the vulnerable. In 2004, maximum penalties were increased, and section 380.1 added, to include aggravating circumstances. In 2011, section 380 (1.1) was added to allow the imposition of a stricter minimum sentence as indicated above, and section 380.1 amended to include additional aggravating factors. This may suggest a positive acknowledgement to an ever-increasing problem in offending, and the government's reaction to it. However, it is debatable whether increasing the length of sentences and adding additional aggravating factors will provide a basis to deter those thinking about committing fraud in online environments.

The Competition Bureau ('CB') was formed, to work alongside other bodies, such as the Canadian Anti-Fraud Centre ('CAFC') and the Royal Canadian Mounted Police. The CB was designed to educate Canadians, helping them spot the signs of fraud, and advising on protection from it. Canada's CB model has been adopted in some form, in twenty-nine other countries including the US and Australia. The system itself and the way information is imparted to citizens seems globally popular, but how affective that model really is, remains questionable.

The CB offers considerable advice and encourages the reporting of fraud. However, it is important to note that estimated statistics show that between January 2014 and December 2016, Canadians lost more than $290 million to fraud. In addition, the agencies responsible for fraud detection and prevention seemingly are not meeting targets, and only approximately 5 per cent of offences are reported. This raises a number of key questions: (i) whether this is a result of a lack of faith in these bodies; (ii) whether the public are simply not responding and not reporting offences; (iii) whether the amount of information available is so vast that it leaves victims and readers feeling overwhelmed, thus 'giving up' and not following advice; and (iv) how effective in reality are these bodies.

Cross and Kelly[27] observe the impact of online fraud in particular in Canada, Australia and the United Kingdom. Their discussion on victim impact makes powerful reading, as it is clear that fraud results in both physical and psychological consequences. The particular challenges faced in detecting, investigating and making arrests for online fraud and contrasting with traditional offending are noted. They observe a characterisation of, or versions of, 'The Little Black Book of Scams' used widely across the jurisdictions, as 'white noise'[28] Cross and Kelly assert this because of the levels of complex 'information overload' contained in it.[29] Indeed, during the research done for this chapter, and prior to the discovery of the 'white noise' theory, the authors experienced this feeling, equally exasperated by the volume of somewhat repetitive material on offer and lack of solid, clear and simple information available.

The Canadian problem mirrors the UK position. Canadians are reluctant to report fraud. This may be due to embarrassment at being 'caught' by a scam; the low value of the fraud. Perhaps more worryingly, Canadian businesses are seemingly reluctant to expose their weaknesses to fraud, and therefore are also failing to report offences committed. The Canadian Code seems unable to keep pace with online fraudsters. It raises the question as to whether such frauds are not viewed as 'real' offences and the focus placed on more serious crimes. The CB and other agencies say not.[30] The strategy adopted by the various bodies seems to be resulting in some increase of reporting. The CB and CAFC having in 2016 received nearly 90,000 complaints, contrasted with the 2015 figures of just under 70,000 reported.[31] Whilst encouraging, the problem seems likely to continue. Cross and Kelly acknowledge the importance of enforcement, but note that prevention is the real key to reducing online offending.[32] They consider present levels of public information supplied by the crime prevention bodies in the jurisdictions, noting this needs to be 'appropriate and effective'.[33] This observation seems correct and is supported by the authors of this work. If online fraud in particular, is to be tackled effectively wherever it occurs, what is needed is a unified, clear and simple approach across all jurisdictions.

What, if any, lessons may be learned from the Canadian model? The introduction of a minimum sentence for high value fraud, akin to section 380 (1.1), might act as a deterrent. Many instances of fraud in the UK may not qualify, but if offences were viewed holistically, there may be merit in considering this course. Additionally, imposition of aggravating factors could serve as a useful vehicle in fraud prevention.

5.4.2 The Australian model

Australian law relating to fraud and deception is found in different places, including State law. Under the Criminal Code offences cover many guises of deception and fraud. For the purposes of this discussion the Criminal Code and its amendments are examined. Amendments to the Code are found in The Criminal Code Amendment (Theft, Fraud, Bribery and Related Offences) Act 2000 Part 7.3 Fraudulent Conduct. A new Chapter was inserted into the Code, and replaced some offences found in The Crimes Act 1914, such as; section 29A False Pretences; section 29B False Representation; section 29D Fraud. There are similarities observed between the UK deception offences and the Australian offences. The concept of dishonesty for most of these offences is defined in the Australian Act at section 130.3. An overlap is observed between some offences; the wide general dishonesty offence; section 135.1, obtaining property; section 134.1, or a financial advantage by deception; section 134.2, and additionally the obtaining of a financial advantage; section 135.2.[34]

There are many similarities between the Australian model and those observed in the Canadian model. The Australian Competition and Consumer Commission ('ACCC') runs SCAMWATCH, informing Australians on how to avoid scams. Reporting is available via their website.[35] Reports are kept, but SCAMWATCH does not respond to reports. This is somewhat puzzling, and to those reporting frauds this may feel somewhat futile. Organisations such as the Australian Cybercrime Online Reporting Network ('ACORN'), administered by the Australian Crime Intelligence Commission, were set up to allow reporting to one body, to strengthen the response to crimes affecting Australia and combat fraud. Operating since January 2015, ACORN was modelled on reporting systems, such as Action Fraud in the UK and the CAFC in Canada. Similar to the Canadian model, it works alongside other agencies to prevent opportunities for emerging fraudulent criminality and to fill gaps in intelligence. It is important to note that the ACCC/SCAMWATCH website warns of bogus calls and emails alleging the caller or writer to be from ACORN or SCAMWATCH.[36] This raises the question of whether this scam has been developed due to the vast array of bodies and methods of reporting fraud. Although aimed primarily at researching the effect upon victims of online fraud, it is interesting to note the findings of a recent report written for the Criminology Research Advisory Council by Cross, Richards and Smith.[37] The authors of the report interviewed 80 victims of online frauds and scams with a loss value of over $10,000. Some of those interviewed expressed frustration about where to report an offence and being passed from one organisation to another with little result.[38] The overlap between the organisations and the amount of information proffered was also criticised.[39] Victims also noted the lack of clear direction on what to do next.[40] The report resulted in the setting up of ACORN in response to concerns over where to report offences. However, it seems likely that many other problems from a victim perception continue. Somewhat shockingly, some victims stated they were blamed by the agencies they contacted for what had happened to them, noting this felt as bad as the fraud committed.[41] Other interviewees emphasised the lack of clear answers to questions from agencies.[42] These victims noted that even if an unfavourable outcome had resulted, that would have been preferred. The research revealed that the Australian police bodies still see this type of offending as lower down the scale of crimes to be solved.[43] This is not reassuring to those who report crimes. Whilst such attitudes remain, the likelihood of combating offending seems remote.

A familiar, somewhat frayed thread appears to run through the Australian reporting mechanism. Despite the myriad of ways that exist to report fraud and considerable information that is available, many citizens do not report it. The volume of information available and bodies to report it to is laudable, but it appears the volume of these may serve to put off victims, rather than encourage them to take action.

During the period, 1 July 2016 to 30 June 2017 3,350 indictable and 914 summary fraudulent conduct offences were charged under the Commonwealth Criminal Code Act 1995.[44] These statistics do not cover unreported crimes. It is suggested that only twenty-five per cent of frauds are reported, and indications are that fraud and deception offences are Australia's most expensive' category of offending.[45]

Broadhurst[46] reminds us that 'crime follows opportunity'.[47] The use of the internet means that boundaries are exceeded and crimes easily committed. Broadhurst notes that in November 2015 93 per cent of the Australian population were internet users.[48] He comments that scams and frauds were the most common cybercrime reported to the Australian police.[49] ACORN in its first year, received reports of 39,491 cybercrimes in 2015.[50] There is no doubt that offending is rife. Response to this ever growing and evolving offending can be seen in increased sentencing and penalties. Although Broadhurst has as his focus, the law in Australia, this position could be applied to the other jurisdictions discussed in this paper. Broadhurst acknowledges the adoption of cross-jurisdictional agreements is necessary to prevent cyber fraud.[51] He considers the mutually beneficial nature of an international and joint approach to tackling cybercrime.[52] He reminds us that the likelihood of detection and prosecution remain low due to cross-border policing limits.[53] Online offending he states, is popular because of the ease of access to millions of victims by use of the internet and technology.[54] Broadhurst explains, offending can exist entirely online, but notes it greatly effects all of us.[55] He comments that adoption of the Council of Europe's Cybercrime Convention in 2001 (in Europe) and the signing of the United Nations Office on Drugs and Crime ('UNODC') in 2013 (in jurisdictions including Australia) is welcomed.[56] However, he highlights the lack of unified and internationally enforceable laws to address the problem. Broadhurst comments on the importance and priority of increasing deterrence, strengthening mutuality of legal assistance across borders and ensuring standards and guidelines for pre-designed incorporated cybersecurity of new products before release into the public sphere, combined with promoting enhanced cyber-safety awareness and crime prevention.[57] The authors of this work, suggest, as Broadhurst does, that much more is urgently needed. It seems no new lessons may be learned from the Australian model, and the recurrent problems continue.

5.4.3 The New Zealand model

The Crimes Act 1961 partly codifies criminal offences in New Zealand, though other common law offences and defences remain. The Crimes Act 1961, Part 10, was repealed on 1 October 2003, and replaced by section 15 of the Crimes Amendment Act (2003 No 39). This was substituted by Part 10, Crimes against rights of property, including s240, obtaining by deception or causing loss by deception. The focus of these provisions appears to be directed at the monetary value of the crime itself, than the wrong done to the victim or society. It is interesting to note the definition of dishonesty in section 217 of the Crimes Act 196, appears an entirely subjective test. This seems in direct contrast with the latest United Kingdom decision in *Ivey v Genting Casinos (UK) Ltd t/a Crockfords*.[58]

To examine the level of the fraud and online fraud problem in New Zealand it is useful to note that in 2016, 771 offences of fraud and deception were charged. Of those charged only 371 were convicted. To address the problem, the government of New Zealand provides numerous sources of available information to advise its citizens on protecting themselves against fraud, online fraud, and scams.[59] One of the bodies, SCAMWATCH (discussed above in relation to the Australian model), seeks to assist citizens on fraud prevention in New Zealand. Data provided on the SCAMWATCH website notes that in 2016, 7,000 incidents were reported to NETSAFE (another, independent online safety body, set up by the police, and other providers, to accept reports of frauds and advise on the latest scams). It is noted that over 11.7 million dollars were lost to such scams. The Orb, yet another reporting mechanism, allows reports to be made to NETSAFE, in association with the New Zealand Police. The Australia Scams Awareness Network ('ASAN'), comprising of government regulatory agencies and departments in Australia and New Zealand, also exists to raise awareness about current scams. The ASAN has a large list of members and partners on its website, which could seem rather daunting to those trying to find out what to do after being scammed. There seems to be plenty of support mechanisms and opportunities to report incidents, but again, a recurring theme is evident. Various forms of information is being provided, support and advice offered, yet the problem persists. Is this again related to the overlapping nature of the bodies, the mass of information available information that may confuse the public rather than assist? One thing that seems clear is that the level of fraud/deceptions and scams is increasing, but is the legislative structure working? It appears that the available law is again not keeping pace with offending.

5.4.4 Some observations from Canada, Australia and New Zealand

Holistically and at a global level, systems such as the United Nations report-ing system, Sharing Electronic Resources and Laws On Crime ('SHERLOC'), may be a useful as a vehicle for information and sharing of ideas between member nations.[60] The use of the repository to combat fraud, and in particular cyber fraud seems potentially useful. Whether it is helping to reduce offend-ing, is less clear, given the continuing rise in such offending in the jurisdictions considered in this work.

What is clear is the need for a global attack on the fraudsters. The Budapest Convention on Cybercrime of 2000 opened the forum for discussion, prioritising the need for a harmonious common criminal policy on cybercrime. Whilst this is a starting point, there still seems to be much more to be done.

Lack of resources, coupled with ineffective enforcement mechanisms, seems to be at the heart of the problem. This appears to be rooted in a general apathy of governments to tackle the problem head on. It has been observed that common problems overlap the jurisdictions. A core problem is the prevalence of under reporting of instances of fraud, where victims seem to share a mutual embarrassment of being 'scammed'. A further issue appears to be a lack of resources to tackle fraud perpetrated in online environments which leads to an ineffective solution to manage the extent of the problem. The general inertia towards reporting the more minor incidents by victims, businesses having their security systems scrutinised is also noted. Governments appear unable or perhaps unwilling to prevent the cycle of frauds. Why is there a lack of international coordination to deal with online fraud in particular? Is it related to varying levels of readiness or willingness to deal with the issue?

Governments and private companies are responding with differing levels of interest, however articulated. Governments may be unwilling to risk loss of trade by the imposition of strict fraud and cyber fraud laws capable of preventing it. Or, they may fear a loss of trust in a global economy. Private companies not wishing to highlight their own security risks may result in incidents suffered going unreported.

The key to reducing cyber fraud in particular seems to be working closely together across jurisdictions to combat the global nature of it. Addressing the issue in each country appears ineffective given the reach of the problem. Perhaps a form of mandatory information sharing might be a way forward? This would, of course, not be without its problems and resourcing would be core to its success.

It is suggested, however the law is presented or dressed, there is an inability to deal with its prevalence. Some differences are observed by the input of agencies set up to crack fraud, but it is difficult to say that what is being done is enough.

5.5 Conclusion

The discussion in this chapter has argued that the criminal law has long been in a state of flux in the UK and in other common law jurisdictions such as Canada, Australia and New Zealand. This state of flux may in part be attributable to the fact that those engaged in perpetrating acts of fraud continually change their modus operandi. Specifically, with new emerging technologies, offenders have demonstrated an ability to develop the way they commit fraud by fully utilising the anonymity the internet can provide these offenders who can now perpetrate these fraudulent acts from locations far outside of the jurisdiction of the UK.

The common theme across each part of this chapter is that there is a significant amount of law at the domestic and international levels that are all aimed at presenting the solution to manage the prevalence of fraud. However, the current construction of law and policy on fraud creates a significant amount of what can only be referred to as being chatter or white noise on dealing with fraud. The discussion in this chapter has revealed that part of the problem with the current statutory frameworks in the countries considered above, is that it fails to appreciate the very nature of fraud as it is currently being perpetrated. Essentially, on the basis of the discussion in this chapter, it is contended that the law is out of step with current manifestations of fraud. It may be argued that this is in part due to the fact that the current definition of fraud in the UK has emerged out of a retrospective examination of previous identified weaknesses in the statutory construction of fraud offences.

If fraud is to be managed by the criminal law, it is contended that at minimum there is a need for a statutory framework that is capable of constructing an offence of fraud regardless of how criminals engage in committing fraud. Currently, those who commit fraud in online environments have the capacity to be prosecuted under different statutes including the Theft Act 1968, the Fraud Act 2006 and the Computer Misuse Act 1990. This collection of statutes creates a scattered approach to managing the occurrence of fraud that fails to capture modern manifestations of fraud adequately. In conclusion, it is argued that the law now needs to become much more anticipatory in nature so that it can keep up to date with modern manifestations of fraud. Further, as modern manifestations of fraud now occur outside of the jurisdiction, there is a stronger need for the international law to become the foundation to assist in defining offences and enforcing offences given the fact that modern manifestations of fraud are now essentially borderless. As it currently stands, the Fraud Act 2006 cannot on its own be considered as being capable of assisting in the prevention and detection of fraud capable of being perpetrated in online environments.

Notes

1 Visiting Lecturer in Law, King's College London.
2 Judicial Research Fellow, The Courts Service (Ireland) and Doctoral Researcher at the University of Birmingham.
3 D Garland, *The Culture of Control* (Oxford University Press, 2001), 29–40.
4 Office for National Statistics (ONS), *E-commerce and ICT activity: 2016* (ONS, 2017).
5 Y Cao, Y Lu, S Gupta and S Yang, 'The effects of differences between e–commerce and m–commerce on the consumers' usage transfer from online to mobile channel' (2018) 13(1) *International Journal of Mobile Communications* 51, 55–59.
6 C Cadwalladr and E Graham-Harrison, 'Revealed: 50 million Facebook profiles harvested for Cambridge Analytica in major data breach', *The Guardian* 17 March 2018.
7 D Curran, 'Are you ready? Here is all the data Facebook and Google have on you', *The Guardian*, 30 March 2018.
8 P Hunton, 'The growing phenomenon of crime and the Internet: a cybercrime execution and analysis model' (2009) 25 *Computer Law & Security Review* 528, 530–531.
9 R Bryant, *Investigating Digital Crime* (Wiley-Blackwell Publishing, 2008), 32–35.
10 Fraud Act 2006, ss.1–4.
11 [1977] 1 WLR 298.
12 [1974] AC 370.
13 [1973] RTR 8.
14 [1996] 3 All ER 281.

15 B Summers, 'The Fraud Act 2006: has it had any impact' (2008) 75 *Amicus Curiae* 10, 12–14.
16 Hunton, 'The growing phenomenon of crime and the Internet' (n 8) 532.
17 M Cross, *Scene of the cybercrime* (Styngress Publishing, 2008) 22–29.
18 D Wall, Cybercrime: the transformation of crime in the information age (Polity Press, 2007), 15–19.
19 B Sandywell, 'On the globalisation of crime: the Internet and new criminality' In Y. Jewkes & M. Yar (eds) *Handbook of internet crime* (Willan Publishing, 2010), 39–43.
20 S Gordon and R Ford, 'On the definition and classification of cybercrime' (2006) 2(1) *Journal in Computer Virology* 13, 15–16.
21 Garlik. *UK cybercrime report 2009*, September 2009. Retrieved from <www.garlik.com/press.php?id1/4613-GRLK_PRD> accessed 1 March 2018.
22 P Grabosky, R Smith and G Dempsey, *Electronic Theft: Unlawful Acquisition in Cyberspace* (Cambridge University Press, 2001), 24–26.
23 Bryant, Investigating Digital Crime (n 9) 37–39.
24 N Fletcher, 'Challenges for regulating financial fraud in cyberspace' (2007) 14(2) *Journal of Financial Crime* 190, 195–196.
25 Hunton, 'The growing phenomenon of crime and the Internet' (n 8) 532.
26 See <lois.justice.gc.ca> (Justice Laws Website), accessed 1 March 2018.
27 C Cross and M Kelly, 'The Problem of "white noise": examining current prevention approaches to online fraud' (2016) 23(4) *Journal of Financial Crime* 806, 810.
28 ibid, 807.
29 ibid.
30 See <www.competitionbureau.gc.ca/eic/site/cb-bc.nsf/eng/04201.html> accessed 1 March 2018.
31 See <www.competitionbureau.gc.ca/eic/site/cb-bc.nsf/eng/04201.html> accessed 1 March 2018.
32 Cross *et al* 'The Problem of "white noise"' (n 27) 807.
33 ibid, 807.
34 See <www.legislation.gov.au> accessed 1 March 2018.
35 See <www.scamwatch.gov.au/report-a-scam> accessed 1 March 2018.
36 See <www.scamwatch.gov.au/site-search/Acorn> accessed 1 March 2018
37 C Cross, K Richards and R Smith, *Improving responses to online fraud victims: An examination of reporting and support* (Criminology Research Advisory Council, 2016).
38 ibid, 6.
39 ibid, 5–6.
40 ibid, 51–52.
41 ibid, 48–54.
42 ibid, 53–54.
43 ibid, 48–50.
44 See <www.cdpp.gov.au/statistics/additional-tables> accessed 1 March 2018.
45 See <www.police.wa.gov.au/Crime/Fraud> accessed 1 March 2018.
46 R Broadhurst, 'Cybercrime in Australia' in A Deckert and R Sarre (eds), *The Palgrave Handbook of Australian and New Zealand Criminology, Crime and Justice* (Palgrave Macmillan, 2017), 221–225.
47 P Grabosky and R Smith, *Crime in the digital age: Controlling telecommunications and cyberspace illegalities.* (Transaction Publishers, 1983).
48 Broadhurst, 'Cybercrime in Australia' (n 46) 221–225.
49 ibid, 225.
50 <www.acorn.gov.au/resources> accessed 25 April 2018.
51 Broadhurst, 'Cybercrime in Australia' (n 46) 221–225.

52 ibid.
53 ibid.
54 ibid, 229.
55 ibid.
56 ibid, 232.
57 ibid.
58 [2017] UKSC 67.
59 See <www.police.govt.nz/advice/email-and-internet-safety/internet-scams-spam-and-fraud> accessed 1 March 2018.
60 See <www.unodc.org/cld/v3/sherloc/index.jspx?tmpl=cybrepo> accessed 1 March 2018.

Bibliography

Broadhurst, R., Cybercrime in Australia. In: Deckert A., Sarre R. (eds) *The Palgrave Handbook of Australian and New Zealand Criminology, Crime and Justice* (Palgrave Macmillan, 2017)

Broadhurst, R., 'Developments in the Global Law Enforcement of Cyber-Crime' (2006) 29(3) *Policing: An International Journal of Police Strategies and Management* 408

Bryant, R., *Investigating Digital Crime* (Wiley-Blackwell Publishing, 2008)

Cadwalladr and E. Graham-Harrison, 'Revealed: 50 million Facebook profiles harvested for Cambridge Analytica in major data breach', *The Guardian* 17 March 2018

Cao, Y., Y. Lu, S. Gupta and S. Yang, 'The effects of differences between e–commerce and m–commerce on the consumers' usage transfer from online to mobile channel' (2018) 13(1) *International Journal of Mobile Communications* 51

Cross, M., *Scene of the cybercrime* (Styngress Publishing, 2008)

Cross and M. Kelly, "The Problem of "white noise": examining current prevention approaches to online fraud" (2016) 23(4) *Journal of Financial Crime* 806

Curran, D., 'Are you ready? Here is all the data Facebook and Google have on you', *The Guardian*, 30 March 2018

Davies v Flackett [1973] RTR 8. Parliament

DPP v Ray [1974] AC 370

Fletcher, N., 'Challenges for regulating financial fraud in cyberspace' (2007)14(2) *Journal of Financial Crime* 190

Garland, D., *The Culture of Control* (Oxford University Press, 2001)

Garlik. *UK cybercrime report 2009*, September 2009

Gordon, S. and R. Ford, 'On the definition and classification of cybercrime' (2006) 2(1) *Journal in Computer Virology* 13

Grabosky, and R. Smith, *Crime in the digital age: Controlling telecommunications and cyberspace illegalities.* (Transaction Publishers,1983)

Grabosky, P., R. Smith and G. Dempsey, *Electronic Theft: Unlawful Acquisition in Cyberspace* (Cambridge University Press, 2001)

Hunton, P., 'The growing phenomenon of crime and the Internet: a cybercrime execution and analysis model' (2009) 25 *Computer Law & Security Review* 528

Ivey v Genting Casinos (UK) Ltd t/a Crockfords [2017] UKSC 67

Office for National Statistics (ONS) *E-commerce and ICT activity: 2016* (ONS, 2017)

Ormerod, D., 'The Fraud Act 2006 – Criminalising Lying?' [2007] *Criminal Law Review* 193

R v Rashid [1977] 1 WLR 298

R v Roziek [1996] 3 All ER 281

Sandywell, B., 'On the globalisation of crime: the Internet and new criminality'. In Jewkes Y and Yar M (eds) *Handbook of internet crime* (Willan Publishing, 2010) 38–66

Summers, B., 'The Fraud Act 2006: has it had any impact' (2008) 75 *Amicus Curiae* 10

Wall, D., *Cybercrime: the transformation of crime in the information age* (Polity Press, 2007)

6 The Fraud Act 2006

A decade of deception?

Maureen Johnson[1]

6.1 Introduction

Ten years ago, the Fraud Act 2006[2] was enacted to introduce a general fraud offence into English criminal law following the recommendations in the 1999 Consultation Paper[3] and the Law Commission's report on Fraud[4] in 2002. Prevalent in the academic discussion and criticism of the new Act at the time were three issues, that of the application of the offence of fraud to online criminality, the conversion of the offence to an inchoate liability, and the inclusion of dishonesty as an element of the new offence.[5] The Fraud Act's tenth birthday provides an ideal opportunity to examine the use to which the Act has been put, and decide if the modus operandi of the fraud offence appears to have lived up to its progressive, post-modern expectations.

The Law Commission's 2002 report considered that the deception offences in the Theft Acts 1968 and 1978 lacked the flexibility to ensure that financially motivated crime carried out with the aid of modern technology could be effectively targeted. This was particularly so after the decision in *DPP v Ray*[6] which established that a 'deception' – for the purposes of the Theft Acts 1968 and 1978 – had to be played upon a human mind. When a human mind was not involved, perhaps when a stolen bank card was used to withdraw funds at an ATM, the deception offences could not be charged.[7]

Further, the re-categorisation of the offence as a 'conduct', as opposed to a 'result' crime,[8] was to enable the law to step in at an early stage to prevent criminality and to protect potential victims. The fraud offence[9] under section 1(2)(a)–(c) of the Fraud Act 2006[10] are all inchoate offences, as it is the intention to obtain benefit which is prohibited rather than the actual acquisition of property, as used to be the case under the Theft Acts mentioned above.

The requirement of dishonesty as an important element of the new fraud offences was also questioned both before and after the enactment of the Fraud Act 2006, as reliance on the common law *Ghosh*[11] test was felt to be potentially problematic.[12]

The only remedy for these concerns was patience, but there are now ten years of the Fraud Act 2006's operation to look back on, and sufficient case law to enable genuine analysis of the use to which section 2[13] of the Fraud Act 2006 is being put.

6.2 The Fraud Act 2006

The concept of fraud in English law is longstanding, and the main problem with the offence is beautifully summarised by Lord Hardwicke speaking at a trial for civil fraud in 1759 and quoted in the Law Commission's report:

> Fraud is infinite, and were a Court of Equity once to lay down rules, how far they would go, and no farther, in extending their relief against it, or to define strictly the species or evidence of it, the jurisdiction would be cramped, and perpetually eluded by new schemes which the fertility of man's invention would contrive.[14]

In English criminal law the words 'fraudulently' and 'defraud' were used extensively in the Larceny Act 1916, which was replaced by the Theft Act 1968, the concept of larceny being repealed on 1 January 1969.[15] The Theft Acts 1968 and 1978 in turn had six sections which relied upon the concept of 'deception' for their execution and these were repealed by the Fraud Act 2006. These six offences[16] were complex and difficult to explain to juries and judges alike, and when the Fraud Act 2006 was passed, it received a cautious welcome from criminal lawyers and academics[17] who doubtless envisioned a more straightforward and serviceable way to convict those accused of enriching themselves by means of (largely) financial trickery.

There were concerns[18] about the lack of key definitions, such as 'fraud' or 'false', but the idea that it would herald a new era in the prosecution of technological frauds was generally applauded,[19] particularly with the demise of the *actus reus* of 'deception' which – it was accepted – could not apply to a machine.[20] Freed from the constraint of deception, the new general offence of fraud, now a conduct and not a result crime, was to be fit for purpose in the information age, in a world of phishing[21] and pharming,[22] of distributed denial of service attacks and identity theft. It was felt at the time[23] of the enactment that section 2 would be the most relied upon section of the short act, relevant, according to David Ormerod, to 'criminalising lying'.[24]

One of the major concerns about the Fraud Act 2006 was the conversion of the crime of deception, a result crime with a need to prove the obtaining of a benefit, into an inchoate offence, removing the need for an actual harm to the victim or actual benefit to the defendant. Inchoate offences, characterised by the lack of direct harm caused, are perhaps most familiar in UK as the generic inchoates, under the law of attempts,[25] conspiracy[26] and assisting or encouraging crime,[27] all of which are now statutory offences, in spite of having a fairly recent history in the common law. Inchoate offences draw their legitimacy from the prevention of a risk of an identifiable wrong, and the culpability of the defendant in intending that the crime be carried out. A legal moralist will insist[28] that this intention is sufficient for criminal liability to arise, irrespective of the lack of harm occurring. This is the culpability centred view of criminality – if obtaining property by trickery is wrong, intending to obtain property by trickery, even without more, is just as wrong. Especially if a person has done all they can to bring the crime about. In contrast, the harm centred[29] view holds that it is actual harm that should be punished, and if none has occurred then criminalisation is unnecessary. In order to make sense of English law's traditional inchoate rationale, as evidenced by the Fraud Act 2006, it is necessary then to adhere to the culpability centred view of criminalisation[30] – a person is bad if their intentions are bad and these intentions come to the attention of another, either by overt acts, or via speech, classically through conspiracy or encouraging crime. In order to 'balance out' the minimal or objectively innocent *actus reus* which applies to the inchoate offences, there has traditionally been a strong *mens rea* requirement, usually intention, that the ulterior crime be committed. This has been reduced to recklessness for the assisting or encouraging offences in the Serious Crime Act 2007. The fact that the *actus reus* of fraud was felt to be so easy to commit threw great weight onto the *mens rea* of the offences, again, especially section 2, and the issue of dishonesty was much discussed and widely disapproved of as a requirement that was difficult to explain to juries and relied on a circular, common law definition.[31]

Whatever the anticipatory criticisms or plaudits aimed at the Fraud Act 2006, the only way to really analyse the new concepts required patience. As the Act has now been on the statute books for ten years and has built up a jurisprudence of its own, it is possible to begin an evaluation of its effectiveness, through a discussion of these three questions:

1   Is the Fraud Act 2006 being used to stop the progress of fraudulent behaviour carried out with the aid of a computer?
2   Has the Fraud Act 2006 been used to convict and punish those who intend to cause harm before the harm has actually occurred – in its inchoate liability?[32]
3   Has the question of a defendant's dishonesty proven to be a problem, given the difficulties of convicting individuals based on the controversial *Ghosh*[33] definition?

The Fraud Act 2006 may be discovered to have had little effect on the criminal justice process, or it may be that the lightning fast technological advances and the increasingly mobile legal landscape have already outpaced the aspirations of the Act while it is still in its comparative infancy.

6.3 Empirical research

Research conducted by the author as part of a Doctoral thesis consisted of searching legal databases – in this case Westlaw and Lexis – for cases containing the relevant provisions and this has enabled an overview of the appeal cases dealing with the section 2 offence. All results between the year 2006 and the present day (2016) were then reviewed. Included in the results are any subsequent appeals, and the sentence that has been handed down in a particular case.

As an example, the first search in the data base was 'Fraud Act 2006' and the second – within those results – was for 'section 2'. Although this method will only deal with appeal cases, it will be sufficient to give an overview of the type of cases prosecuted, the reasoning behind judicial decisions and sentencing, and the views of the appellate courts. By examining *every* appeal case concerning section 2 of the Fraud Act 2006 in the prescribed periods – and therefore the entire population of examinable materials, any implication of bias is refuted. The appellate courts' decisions will also highlight the definitional and operational problems of the new offences as observed by the judiciary and practitioners. All the cases have been heard in the Court of Appeal or the Supreme Court (formerly the House of Lords) in England and Wales Cases heard in Scotland, Northern Ireland, or cases involving court marshal have not been included.

Of the cases analysed in the research which involved conviction for an offence under section 1(2)(a) of the Fraud Act 2006 – fraud by false representation – it was discovered that only ten per cent of the frauds that were prosecuted were carried out 'online' in the classic computer crime way we have been lead to believe is so prevalent. Although section 2 of the Fraud Act 2006 is an inchoate offence in that it does not need the defendant to gain – just that the intention to gain (or to cause loss) is present, in the cases reviewed as coming before the Criminal Division of the Court of Appeal, in the years between 2006 and the present, almost all the defendants had – in fact – gained (usually) a pecuniary advantage. The Fraud Act 2006, although largely drafted to bring fraud into the inchoate offence arena, does not seem to be used in that way to bring prosecutions. Analysis of case facts conducted as part of my Doctoral research show that a prosecution is only started when property has passed in much the same way as the old deception offences used to operate.

Using data from freedom of information requests made to all 43 UK police forces over a four year period and research into the individual application of section 2 by the Crown Court and Court of Appeal, this chapter asks, as far as the man in the street is concerned, if the offence under section 2 has been the E-crime prosecutor's champion, in heralding a bold new era of fraud conviction, or whether the reality has been rather more prosaic.

Media[34] reports lead us to believe that fraud, particularly internet fraud, is rocketing out of control and that hundreds of thousands of individuals are losing millions of pounds annually.[35] The Experian website calculates that fraud costs the UK economy £193 billion a year – equating to more than £6,000 lost per second every day,[36] and the National Audit office states on its website: 'Online fraud is now the most commonly experienced crime in England and Wales, but has been overlooked by government, law enforcement and industry'.[37]

These high-tech offences are specifically the ones that the newly inchoate Fraud Act 2006 was meant to target. So does this mean that thousands of cases are being prosecuted under the Fraud Act 2006 every year? The big problem here was how to find this out.

Figures on crime levels and trends for England and Wales based primarily on two sets of statistics: the Crime Survey for England and Wales[38] ('CSEW') and police recorded crime data.[39] The CSEW asks members of the public to self-report 'crimes' that have affected them in the previous year, but currently only asks about Fraud and computer misuse offences on an 'experimental' basis, making the comparison with previous years difficult.

Based on experimental statistics from new fraud and computer misuse questions that were added to the CSEW from October 2015, adults aged 16 and over self-reported that they had experienced an estimated 5.6 million fraud and computer misuse incidents in the 12 months prior to interview; 3.6 million of these were fraud incidents and 2.0 million were computer misuse incidents.[40] While the CSEW estimates will include crimes that have not been reported to the authorities, being a household survey, they will not capture fraud against organisations.

To make things even more complicated, a body called Action Fraud[41] has recently taken over the official recording of fraud offences on behalf of the 43 individual police forces in England and Wales. Official figures from 2006 to 2011 were those recorded by police forces, but from 2011 onwards the official figures were recorded by Action Fraud – this is likely to mean that year on year comparisons are again difficult to make. In order to help individuals to report fraud accurately, the Action Fraud website lists 150 different types of fraudulent behaviour, from the fairly self-explanatory cheque fraud, spam emails and romance fraud, to the more obscure, such as 'smishing' – obtaining personal details by SMS message', 'vishing' – obtaining personal details by phone, 'tabnapping' – a type of phishing scam that fraudsters use to get people's personal information and 'health in pregnancy grant fraud'. This website encourages the public to self report and self select what sort of fraud they think has occurred, and they are then given a police crime number. Although there is no evidence to support a deliberate misuse of such a system, such self-reporting is open to misinterpretation, particularly in a technically complex area such as this. The CSEW for the year ending 2016 states:

> The extent of fraud is difficult to measure because it is a deceptive crime; victimisation is often indiscriminate, covering organisations as well as individuals. Some victims of fraud may be unaware they have been a victim of crime, or that any fraudulent activity has occurred for some time after the event. Others might be unwilling to see themselves as victims or reluctant to report the offence to the authorities, feeling embarrassed that they have fallen victim. The level of fraud reported via administrative sources is thought to significantly understate the true level of such crime.[42]

One of the first issues that arose in the course of this research, was how to establish – at least – a semi–factual base in order to try to quantify the number and nature of the uses to which the Fraud Act 2006 has been put.

The origins of this research began in 2011 and were aimed at tracking the progress of newly enacted inchoate provisions. The four inchoate offences selected were; section 2 of the Fraud Act 2006, the possession offence[43] under

Table 6.1 Projected figures for the whole of England and Wales. The figures have been rounded up or down either side of the 0.5 percentage

Year ending	Arrests under s2 Obscene Publications Act 1959 (1)	Arrests under s63 of the Criminal Justice and Immigration Act 2008 (2)	Arrests under s62 of the Coroner's and Justice Act 2 009 (3)	Arrests under s2 Fraud Act 2006 (4)
2011	21	164	72	20,606
2015	236	1609	686	15,201
% increase/ decrease	1023.8	881.1	582.8	−26.2

section 62 of the Coroner's and Justice Act 2009, and the possession offence[44] under section 63 of the Criminal Justice and Immigration Act 2008, and intent to distribute offence[45] under section 2 of the Obscene Publications Act 1959. A Freedom of Information request was submitted to all 43 Police forces in England and Wales asking for the number of arrests under the relevant provision in the 12 months from June 2010 to June 2011. This exercise was then repeated four years later covering the period from June 2014 to June 2015 and the figures compared.

When making the Freedom of Information requests, the focus on the number of arrests and not convictions was deliberate as it is in this number that it is possible to see the actual use to which the statute is being put, to allow prosecutors to seize items or question suspects. Thereafter, whether a charge is brought or a conviction obtained is due to an enormous range of variables, such as the Crown Prosecution Service, a national body, making a decision – based on the evidence and likelihood of conviction – whether to proceed with a prosecution, or whether, at any point in the progression of the case, a charge is dropped for a technicality, lack of evidence or lack of public interest. In the light of this it can be seen, that the number of arrests made was felt to be the purest way to determine the usefulness of the statute itself.

The research was intended to track the (purported) rise in the use of inchoate offences in the English criminal system. The expected exponential increase was observed in three of the offences (1) to (3) above, but surprisingly, not in (4), the fraud by false representation offence.

It becomes apparent from this empirical research that the numbers of arrests for fraud under section 2 of the FA is on the decrease, roughly in line with the average decrease in criminal offences generally over that time period as presented by the Office of National Statistics,[46] which is about 22–24% over the four-year period, although different ways of calculating and recording offences makes this figure notoriously difficult to compare like for like. This seemed to be at odds with the figures from the CSEW, and an apparent anomaly which needed to be investigated further. This being so, the next stage was to find out what sort of behaviour was being targeted by the Fraud Act 2006, principally under section 2. Again, accurate accounts of first instance case law are difficult to come by where cases are not reported, as is the norm for the vast majority of criminal cases heard in the Magistrates Courts and Crown Courts up and down the country. Research into the number of fraud by false representation (section 2) cases heard in the St Albans' Crown Court in 2011 revealed that there were 31 cases heard, and in the year 2015 there were 27 cases where a charge was brought under section 2, which does not seem excessive given the 3.6 million 'self-reported'[47] cases in the CSEW report. There are 77 branches of the Crown Court in England and Wales, but even detailed research into these would give no idea of the cases heard in the 330 Magistrates Courts, where more than 95% of criminal cases are tried. As section 2 is a triable-either-way offence, capable of summary trial at the Magistrates Court or trial on indictment at the Crown Court, even a crude estimate of the number of cases involving section 2 of the Fraud Act 2006 would be very difficult, and subject to an unacceptable degree of error.

However, by turning to reported case law and conducting a search of Court of Appeal cases between the year 2006 and 2016 it was possible to see how many of them were concerned with section 2 offences, and also the details of the criminal behaviour that led to the conviction. There were 102 Court of Appeal cases concerning section 2 in this ten-year period. The results of an analysis of these cases may give an insight into the answer to the three questions set out above.

Question 1

Is the Fraud Act 2006 being used to stop the progress of fraudulent behaviour carried out with the aid of a computer?

To answer this question, it is necessary to be able to define computer fraud, which is already a difficult concept, with myriad contenders. For clarity, it will be defined as a fraud that takes place without the deception of a human being[48] – the so called 'lacuna' which was one of the reasons that the Fraud Act 2006 was enacted.[49] It will not include a fraud that happens to use the internet or emails as a way of communicating with a person with a view to committing a fraud, an old offence, committed through a new medium. For instance, in one of the appeal cases examined, Katie Ringer[50] conned male friends on the internet by pretending to raise funds for the funeral of a fictitious still born child and a child she – falsely – claimed was sick and needed treatment abroad. She obtained upwards of £3,000 but she clearly deceived people in the process and not just a computer, so this is a crime that would have probably proceeded under obtaining property by deception in the repealed section 15 of the Theft Act 1968. A review of the 102 appeal cases concerning section 2 revealed precisely none that took place without the deception of a real, live human being.

It seems then that the idea of the Fraud Act 2006 as being a statute that would combat computer crime by doing away with the lacuna where there was no 'human mind' to be deceived has failed to live up to its promise. It is unlikely, given the huge amount of 'computer frauds' (as described above about 3.6 million per annum) which take place that every case involves human agency, and the Fraud Act 2006 clearly makes it possible for these criminal actions to be charged. The real issue with these cases is not the lack of a suitable charging mechanism, but lack of available evidence, frauds being committed from outside England and Wales, and lack of reporting to the relevant authorities. Businesses such as banks and credit card providers have always preferred to keep fraudulent activity 'in house', by reimbursing affected customers and taking steps to bring the fraudulent activity to an end – such as cancelling a cloned debit or credit card and issuing a new one to the compromised customer. The criminal justice system is rarely engaged in these cases, which have almost taken on the mantle of a tortious activity, with reparation made to the party who has lost money in a way that has become so common that most people barely think of themselves of victims of a criminal enterprise at all.

Question 2

Has the Fraud Act 2006 been used to convict and punish those who intend to cause harm before the harm has actually occurred – in its inchoate liability?

The inchoate liability imposed under section 2 is on the grounds that no property has actually been gained or lost, but there was the intention to cause gain or loss[51] and the defendant was dishonest in making the false representation.[52] This is classic inchoate liability where there may be no 'victim' who has actually been harmed, but the defendant's intention to do so is enough to convict her. Out of the 102 cases reviewed, only two cases concerned a count which could be labelled as inchoate, albeit that other counts in the same case were completed frauds, where property had passed. In *R v Christopher Osbourne*,[53] a man was charged with section 2 offences for presenting an altered and photocopied sick note – which had been written for his daughter – in order to get out of a community sentence imposed for another offence. He was also charged with posing as his own stepson to obtain a loan for a family holiday, but in this he was unsuccessful. Mr Osbourne was given a community order and required to do 180 hours unpaid work. In the second case of *R v Veronica Dittman*,[54] a woman (Anderson) was charged with a section 2 offence for attempting to take a practical driving test in the place of her friend (Dittman), having already – it was claimed – taken the theory test for her as well. Ms Dittman was sentenced to two months imprisonment for her part in the fraud. In both of these cases it is likely that, had section 2 of the Fraud Act 2006 not been available, the charges could have been brought under section 1 of the Criminal Attempts Act 1981 for a crime of attempted deception under one of the Theft Act 1968 offences. For an attempted crime to be proven, there must be an intention to carry out the ulterior offence, and there must have been an act which was 'more than merely preparatory' towards the completion of the ulterior offence. The definition of 'more than merely preparatory' is notoriously difficult,[55] but there is no reason to suppose that an individual such as Ms Dittman, by arranging for Anderson to present herself, with Dittman's documentation, on the day of the test, while Dittman herself kept away from the test centre, had not 'embarked upon the crime proper'[56] and therefore an attempted offence would have been made out. In the event that an attempted crime could not be made out in Ms Dittman's circumstances, there seems to be little doubt that a statutory conspiracy under section 1(1) of the Criminal Law Act 1977 is present. A statutory conspiracy requires an intention that the offence is carried out, and an agreement on the part of the defendants that a course of conduct shall be pursued which, 'if the agreement is carried out in accordance with their intentions . . . will necessarily amount to or involve the commission of any offence or offences by one or more of the parties to the agreement'.[57]

Question 3

Has the question of a defendant's dishonesty proven to be a problem, given the difficulties of convicting individuals based on the controversial Ghosh[58] definition?

In only one of the cases reviewed was the defendant's dishonesty an issue. This case concerned an application for extradition from the United Kingdom to the United Arab Emirates based on a mortgage fraud entered into in the UAE. In *The Government of the United Arab Emirates v Sheeraz Amir*[59] a man presented a cheque which was subsequently not honoured. The judge in the case was clear that the failure to honour a cheque was not an offence under section 2 of the Fraud Act 2006, but an earlier representation that the cheque would be honoured, if made dishonestly, would fall foul of section 2. The definition of dishonesty is still largely a common law concept taken from the judgment in the case of *Ghosh*:[60]

> In determining whether the prosecution has proved that the defendant was acting dishonestly, a jury must first of all decide whether according to the ordinary standards of reasonable and honest people what was done was dishonest. If it was not dishonest by those standards, that is the end of the matter and the prosecution fails. If it was dishonest by those standards, then the jury must consider whether the defendant himself must have realised that what he was doing by those standards dishonest.[61]

Where the answer to both questions is 'yes', then the defendant will be found to be dishonest. In spite of its longevity, the *Ghosh* test is an unsatisfactory one, given the impropriety of trying to define a negative concept by relation to its positive counterpart, and the clear lack of a 'standard' of honesty amongst any given population.[62] Nevertheless, it is this test which is used in order to define dishonesty[63] in relation to the Fraud Act 2006, and in a case such as *The Government of the United Arab Emirates v Sheeraz Amir*, at first instance, it would be for the jury to apply the test and conclude the state of the defendant's mind in this situation. In *The Government of the United Arab Emirates v Sheeraz Amir* itself, being an appeal case, no such application was necessary anyway. The fact that the issue of dishonesty was considered only once in the 102 cases analysed might lead to the belief that – awkward as it is – the inclusion of the *Ghosh* test as the test for dishonesty in the Fraud Act 2006 is not a cause for concern as the direction seldom needs to be given. In most cases, where there is no *Ghosh* direction given by the judge, it is likely that the defendant's dishonesty is not a question on which the jury needs any guidance.

In fact the cases reviewed revealed a disappointingly mundane group of offences. Mortgage fraud, stolen or invalid cheques, insurance fraud by forging medical certificates or overstating the damage of vehicles in a collision, and 'builders' and rogues who targeted elderly or vulnerable people. A Mr Wright[64] raised over £1 million for sick children, not all of which he spent on sick children, a Mr Formhals[65] operated a website selling 'Churchill' memorabilia of dubious provenance, most of which he had signed himself. Annie Hoxhalli[66] took a £30 tee-shirt back to Top Shop for a refund when she actually bought it from somewhere else. In short, just the sort of offences which were the remit of the deception offences before 2006, not inchoate offences which enabled the law to intercept a criminal before harm was done, not technologically complex offences where computer experts manipulated code or artificial intelligence for personal gain, and not those where the troublesome definition of dishonesty has caused any problems at all.

6.4 Conclusion

Ten years is not a long time in the life of an English statute. In cases involving the validity of guarantees in particular, section 4 of the Statute of Frauds 1677 makes regular appearances, and the 150-year-old Offences Against the Person Act 1861 is one of the most used statutes in English criminal law. The Fraud Act 2006 then, is still a youngster, but maybe it has not lived up to the lofty expectations of lawyers and academics of ten years ago. It has not been decried as unjust in its application, nor does it seem to have been ground-breaking in convicting defendants who would otherwise have been able to escape liability by an innovative use of technology. The Fraud Act 2006 in its ordinary, criminal law persona is still covering much the same ground as the sections of the Theft Acts 1968 and 1978 which it was responsible for repealing in January 2007 and in spite of 'self-reported' and 'estimated' fraudulent incidents running into the millions in England and Wales, cases reported to the police, individuals arrested and convictions secured, are numbered much more soberly. This would seem to indicate that all is well with the Fraud Act 2006 – that it is operating as a solid and pragmatic statute, capable of application to the everyday crimes committed by ordinary people in a straightforward way, without the complications of the deception offences. That the Fraud Act 2006 does not appear to have taken the law into new and controversial areas should be a cause for satisfaction, not regret.

Notes

1 Senior Lecturer in Law, University of Hertfordshire.
2 A full version of the Fraud Act 2006 can be found at <www.opsi.gov.uk/acts/acts 2006/ 20060035.htm> accessed 1 May 2018.
3 No 155 of 27 April 1999 Legislating the Criminal Code: Fraud and Deception available at <www.lawcom.gov.uk/docs/cp155.pdf> accessed 1 May 2018.
4 Law Com No 276 Cm 5560 is available at <www.lawcom.gov.uk/docs/lc276.pdf> accessed 1 May 2018.
5 M Johnson & KM Rogers, 'The Fraud Act 2006: The E-Crime Prosecutor's Champion or the Creator of a New Inchoate Offence?' (2007) 21 (3) *International Review of Law, Computers and Technology* 295.
6 *DPP v Ray* [1974] AC 370. Lord Morris stated (at page 384): 'For a deception to take place there must be some person or persons who will have been deceived.' Further, in Re London and Global Finance Corporation Limited [1903] 1 Ch 728, Buckley J stated (at page 732): 'To deceive is . . . to induce a man to believe that a thing is true which is false, and which the person practising the deceit knows and believes it to be false.'
7 A charge of theft could still be brought if the offence was completed, but technically this would be a theft against the bank, not the customer.
8 D Ormerod, 'The Fraud Act 2006 – criminalising lying?' [2007] Crim LR 193.
9 Strictly speaking there is only one fraud offence, committed in three ways, under sections 2, 3 and 4.
10 P Kiernan and G Scanlan, 'Fraud and the Law Commission: the future of dishonesty' (2003) 10(3) *Journal of Financial Crime* 199.
11 Although see the case of *Ivey v Genting Casinos Ltd* [2017] UKSC 67 which throws doubt on the validity of the *Ghosh* test.
12 Ormerod (n 8).
13 The charge for false representation is under section 1(2)a of the Fraud Act 2006, which refers to a breach of section 2. The offence of false representation will be referred to as a section 2 offence throughout this chapter.
14 The Law Commission *Fraud* (Report No. 276), July 2002. The Report is available at: <www.lawcom.gov.uk/lc_reports.htm#2002> page 16, para 3.14 originally see Letter of Lord Hardwicke to Lord Kames, dated June 30, 1759, printed in Parkes, *History of the Court of Chancery* (1828), 508, quoted in Snell, *Principles of Equity* (25th ed. 1960), 496.
15 Except in the Baliwick of Jersey, where larceny is still a common law offence.
16 Obtaining property by deception: section 15 of the Theft Act 1968, obtaining a money transfer by deception: section 15A, Theft Act 1968, obtaining a pecuniary advantage by deception: section 16, Theft Act 1968, procuring the execution of a valuable security by deception: section 20(2), Theft Act 1968, obtaining services by deception: section 1, Theft Act 1978 and evading liability by deception: section 2, Theft Act 1978.

17 'With identity theft and credit card scams a growing concern, the new legislation is likely to be welcomed by the financial and banking sector and, once passed, should result in a considerable increase in the number of prosecutions of technology related crime.' S Barty and P Carnell, 'Fraud Bill offers new protection against technology abuse' (2005) 6(7) *World Internet Law Report* 20, 21.

18 Johnson and Rogers (n 5) 295–304.

19 D Bainbridge, 'Criminal law tackles computer fraud and misuse' (2007) 23(3) *Computer Law and Security Report* 276, 280.

20 *DPP v Ray* (n 6).

21 Defined by the *Oxford English Dictionary* as 'the fraudulent practice of sending emails purporting to be from reputable companies in order to induce individuals to reveal personal information, such as passwords and credit card numbers.'

22 Defined by the *Oxford English Dictionary* as 'the fraudulent practice of directing internet users to a bogus website what mimics the appearance of a legitimate one, in order to obtain personal information such as passwords, account numbers etc.'.

23 Ormerod (n 8).

24 ibid.

25 Section 1 of the Criminal Attempts Act 1981.

26 Section 1 of the Criminal Law Act 1978.

27 Sections 44–46 of the Serious Crimes Act 2009.

28 M Moore, *Placing Blame; A theory of Criminal Law* (Oxford 1997).

29 J Feinberg, *The Moral Limits of the Criminal Law* Vols 1–4 (Oxford 1984–1988).

30 J Herring, *Great Debates in Criminal Law* (3rd ed Palgrave 2015).

31 E Griew, 'Dishonesty: the objections to Feely and Ghosh' (1985) Crim LR 341.

32 Inchoate means incomplete, and is a form of criminal liability based on (usually) the intention to commit a crime together with steps taken towards committing it, but where the offence is not – for some reason – completed.

33 *R v Ghosh* [1982] QB 1053.

34 See *BBC News* website, 21 July 2016 <www.bbc.co.uk/news/uk-36854413> accessed 1 May 2018.

35 *The Times*, 26 November 2017, Eight Ways to Beat Fraud this Christmas <www.thetimes.co.uk/static/connected-families/the-most-fraudulent-christmas-ever/> accessed 1 May 2018.

36 D Eaves <https://experianhostedcontent.co.uk/blogs/latest-thinking/identity-and-fraud/fraud-costs-uk-economy-193-billion-year-equating-6000-lost-per-second-every-day/> accessed 1 May 2018.

37 A Morse, head of the National Audit Office, 30 June 2017 <www.nao.org.uk/report/online-fraud/> accessed 1 May 2018.

38 See <www.crimesurvey.co.uk/SurveyResults.html> accessed 1 May 2018.

39 See <www.gov.uk/government/statistics/police-recorded-crime-open-data-tables> accessed 1 May 2018.

40 See <www.ons.gov.uk/peoplepopulationandcommunity/crimeandjustice/bulletins/crimeinenglandandwales/yearendingsept2016> accessed 1 May 2018.

41 See <https://actionfraud.police.uk/> accessed 1 May 2018.

42 Crime Survey of England and Wales – year ending September 2016 page 39.

43 Section 62 of the Coroners and Justice Act 2009 prohibits the possession of 'illegal images of children'.

44 Section 63 of the Criminal Justice and Immigration Act 2008 prohibits the possession of images of 'extreme pornography' usually involving real or simulated violence.

45 Section 2 of the Obscene Publications Act 1959 prohibits the publication of an obscene article.

46 Office for National Statistics, <www.ons.gov.uk/peoplepopulationandcommunity/crimeandjustice/bulletins/crimeinenglandandwales/2015–10–15#overview> accessed 1 May 2018.

47 See <www.ons.gov.uk/peoplepopulationandcommunity/crimeandjustice/bulletins/crimeinenglandandwales/yearendingsept2016> accessed 1 May 2018.
48 Such as the use of a stolen or cloned credit card to withdraw money from an Automated Teller Machine or to purchase goods from an online retailer.
49 Law Com No 276 Cm 5560 is available at <www.lawcom.gov.uk/docs/lc276.pdf> accessed 1 May 2018.
50 *R v Ringer (Katie)* [2016] EWCA 241.
51 See section 5 of the Fraud Act 2006.
52 Section 2(1)a of the Fraud Act 2006.
53 *R v Osbourne* [2008] EWCA Crim 3004.
54 *R v Dittman* [2012] EWCA Crim 957.
55 See, for instance, the cases of *Campbell* (1991) Crim LR 268 and *Geddes* [1996] Crim LR 894.
56 *Jones* [1990)] 1 WLR 1057.
57 Section 1(1) of the Criminal Law Act 1977.
58 *Ghosh* (n 33).
59 *The Government of the United ARAB Emirates v Sheeraz Amir* [2012] EWHC 1711.
60 *Ghosh* (n 33).
61 ibid, 1046 (Lord Lane CJ).
62 See E Griew 'Dishonesty: the objections to Feely and Ghosh' (1985) Crim LR 341.
63 See now the case *of Ivey v Genting Casinos Ltd* [2017] UKSC 67 for a potentially reformed test for dishonesty. Nevertheless, all the cases referred to in this chapter were considered under the *Ghosh* test, before the case of *Ivey*.
64 *R v Wright (Kevin)* [2014] EWCA Crim 376.
65 *R v Formhals (Allan)* [2013] EWCA Crim 2624.
66 *R v Hoxhalli (Annie)* [2016] EWCA Crim 724.

Bibliography

Action Fraud
Bainbridge D, 'Criminal law tackles computer fraud and misuse' (2007) 23(3) *Computer Law and Security Report* 276, 280
Barty S and Carnell P, 'Fraud Bill offers new protection against technology abuse' (2005) 6(7) *World Internet Law Report* 20
Coroners and Justice Act 2009
Crime in England and Wales
Crimesurvey.co.uk
Criminal Justice and Immigration Act 2008
DPP v Ray [1974] AC 370
Experian.co.uk
Feinberg J, *The Moral Limits of the Criminal Law* Vols 1–4 (Oxford 1984–1988)
Fraud Act 2006
Gov.uk
Griew E, 'Dishonesty: the objections to Feely and Ghosh' (1985) Crim LR 341
Herring J, *Great Debates in Criminal Law* (3rd ed Palgrave 2015)
Ivey v Genting Casinos Ltd [2017] UKSC 67
Johnson, M and Rogers KM, 'The Fraud Act 2006: The E-Crime Prosecutor's Champion or the Creator of a New Inchoate Offence?' (2007) 21(3) *International Review of Law, Computers & Technology* 295
Kiernan P and Scanlan G, 'Fraud and the Law Commission: the future of dishonesty' (2003) 10(3) *Journal of Financial Crime* 199

Moore M, *Placing Blame; A theory of Criminal Law* (Oxford 1997)

National Audit Office.org.uk

Obscene Publications Act 1959

Office of National Statistics

Ormerod D, 'The Fraud Act 2006 – criminalising lying?' (2007) Crim LR 193

Re London and Global Finance Corporation Limited [1903] 1 Ch 728

R v Campbell [1991] Crim LR 268

R v Dittman [2012] EWCA Crim 957

R v Formhals (Allan) [2013] EWCA Crim 2624

R v Geddes [1996] Crim LR 894

R v Ghosh [1982] QB 1053

R v Hoxhalli (Annie) [2016] EWCA Crim 724

R v Jones [1990] 1 WLR 1057

R v Ringer (Katie) [2016] EWCA 241

R v Osbourne [2008] EWCA Crim 3004

R v Wright (Kevin) [2014] EWCA Crim 376

The Government of the United ARAB Emirates v Sheeraz Amir [2012] EWHC 1711

Serious Crimes Act 2009

The Times, 26 November 2017, 'Eight Ways to Beat Fraud this Christmas'

7 Criminal fraud legislation since 2006

David Kirk[1]

7.1 Introduction

Fraud investigation and prosecution has gone through much development and change since the early 1980s. The Roskill Committee Report on Fraud Trials in 1986, which led to the creation of the Serious Fraud Office ('SFO') in 1988, reflected a growing concern that fraud was endemic in the City of London and in large corporations. The SFO has taken on the challenges of serious and complex fraud cases over the last 30 years, and although its results have been mixed, it has been successful in holding big business to account. Since the late 1980s the resources allocated by police forces in the UK to fighting fraud has fluctuated. The momentum has generally been downwards, with local fraud squads diminishing in size and number, and fraud generally slipping down the increasingly long list of priorities. In 2005 the then Attorney General, Lord Goldsmith, set up a 'Fraud Review' with the purpose of examining the priorities that ought to be allocated to an adequate counter fraud response. The review led to an increase in counter fraud activity, including the setting up of the National Fraud Authority to observe and report on fraud issues. Almost immediately this work was, to a significant extent, overtaken by the global financial crisis of 2008. The crisis laid bare some extremely bad conduct at the heart of the world's economies, and set in train a challenge to the authorities: how can such conduct be curbed and punished? At the same time the methodology of fraud was developing into a global menace which recognised few borders: cyber-crime was one major new threat. This had the additional threat that it had the backing of, and provided benefit to, organised criminals. The government has taken some steps to meet these, and other, new threats, but to most observers the resources and skills allocated to the fight against fraud are inadequate. Recent legislation has sought to provide the tools to stem the alarming increase in loss through fraud both to the economy as a whole, and to individual victims. This chapter addresses the merits and the impact of this legislative programme.

7.2 The Fraud Act 2006

The Fraud Act 2006[2] set out to define fraud and characterise specific fraudulent activity, providing a sound basis for tackling fraud, and a sentencing matrix that reflected the seriousness of the offending. It was part of a project to bring counter-fraud action up to date. The Attorney General's Fraud Review, also published in 2006, placed emphasis on developing and maintaining a coherent counter fraud strategy from investigation to trial, coupled with an accurate assessment of fraud risk and extent of damage.[3] Both are examples of proactive policy initiatives. Both showed how to apply intelligent responses to current problems, the Fraud Act 2006 repealing the eight deception offences within the Theft Act 1968 and the Theft Act 1978 in order that fraud could be more effectively prosecuted, and the Fraud Review applying experience and sense to the systems of investigation and prosecution that were significantly failing.

The implementation of the Act and the publication of the Review preceded the global financial crisis by about 18 months. From 2008 onwards attention turned, understandably, to studying the causes of the crisis, and the steps that could be taken to avert a repetition of the banking failures which had such a catastrophic impact on national economies around the world. This chapter, as well as looking back at the first ten years of the Act, will therefore consider the counter-fraud legislation that has been enacted in the wake of the crisis to deal with complex City, financial services and corporate fraud.

The Act is short and to the point. It has 15 sections and 3 schedules. It is self-contained, in other words it does not cross-refer to other legislation, or to guidelines that must be published to explain the meaning and impact of a section. It is intended to deal with the kind of ordinary everyday fraud that is committed by career criminals, often part of an organised crime gang, and by opportunists who take advantage of vulnerable and careless victims. It can also be brought into play in dealing with global, financial crime problems, but as we will see, city fraud requires a more complex approach.

The basic deception offences, which form the backbone of the Act, have been updated from sections 15 and 16 of the Theft Act 1968, and are a vital part of the armoury of fraud investigators and prosecutors. Individual citizens must be protected from determined fraudsters who are committing fraud offences through boiler rooms, land banking, pension release, phishing, hacking and increasingly sophisticated digitally enabled and cyber crime attacks. Recent figures would suggest that losses through this kind of fraud exceed £150 billion per year, and that a significant proportion of the population falls victim to scams of one sort or another in any one year.[4] The problem of dealing with this sort of crime is that the resources available to deal with it are woefully inadequate. In other words, the legislation is in place, including the Act, and it is fit for purpose, but tackling high volume fraud is not a priority for law enforcement. If you are the victim of a fraud, you call the police, and are referred to Action Fraud, but you are unlikely to hear from the authorities again. You are more likely to get financial redress from the bank which facilitated a transaction, or from your insurance company. Few individuals will be prosecuted.

The Act creates a single offence of fraud which can be committed in three ways:

1 Fraud by false representation (section 1(2)(a));
2 Fraud by failing to disclose information (section 1(2)(b)); or
3 Fraud by abuse of position (section 1(2)(c)).

There must be dishonesty (as defined by the well-known *Ghosh*[5] test, and reinterpreted in 2017 by the Supreme Court in *Ivey v Genting Casinos Ltd*[6]), and there must be an intent to make a gain or cause a loss.

Other offences relate to possession of (section 6) or making or supplying (section 7) articles for use in fraud; fraudulent trading (sections 9 and 10); and obtaining services dishonestly (section 11).

The Act does not interfere with the offence of conspiracy to defraud, a common law offence preserved by the Criminal Law Act 1977.

The efficacy, or otherwise, of a piece of legislation may be judged by a number of factors, including how often prosecutors include it in indictments,[7] and the extent to which the Court of Appeal Criminal Division is called upon to arbitrate on points of law arising from the provisions in the Act. On the latter point, it may be said that the deception offences in the Theft Act 1968 created a good deal of case law. By contrast, over the first 10 years of its existence on the statute book, the Fraud Act 2006 has given rise to very little litigation. *Archbold* devotes only 12 pages to the Act in its 2018 edition, and no decisions of any significance arising from cases brought under the Act are cited.[8] Much of the reason for this is no doubt that the extensive litigation produced by the Theft Act 1968 decided a range of deception issues. It is, of course, also possible that the fact that law enforcement in the UK has focused less on non-violent property offences means that there are fewer false representation cases being tried in the Crown Court.

However, in order to deal with the more complex world of financial services misconduct it is perhaps necessary to create more sophisticated responses to evolving problems. In the last five years a number of reactive measures have been enacted to tackle what appeared to be the causes of the 2008 global financial crisis, including reckless banking, poor systems and controls, benchmark manipulation and poor management.

The global financial crisis has prompted law enforcement in most jurisdictions to try to 'do something about' the misconduct that got us all into such an economic mess. The bankers have been blamed by media, politicians and public, and attempts have been made to seek retribution, but little has been achieved. The public have wanted to see wealthy bank directors strung up, or at least put in the stocks, for failing to spot the danger signs in the levels of toxic debt on their balance sheets, and for otherwise profiting from their egregious recklessness. But no one has been prosecuted.[9]

The easiest target of those who sought to ensure that it would never happen again was of course the banking sector. In the UK, the Parliamentary Committee on Banking Standards ('PCBS') examined the facts post crash, and reported in

2012. The Committee had no doubt that senior bankers needed to be held to account.[10] Therefore, the measures introduced since the crash have included accountability as a major element.

7.2.1 Senior Managers and Certification Regime

The Senior Managers and Certification Regime is being rolled out by the UK Financial Regulator across the financial services sector, with senior managers having to take a direct line responsibility for compliance issues in their business. How this will work in practice remains to be seen, but early indications are that the regime is causing much soul-searching and concern at board level, and is having an impact on corporate culture and management behaviour.

7.2.2 Reckless management of a bank

One interesting outcome of the PCBS's deliberations was the introduction of section 36 of the Financial Services (Banking Reform) Act 2013: offence relating to a decision causing a financial institution to fail. If you are a senior banker of a regulated firm who makes a decision that causes the bank to fail, or fails to stop such a decision being taken, knowing that there is a risk that the decision will cause the bank to fail, then you are guilty of a criminal offence.

It seems highly unlikely that such an offence will ever be charged, and if charged, that a conviction will result. The nature of decision-making at senior level in a bank is not a solitary occupation. There will be teams of internal and external advisors, as well as fellow board members, who will play their part in reaching a decision, and the analysis of that process will almost certainly be difficult to characterise as reckless. In addition, it is hardly likely that a large financial institution will fail because of a single internal decision: failure will also be caused by external factors, including unforeseen changes in the economy.

The banks which built up dangerous levels of toxic debt in the run up to the financial crisis were all following a policy which, at some stage, had seemed like a very good idea. Just as with the Libor scandal, it was not an isolated bank which made a reckless decision. On the contrary, all the major banks were marching to the same tune. It may therefore be asserted that the joint thinking of many senior bankers – across Europe and the United States – which has not been challenged by the regulator, and which for some time appears to have been producing profits, as well as, for example, supporting home ownership ambitions championed by successive governments, cannot be judged to be a breach of the section.

While it is not difficult to predict that this offence will never be successfully prosecuted, it is also fair to say that the existence of the offence will create an additional column in the risk register: which senior board member wants to take the risk that his decision will be judged to have been reckless? In providing an opportunity to review risk, like the Senior Managers and Certification Regime, it will remind senior directors of their duties.

7.2.3 Benchmarks

Another highly significant post financial crisis fraud issue was the exposure of Libor, Forex and other benchmark manipulation by banks around the world. In response to this scandal, Parliament enacted section 91 of the Financial Services Act 2012: misleading statements in relation to benchmarks. It is perhaps an example of an *ex post facto* legislative response since benchmark manipulation, having been exposed by investigations by a number of regulators, including the Financial Conduct Authority, is unlikely to be practiced again. Regulatory action against several banks saw the level of administrative fines in the UK rise to £1.4 billion in 2014/15 from £420 million in the two previous years.[11] There were a number of prosecutions, brought by the Serious Fraud Office, and in one case[12] a prison sentence of 14 years was handed down. Although this was reduced on appeal to 11 years, it was clear that Libor manipulation was treated with the utmost seriousness by the courts. The defendants were all charged with conspiracy to defraud. The section 91 offence was not, of course, in force at the time of the offending.

7.2.4 Offences under the Bribery Act 2010

Although the Bribery Act 2010 was not in any way a response to the financial crisis, it was introduced at a time when businesses were overwhelmed with problems. Not only was the economy extremely weak in the wake of the crisis, but now there was new legislation which refocused attention on the thorny topic of international corruption, and made it even more difficult to do business in many parts of the world. The Law Enforcement fanfare which greeted the UK Bribery Act was considerable, and the UK has been congratulated for taking a bold step in the international war on bribery. In particular, section 7 of the Act represented a step-change in the approach to corporate misconduct by creating a corporate offence of failing to prevent corruption. This was a wholly new concept in criminal law terms. It represented a move away from the traditional approach to corporate criminal liability of the 'identification doctrine' where the directing mind and will of a company has to be identified with misconduct committed by, or on behalf of, a corporation. It has prompted companies to review their procedures, and to ensure that they have adequate systems in place to prevent bribery. In other words, the Act has created a climate for better business ethics.

7.2.5 Failing to prevent the facilitation of tax evasion

On the back of this new offence, the Criminal Finances Act 2017 has introduced a similar offence of failing to prevent the facilitation of UK tax evasion.[13] A defence of having reasonable procedures in place to prevent the facilitation of tax evasion, similar to the section 7 of the Bribery Act 2010 defence, can be deployed.[14]

Attempts were made to add an amendment to the Criminal Finances Bill creating another offence, of failing to prevent economic crime. This must wait for another legislative opportunity. The Serious Fraud Office would have liked to be able to deploy such an offence against the banks which permitted, and possibly encouraged, benchmark manipulation in relation to Libor and Forex. However, they were forced to decide that they could not take action under the 'identification doctrine' because evidence of senior management knowledge of misconduct did not exist.

The concept of the 'failure to prevent' offence looks good on paper, and undoubtedly has the potential benefit, like section 36 of the Financial Services (Banking Reform) Act 2013, of concentrating the minds of senior management on the consequences of the decisions they take. On the face of it, the elements of the offence are simple: bribery or tax evasion takes place somewhere in the business, either in England and Wales, or in any other jurisdiction in the world, because the company has failed to put systems in place to prevent it.

One problem with this approach is that it is not always easy to define what an 'adequate' (Bribery Act 2010) or 'reasonable' (Criminal Finances Act 2017) preventative procedure might look like. Both Acts have required the relevant government department to produce guidance, and in each case nearly 50 pages of guidance has been produced to explain what sections 7 and 45 mean. In practice, however, it may be difficult to satisfy the Serious Fraud Office or Her Majesty's Revenue and Customs that you put in place procedures which should have prevented the offence being committed. The range of risk that should have been foreseen will depend on circumstances. Staff training is an essential part of any compliance programme. The whistleblowing hot-line must be fit for purpose, including providing protection for whistleblowers. While the compliance advice that can be purchased from lawyers and accountants, may show that a company has taken the problem seriously, it will not always be a complete answer to an allegation that proper systems and controls were not in place.

It may also be said that, while defining bribery risk, particularly in terms of the known risk of bribery in specified countries, is relatively easy, defining the limits of tax avoidance and tax evasion will almost always be complicated. Most corporate tax schemes will have been put in place in reliance on expensive advice from specialist external lawyers and accountants, who will have given very careful consideration to the relevant tax provisions. Senior management, and the finance department, are likely to take careful note of the advice given without being in a position to judge the intricacies of its legality. But they can be fairly sure that the advice does not propose that a scheme should be put in place that amounts to tax evasion. Therefore, it is very unlikely that the kind of aggressive corporate tax avoidance that has been so much in the news over the last few years will be affected by this measure. Tax evasion is fraudulent and dishonest conduct perpetrated by individuals who can be easily identified, and against which a variety of existing criminal offences can be deployed.

We will probably never know for sure, therefore, how effective this new type of provision is, because these two sections are unlikely to be challenged in the Court of Appeal. Corporates will seek to settle any enforcement action as quickly and cheaply as possible., because settling the case, particularly with a Deferred Prosecution Agreement, will cause less reputational damage, and it will allow the company to return to business as usual.

7.2.6 Unexplained Wealth Orders

The Criminal Finances Act 2017 creates a new form of confiscation, to add to an already long list of attempts to part criminals from their ill-gotten gains: the Unexplained Wealth Order.[15] This enables various law enforcement authorities to apply to the High Court for an Order in respect of any property. The Order requires 'the person whom the Authority thinks holds the property'[16] to provide certain information about it, including how it was paid for. The Court must be satisfied that there is 'reasonable cause to believe' that the respondent owns the property, which must be worth more than £50,000.[17] The Court must also have reasonable grounds for believing that the respondent could not have afforded to buy the property out of his or her assets. This looks simple enough, but one wonders whether in practice it will work as intended. The Civil Recovery Order introduced by the Proceeds of Crime Act 2002[18] has had a checkered history,[19] and it will be interesting to see how the High Court deals with applications under the 2017 Act.

7.2.7 Deferred Prosecution Agreements[20]

At the same time, a new way of litigating the failure to prevent offence – and indeed other corporate offences – has been introduced: the Deferred Prosecution Agreement ('DPA'). The DPA, which is a form of alternative dispute resolution imported from the US, is in essence a process which punishes corporate wrongdoing without creating the risk that the punishment will destroy the company and cause harm to innocent third parties like employees, investors and creditors.[21] It is also another way to improve corporate conduct by persuading companies that reporting their own misdemeanours to the authorities is a sensible alternative to ignoring the problem and allowing the misconduct to continue. It can be followed up by remedial processes, which will be overseen by court appointed monitors. This all demonstrates contrition and will lead to better corporate governance.

The main problem, however, with the 'corporate offence' approach to fraud is that companies cannot go to prison. The only possible sentence is a fine which can be said to have little or no impact, and impact, or deterrence, is an essential part of the criminal process. In the public consciousness it is very unlikely that it will be perceived that a company that receives a reduced fine and no conviction after negotiating a DPA has been punished. Individuals run companies, and individuals, so it is said, should be punished. A corporate fine is just the 'cost of doing business'. At the same time, the process of bringing a DPA before the court is cumbersome and time-consuming, and there is arguably little benefit for Law Enforcement in terms of cost reduction and freeing up resources for other investigations.

7.3 Conclusion

What effect has this legislative and procedural activity had on the business community? The combination of the Senior Management and Certification Regime, DPAs, 'failure to prevent' corporate crimes, and well-intentioned but unprosecutable offences may be said to amount to a package of measures that might, in the long term, improve conduct and, at the same time, reduce the risk of serious damage to the economy and consequent recession. Undoubtedly, there has been an increase in focus on the systems and controls of large businesses. Senior management has been forced to concentrate on governance and compliance issues. There are new approaches to anti-money laundering processes. The private sector is working more closely than ever with law enforcement, to the positive benefit of both sides. But will all this prevent another recession which is largely caused by the familiar combination of corporate greed and misconduct, but which will inevitably be different in scale and scope from any predecessor? Already, the idealistic fervour that saw attempts being made to 'do something' about bad bankers is now being met by the inevitable countercurrent: we must allow businesses to take risks and we must not tie them up in regulatory red tape that prevents creative thinking and profit making.

Against this background, the Fraud Act 2006 looks like good old-fashioned criminal legislation: its aims are clear, and it achieves what it sets out to do, namely to criminalise fraud by fraud offences. It can be used with confidence, and for the purpose of bringing fraudsters to trial. While, of course, it is hoped that there will be an element of deterrent effect, this is not its main aim. By contrast, section 36 of the Financial Services (Banking Reform) Act 2013, section 7 of the Bribery Act 2010, section 45 of the Criminal Finances Act 2017, section 91 of the Financial Services Act 2012, and the Senior Managers and Certification Regime, all seek to improve culture and conduct.

The offences aimed at complex corporate misconduct by senior management of major businesses are sometimes seen as being too difficult and resource intensive to prosecute. There have been occasions when political imperatives have interfered. The Serious Fraud Office, which over the years since 1988 has frequently been threatened with closure, has tried to show that serious and complex fraud can be brought before the courts in an effective way. The roll call of such cases is impressive, and even if the end results have not always been positive, the fact that the SFO has been prepared to take such difficult cases on has acted as a disincentive to corporate misconduct. The extent to which the tide of recent counter fraud legislation will assist the SFO to prosecute complex fraud remains to be seen.

Notes

1 Consultant Solicitor at RS Legal Strategy.
2 The Act came into force on 15 January 2007.
3 Fraud Review: Final Report (Attorney General's Office, 2006) <http://webarchive. nationalarchives.gov.uk/20070222120000/http://www.lslo.gov.uk/pdf/FraudRevie w.pdf> accessed 21 March 2018.
4 C Hodgson, 'More than £150 billion was lost to fraud in 2016' (Business Insider UK, 3 July 2017) <http://uk.businessinsider.com/national-audit-office-rise-in-online-fraud-policing-insufficient-2017–7> accessed 21 March 2018.
5 [1982] QB 1053.
6 [2017] UKSC 67.
7 If there are any statistics about this, I have not been able to find them.
8 PJ Richardson (ed), *Archbold: Criminal Pleading, Evidence and Practice 2018* (66th edn, 2017 Sweet & Maxwell 2017).
9 The Serious Fraud Office prosecution of several Barclays Bank senior managers, which is due to be tried in 2019, is not an example of bosses being prosecuted for causing the 2008 crash. Rather, it is an example of trying to avoid the consequences of it.
10 Parliamentary Commission on Banking Standards, *Changing banking for good* (first report) (2013–14, HL Paper 27-I, HC 175-I).
11 See Financial Conduct Authority, Annual Report and Accounts 2014/15 <www.fca. org.uk/publication/corporate/annual-report-2014–15.pdf> accessed 21 March 2018.
12 *SFO v Tom Hayes,* convicted in August 2015. A confiscation order in the sum of £1.3m was also made against him, and the FCA prohibited him for life from being authorised in the financial sector. Both sanctions have been subject to appeal.
13 Section 45 of the Criminal Finances Act 2017.
14 ibid section 45(2).
15 Section 1 of the Criminal Finances Act 2017 and section 362A of the Proceeds of Crime Act 2002.
16 Section 362A(2)(b) of the Proceeds of Crime Act 2002.
17 ibid Section 362B(2)(a) of the Proceeds of Crime Act 2002.
18 Part V of the Proceeds of Crime Act 2002.
19 In 2014 the Crown Prosecution Service stated that it had only obtained two Civil Recovery Orders: CPS Asset Recovery Strategy, June 2014 <www.cps.gov.uk/sites/ default/files/documents/publications/cps_asset_recovery_strategy_2014.pdf> accessed 21 March 2018.
20 Section 45 and Schedule 17 of the Crime and Courts Act 2013. The Act came into force on 24 February 2014.
21 In the US this process was introduced in the wake of the failure of Enron, and the subsequent demise of Arthur Andersen caused by a threat to prosecute the accountancy firm arising out its dealings with Enron.

Bibliography

Bribery Act 2010
CPS Asset Recovery Strategy, June 2014
Criminal Finances Act 2017
Criminal Law Act 1977

Financial Conduct Authority, Annual Report and Accounts 2014/15
Financial Services Act 2012
Financial Services (Banking Reform) Act 2013
Fraud Act 2006
Fraud Review: Final Report (Attorney General's Office, 2006)
Ghosh [1982] QB 1053
Hodgson, C 'More than £150 billion was lost to fraud in 2016' (Business Insider UK, 3 July 2017)
Parliamentary Commission on Banking Standards, *Changing banking for good* (first report) (2013–14, HL Paper 27-I, HC 175-I)
Proceeds of Crime Act 2002
Richardson, PJ. (ed), *Archbold: Criminal Pleading, Evidence and Practice 2018* (66th edn, 2017 Sweet & Maxwell 2017)
SFO v Tom Hayes (2015) CCA unreported
Theft Act 1968
Theft Act 1978

8 Revisiting dishonesty

The new strict liability criminal offence for offshore tax evaders

Sam Bourton[1]

8.1 Introduction

Tax evasion presents a high cost to worldwide revenues, with losses in the UK alone reaching £5.2bn.[2] Since the recent financial crisis, high public deficits have instigated a new global impetus to combat this financial crime and its deleterious effects on national revenues. This is illustrated by the global proliferation of international agreements, providing for the automatic exchange of information between tax authorities.[3] Soon to come into force, these measures will be 'a real game-changer,' if capable of increasing the compliance information generated from offshore income or accounts to match that received for domestic income.[4] Against this background, the UK Government has recently sought to reform the law and enforcement action taken to combat offshore tax evasion to ensure this new information is utilised to tackle non-compliance effectively.[5] Specifically, the revenue collection authority, Her Majesty's Revenue and Customs ('HMRC'), has been tasked with increasing prosecutions for tax evasion offences to 1165 individuals in 2014/15,[6] with the aim of sustaining this level thereafter.[7] This is in sharp contrast to previous practice, as HMRC rarely instituted criminal proceedings for tax evasion offences, opting instead to settle liabilities by way of cost-effective civil settlement procedures.[8] These targets have been bolstered by the introduction of new criminal offences to tackle tax evasion,[9] including a new criminal offence for offshore tax evaders.[10]

The aim of this chapter is to determine the impact this new offence will have on prosecutions for offshore tax evasion. The chapter begins by outlining the scope of the offence and the proposed rationale for its introduction. The second section considers whether the new offence is likely to meet this objective, by exploring the problems formerly inherent in proving criminal intent for offshore tax evasion offences. This analysis will involve a consideration of the problems engendered by the *Ghosh* and *Ivey* tests of dishonesty in English Law, discussed extensively in relation to fraud and theft offences, with a specific focus on the difficulties encountered in the prosecution of tax evasion offences. The final part of this chapter considers the likely effects of combatting these difficulties using a strict liability offence and examines whether any adverse effects are likely to be tempered by available safeguards and defences.

8.2 The new offence

After an extensive period of consultation, and near unanimous disapproval from respondents,[11] the strict liability criminal offence for offshore tax evaders was enacted in the Finance Act 2016.[12] The offence was introduced in an attempt to remedy some of the challenges involved in tackling offshore tax evasion, providing HMRC with a 'valuable additional tool' to increase the number of successful prosecutions.[13] The realisation of these aims is intended to be fulfilled by the strict liability nature of the offence, which makes 'prosecution easier by removing the need to prove intent,' thereby operating as a deterrent to those seeking to evade their tax liabilities offshore.[14]

The offence is committed when an individual fails to give notice of chargeability to tax,[15] fails to deliver a return,[16] or makes an inaccurate return,[17] in relation to offshore income, assets or activities in excess of the threshold amount,[18] which is currently £25,000 of potential lost tax revenue per year.[19] The offence applies to income tax and capital gains tax and encompasses all offshore income and gains, which are not reportable under the Common Reporting Standard ('CRS').[20] As noted, the offence is one of strict liability, where it is unnecessary to determine the state of mind of the defendant to obtain a conviction.[21] However, it is a defence for an individual to show that they have a reasonable excuse for failing to give the required notice,[22] or delivering the return,[23] or to show that they took reasonable care to ensure the accuracy of a submitted return.[24] The offence is of a summary nature, punishable by a fine and/or a maximum of six months imprisonment.[25]

8.3 Dishonesty

The new offence constitutes an unprecedented change in the common understanding of both the definition and nature of criminal tax evasion. For instance, although in its widest sense tax evasion is a term simply used to describe any 'illegal non-payment or underpayment of tax,'[26] previously, for an individual to be liable to prosecution, he must also have possessed the requisite *mens rea*.[27] In contrast, the new offence does not require any proof of *mens rea*; the act itself now forms the basis of liability. This change was introduced in an attempt to facilitate the prosecution of offshore tax evasion, assisting with the fulfilment of recent targets.[28] In light of this articulated rationale, this section examines the difficulties formerly inherent in proving criminal intent in prosecutions for this crime.[29]

Prosecutions for offshore tax evasion are currently brought under a plethora of statutory and common law offences, including statutory offences of making a false representation,[30] false accounting,[31] and being knowingly concerned in the fraudulent evasion of income tax,[32] and common law offences of conspiracy to defraud and cheating the public revenue.[33] Almost all of these offences require proof of *mens rea*;[34] the appropriate test is whether the defendant acted 'dishonesty'.[35] As such, dishonesty is a primary consideration in many tax evasion cases and is often of fundamental importance to a determination of liability for the offence. For instance, the predominantly used common law offence of cheating the public revenue is considered to be so extraordinarily broad,[36] that dishonesty is often the 'only live issue at trial'.[37] This is because the breadth of the offence means that it *prima facie* encompasses any form of deliberate tax non-compliance, including ineffective tax avoidance schemes, with dishonesty forming the crucial determinant of criminal liability.[38] Further, even where the *actus reus* of a tax evasion offence is narrowly defined, the conduct elements are frequently largely predetermined or admitted, leaving the trial to focus on the issue of dishonesty.[39] In effect, the notion of dishonesty is central to considerations of criminality in tax non-compliance and is considered an essential element of both the nature and definition of the offence.[40]

The appropriate test of dishonesty is that used for many other financial offences, such as theft and fraud.[41] In the case of *Feely*, dishonesty was held to be an ordinary word and thus, not a question of law to be defined judicially,[42] but a question of fact to be determined by a jury applying the current standards of ordinary decent people.[43] Consequently, following the case of *Ghosh*,[44] for over 35 years, the test to be applied was as follows;

1   Was the defendant's conduct dishonest according to the ordinary standards of reasonable and honest people?
2   If it was so dishonest, did the defendant himself realise that what he was doing was by those standards dishonest?[45]

The *Ghosh* test, and its impact on prosecutions, was the subject of well-known and sustained criticism. These criticisms centred on the fact that dishonesty is an unusual requirement in English Law, as the *Ghosh* test required jurors to go beyond ascertaining the defendant's state of mind, to additionally determine whether that state of mind was dishonest.[46] In other words, the jury were not tasked with determining whether the defendant's conduct satisfies the legal definition of an offence; they were asked to characterise his conduct by making a moral judgement.[47]

Commentators suggested that the first limb of the test would result in inconsistent verdicts, as, although dishonesty may be an ordinary word,[48] individuals will differ on its application to specified conduct.[49] This is because, in a diverse society, there is unlikely to be a congruence of views in relation to dishonesty, and thus, no such thing as 'the standards of ordinary decent people'.[50] This potentially led to different outcomes in indistinguishable cases, creating uncertainty regarding the criminality of conduct.[51] Further, the test, in its attempt to cope with a lack of definition, may have given too much discretion to the jury, potentially leading to the conviction of defendants based on irrelevant considerations,[52] or ' "anarchic" verdicts which are not technically perverse'.[53] However, as dishonesty was a question of fact, there was little recourse to review by the appellate courts.[54]

The test was also said to lead to longer and more difficult trials as this ambiguity may prompt the defendant to 'take his chance with the jury'.[55] Here, the defendant is not constrained by a legal definition and may instead opt to take advantage of the uncertainty surrounding how the jury will characterise his conduct.[56] The second limb of the test also presented difficulties in this regard in that, aside from being superfluous,[57] it allowed the defendant to claim that he did not realise his conduct was dishonest, in effect permitting him to advance something akin to a mistake of law as a defence.[58] Here, there may have been substantial difficulties in convicting a defendant who held a genuine belief in their honesty, posing a threat to widely held standards of conduct.[59]

In expressing concerns over the second limb of the test, in the recent case of *Ivey*,[60] the Supreme Court effectively dispensed with the *Ghosh* test.[61] In *Ivey*, the Court held that in determining dishonesty, a jury should first ascertain the defendant's subjective belief as to the facts, and must then consider whether his conduct was dishonest according to the standards of reasonable and honest people.[62] Although this decision removed the second limb of the *Ghosh* test, alleviating the difficulty in prosecuting defendants with warped standards of honesty,[63] *Ivey* does not remedy the concerns expressed over the first limb of the *Ghosh* test, nor the ambiguity and inconsistency likely to stem from its application. As such, it is important to consider the impact of the dishonesty test on the prosecution of tax evasion offences.

8.4 Dishonesty and tax evasion

Ormerod persuasively argues that the dishonesty test 'raises special difficulty in revenue cases'.[64] This is because the aforementioned concerns are said to be exacerbated in 'specialised cases' where juries, for want of experience, cannot appreciate the context in which the activities are undertaken.[65] Tax evasion is a key example of such a specialised case, for although jurors may be able to easily determine dishonesty in some cases, many will involve unfamiliar and complicated tax arrangements.[66] As a result, the jury are unlikely to be able to accurately determine dishonesty in these situations; a problem unaided by the fact that the jury cannot hear evidence on what is considered to amount to dishonesty in this context,[67] including evidence of common market practice,[68] or regulatory attitudes to the conduct in question.[69] These concerns are further exacerbated in relation to offshore tax evasion, where the activities involved are often not only complex and alien to most ordinary jurors, but also, cloaked in secrecy.[70]

It is unclear what effect this ambiguity may have on prosecutions for tax evasion offences, as there is a lack of empirical evidence demonstrating the impact of the dishonesty test.[71] However, it is possible that, in certain cases, the jury's uncertainty in regards to dishonesty will advantage the defendant, as the prosecution will find it difficult to discharge the persuasive burden without clear evidence.[72] Conversely, in others, this uncertainty may benefit the prosecution, in that the jury may view complex tax arrangements as distinct from their own activities and therefore dishonest, without taking an informed view of the situation;[73] particularly, if the activities involved are 'artificial and unreal to the layperson'.[74] Moreover, even if the jury is able to comprehend the context of the activities undertaken, it is unclear what the standards of 'ordinary reasonable and honest people' are in relation to tax evasion. On the one hand, tax evasion was once regarded as a morally ambiguous, socially acceptable crime,[75] which may have made it difficult to persuade a jury to convict in all save the most egregious of cases. However, in recent times, public perceptions of both tax evasion and tax avoidance have altered. Here, as the terms are often conflated by the media and the revenue,[76] and both activities are likely to be seen as contrary to the public good and therefore dishonest,[77] the changing public perception of these activities may enable not only the successful prosecution of tax evasion, but also, the prosecution of a wider range of activities, such as ineffective tax avoidance.[78]

Only one thing is clear; dishonesty is responsible for uncertainty in the process, both for individuals and their advisors,[79] and for prosecutors in deciding whether to bring a criminal charge based on the likely success of the prosecution.[80] Here, it is not inconceivable to think that an authority empowered with the discretion to select an appropriate response to instances of non-compliance,[81] will err on the side of caution in pursuing cost-effective civil penalties, in all but the most straightforward cases.[82] Therefore, it is likely that the requirement to prove the defendant acted dishonestly hinders the prosecution of offshore tax evasion offences, at the very least, because of the inconsistency and uncertainty it creates.

Nevertheless, it is possible that too little faith has been placed in the jury's ability to recognise dishonesty in most circumstances.[83] In these instances, the dishonesty test provides an important function in the criminal law, in that it excludes from the ambit of the offence conduct, which is not morally blameworthy, is too minor to warrant a criminal sanction, or which the defendant genuinely believes he has a legal right to engage in.[84] In this respect, the dishonesty requirement prevents a defendant from being unjustly convicted of a stigmatic offence, with the consequences to his livelihood and reputation this may entail;[85] in other words, the test implements justice over consistency by ensuring that the jury considers all of the circumstances relevant to the specific case.[86] The Law Commission, when examining the law pertaining to fraud, noted that this is an unusual approach with moral culpability usually considered in the requirements of the offence itself and rare instances of blameless conduct dealt with using prosecutorial discretion and sentencing decisions.[87] Indeed, they initially concluded that the availability of these options caused the disadvantages engendered by the test to outweigh these potential advantages.[88]

However, tax evasion is unique in relation to other crimes, in that these alternatives are not satisfactory. First, prosecutorial discretion may not be forthcoming when authorities are tasked with increasing the number of prosecutions for tax evasion.[89] Secondly, the *actus reus* of many tax evasion offences may encapsulate traditionally non-criminal conduct. For instance, a taxpayer who makes an innocent mistake as to their liability, or pursues a tax avoidance scheme, which is later declared ineffective, will often satisfy the conduct elements of a tax evasion offence. Thus, to incorporate moral culpability in the requirements of the offence itself, a form of *mens rea* capable of distinguishing between a) those who seek to act within the boundaries of the law in meeting their tax liabilities, but ultimately fail to do so, and b) those who set out to disregard them, would need to be established. However, no alternative form of *mens rea* accurately captures this distinction. In relation to the new offence, the Fraud Lawyers' Association notes:

> It is not possible to square this definition [tax evasion] with lesser forms of *mens rea*. One only has to consider other offences of dishonesty to make the point. For example, it is not possible to handle stolen goods negligently, or commit insurance fraud carelessly. Any such suggestion would be absurd.[90]

The distinction is fundamental when considering that the conduct element of tax evasion offences is more likely to be committed in a blameless manner. The UK's tax code is one of the longest in the world,[91] and when applied, its notorious complexity is highly likely to result in honest mistakes. In these cases, the dishonesty criterion is preferable to other mental elements, as it permits an examination of the accused's motive, or '"why" the alleged offence occurred instead of just "how" it occurred'.[92] This is essential, as it is the accused's motive which should be pivotal in transforming simple tax noncompliance, into one warranting a criminal response.

In this respect, the recent decision in *Ivey*[93] may also have unforeseen effects on tax evasion prosecutions, in that, if the defendant's subjective belief as to the facts is not adequately considered in the jury's characterisation of the honesty of the conduct concerned, many of the benefits derived from the dishonesty test will be lost.[94]

8.5 Strict liability

In enacting the new offence, the legislature did not remedy the perceived problems caused by the dishonesty test with an alternative test, or form of *mens rea*, but rather, with a strict liability offence.[95] The legislature's decision to impose a strict liability offence was undoubtedly motivated by the advantages conferred by these offences, including their ability to offer greater protection to the public from certain forms of harm.[96] This is because, in dispensing with *mens rea*, it is easier to prosecute those who cause such adverse effects,[97] as this task is notoriously difficult, requiring considerable time and effort.[98] In this respect, these types of offences are particularly beneficial when it is especially difficult to prove criminal intent; for instance, when the offence consists of a failure to comply with a rule or standard,[99] or regulates corporate activity.[100] In addition, strict liability offences decrease the costs involved in prosecuting the offence, by reducing the number of elements to be proved at trial.[101] In turn, the ease of prosecuting strict liability offences is said to deter others from engaging in the prohibited conduct.[102]

However, strict liability offences are often objectionable, as they offend against the principle that criminal offences should require proof of fault.[103] The importance of this principle stems from the fact that it prevents the conviction and punishment of those who have not had the opportunity to conduct their activities within the boundaries of the law, ensuring adherence to the rule of law,[104] and preventing unwarranted intrusions into individual liberty.[105] In addition, the principle of *mens rea* assists in achieving the appropriate application of the criminal law, by protecting those who have acted without fault from the consequences of a criminal conviction.[106] Accordingly, by failing to give effect to this principle, strict liability offences may lead to the unjust conviction of those who are not culpable or blameworthy in committing an offence.[107]

8.6 Strict liability and tax evasion

In effect, the introduction of a strict liability offence for offshore tax evaders is likely to facilitate the prosecution of those who have evaded their tax liabilities offshore, as it will be easier to secure convictions for the offence. Although reform of the dishonesty test, or the substitution of dishonesty for an alternative form of *mens rea*, may also have this positive effect, the creation of a strict liability offence is almost certain to do so. This is because the offence removes all difficulties surrounding proving *mens rea*, such as the persistent problem of illustrating a culpable failure to comply with tax legislation, regardless of how that *mens rea* is expressed. In addition, it is likely to decrease the costs involved in such prosecutions, potentially encouraging HMRC to pursue this route.[108] Finally, the ease of prosecuting the offence, coupled with serious consequences for the evader, is in turn likely to deter others. Therefore, if these anticipated effects are realised, it initially appears that the new offence will have a positive impact.

However, it is also clear that the introduction the offence is likely to result in adverse effects on individuals as, in dispensing with *mens rea*, the offence may be imposed on those who are not culpable or blameworthy in respect of its commission. The examples given in the consultation responses are illustrative in this regard; the new offence may initially apply to individuals who are genuinely unaware of a tax liability that has arisen on offshore income or assets, those who incorrectly believe themselves to be non-resident and thus, not liable to tax, or those who have legitimately attempted to plan their tax liabilities offshore, but have taken an incorrect view of the correct tax treatment, amongst others.[109] In these circumstances, the offence may be said to produce injustice, in that these individuals have not been able to consciously conduct their activities within the boundaries of the law and may be subject to the censure and stigma attaching to a criminal conviction, regardless of their level of fault.

8.7 Safeguards and defences

The offence contains several important safeguards and defences. The offence only applies to the evasion of income, assets or activities, which exceed the threshold amount of £25,000 of lost tax revenue per year,[110] and are not reportable under the CRS.[111] These provisions are likely to be a significant safeguard in restricting the scope of the offence, but alone are not sufficient, as many individuals with significant offshore income, assets or activities may be unaware of their tax liabilities in the UK.[112] Accordingly, the new offence provides that it is a defence for an individual to show that they have a reasonable excuse for failing to give the required notice,[113] or for failing to deliver the return,[114] or to show that they took reasonable care to ensure the accuracy of a submitted return.[115] These defences are familiar in tax legislation and although guidance on their application is yet to be released, it is expected to follow current practice.[116] Here, if construed widely, the defences may enable the court to take into account the state of mind of the defendant,[117] effectively ameliorating 'the harshness of liability without fault'.[118] In addition, these defences may permit a consideration of the individual's personal circumstances and abilities in a way that traditional *mens rea* elements cannot.[119] If this is achieved, the defences may ensure that the offence does not apply to those who have acted without fault in its commission.

However, the question remains as to whether the available defences will ever be able to fully prevent the possibility of criminalising blameless conduct, for there is always a risk that the defendant will not be able to produce evidence of taking reasonable care or having a reasonable excuse, even if he has actually done so.[120] Further, the offence provides that evidence of reasonable care or reasonable excuse is a defence, rather than an aspect of the offence,[121] yet, it is unclear why the defendant should bare this burden.[122] Moreover, even if these defences are widely interpreted, the offence could still potentially capture conduct formerly considered insufficiently culpable to constitute a tax evasion offence,[123] as the availability of defences essentially transforms the offence into a negligence offence, which, although preferable to a 'pure' strict liability offence, nonetheless constitutes a lesser standard of *mens rea*. In effect, it is likely that the safeguards and defences contained in the new strict liability offence are not sufficient to prevent the prosecution of those who have acted without fault in its commission.

8.8 Conclusion

Overall, it is likely that the new offence, by removing the need to prove the defendant acted dishonestly, or indeed any form of *mens rea*, will have the effect of increasing the certainty and consistency of the application of the law pertaining to offshore tax evasion, in turn increasing the success rate of prosecutions for this crime. However, as the new offence does not require criminal intent, it is also likely to criminalise conduct considered to be undertaken without fault, directly conflicting with both fundamental principles of the criminal law and traditional conceptions of tax evasion offences. It remains to be seen whether the safeguards and defences contained in the new strict liability offence are sufficient to prevent this possibility. Nevertheless, it is clear that the need for a strict liability offence has not been made out. Here, it is disappointing that the perceived problems have been addressed with the imposition of a limited, and arguably unjust, strict liability offence, without first considering alternative solutions. This overlooks the nature of criminal tax evasion and fails to address the root of the problem in other tax evasion offences.

Notes

1 Department of Law, University of the West of England.
2 HMRC, *Measuring Tax Gaps 2017 Edition: Tax Gap Estimates for 2015–16* (Official Statistics, 26 October 2017) 5.
3 OECD, Standard for Automatic Exchange of Financial Account Information in Tax Matters (July 2014, OECD Publishing).
4 OECD, 'OECD Delivers New Single Global Standard on Automatic Exchange of Information' (OECD, February 2014). <www.oecd.org/g20/topics/taxation/oecd-delivers-new-single-global-standard-on-automatic-exchange-of-information.htm> accessed 30 March 2018.
5 See for instance, HMRC, 'No Safe Havens 2014' (14 April 2014) <www.gov.uk/government/uploads/system/uploads/attachment_data/file/303012/No_safe_havens_2014.pdf> accessed 30 March 2018.
6 HM Treasury, *Spending Review 2010* (Cmd 7942, 2010) 71.
7 See also HM Treasury, *Summer Budget 2015* (HC 2015–16, 264) 43.
8 HMRC 'Guidance: HMRC Policy' (December 2015) <www.hmrc.gov.uk/prosecutions/crim-inv-policy.htm> accessed 30 March 2018
9 Criminal Finances Act 2017, Part 3.
10 Introduced in the Finance Act 2016, s166 amending Taxes Management Act 1970, s106.
11 Including the Fraud Lawyers' Association, The Law Society, The Bar Council, The Criminal Bar Association of England & Wales, ICAEW, CIOT, ICAS, AAT, and STEP.
12 Finance Act 2016, s166 amending Taxes Management Act 1970, s106; Brought into force following The Finance Act 2016, Section 166 (Appointed Day) Regulations 2017, SI 2017/970.
13 HMRC, *Tackling Offshore Tax Evasion: A New Criminal Offence for Offshore Evaders* (Summary of Responses and Further Consultation, July 2015) 8.
14 HMRC, Tackling Offshore Tax Evasion: A New Criminal Offence for Offshore Evaders (Summary of Responses, December 2015) 3.
15 Taxes Management Act 1970, s106B.
16 s106C.
17 s106D.
18 s106B(1)(b), s106C(1)(c), s106D(1)(b).
19 s106F(2); The Sections 106B, 106C and 106D of the Taxes Management Act 1970 (Specified Threshold Amount) Regulations 2017, SI 2017/988, Reg 3.
20 SI 2017/988 (n19), Reg 2C; OECD (n 2).
21 Taxes Management Act 1970, s106B, s106C, s106D.
22 s106B(2).
23 s106C(2).
24 s106D(2).

25 s106G.
26 A Stevenson (ed), *Oxford Dictionary of English* (3rd edn, OUP 2010) 1823.
27 See Fraud Act 2006, s1; Theft Act 1968, s17; Value Added Tax Act 1994, s72(1), 72(3), 72(8); Taxes Management Act 1970, s106A; Customs and Excise Management Act 1979, s167, s170, s170A and B; conspiracy to defraud preserved by s5(2) of the Criminal Law Act 1977; cheating the public revenue preserved by s32(1)(a) Theft Act 1968, see *R v Hudson* [1956] 1 All ER 814 (CA).
28 HMRC (n13) 3.
29 The propriety or efficacy of prosecuting increasing numbers of tax evaders is not considered here.
30 Fraud Act 2006, s1.
31 Theft Act 1968, s17.
32 Taxes Management Act 1970, s106A.
33 Conspiracy to defraud preserved by section 5(2) of the Criminal Law Act 1977; cheating the public revenue preserved by section 32(1)(a) Theft Act 1968, see *R v Hudson* [1956] 1 All ER 814; indirect tax offences include Value Added Tax Act 1994, s72(1), 72(3), 72(8); Customs and Excise Management Act 1979, s170, s170A and B.
34 With the exception of Customs and Excise Management Act 1979, s167(3), s170A.
35 Either as an express requirement or as an aspect of the word fraudulently *A-G's Reference No1 of 1981* [1982] QB 848 (CA); Others require an intention to deceive Value Added Tax Act 1994, s72(3)(a); knowledge or recklessness s72(3)(b) see also s72(8); or knowledge and intention Customs and Excise Management Act 1979, s170(1).
36 *R v Less The Times*, 30 March 1993 (CA).
37 D Ormerod, 'Cheating the Public Revenue' [1998] Crim LR 627, 630; See also, conspiracy to defraud, Law Commission, *Fraud* (Law Com No 276, 2002) 86.
38 ibid; see also D Ormerod, 'Summary Evasion of Income Tax' [2002] Crim LR 3, 21.
39 P Kiernan, G Scanlon, 'Fraud and the Law Commission: The Future of Dishonesty' (2003) 24 Comp Law 4, 6.
40 G McBain, 'Modernising the Common Law Offence of Cheating the Public Revenue' (2015) 8 *Journal of Politics and Law* 40, 76.
41 *Ivey v Genting Casinos* (UK) Ltd [2017] UKSC 67.
42 Following *Brutus v. Cozens* [1973] AC 854 (HL).
43 *R v Feely* [1973] QB 530 (CA).
44 *R v Ghosh* [1982] 2 All ER 689 (CA).
45 ibid at p1064; the *Ghosh* direction is only given in certain circumstances *R v. Roberts* (1987) 84 Cr App R 117 (CA).
46 Law Commission, Legislating the Criminal Code: Fraud and Deception: A Consultation Paper (Law Com No 155, 1999) 5.11.
47 ibid.
48 *Feely* (n 43); Following *Brutus* (n 42).
49 See the Victorian case of *Salvo*, which rejected *Feely, R v. Salvo* [1980] VR 401, p428; see A Steel, 'The Meanings of Dishonesty in Theft' (2009) 38 CLWR 103.
50 E Griew, 'Dishonesty: Objections to Feely and Ghosh' [1985] Crim LR 341, 344.
51 Creating problems in relation to Article 7 of the ECHR; Law Commission (n 46) p.60–65.
52 D Ormerod, 'The Fraud Act 2006 – Criminalising Lying?' [2007] Crim LR 193, 201.
53 DW Elliott, 'Dishonesty in Theft: A Dispensable Concept' [1982] Crim LR 395, 409.
54 M Jefferson, 'Conspiracy to Defraud and Dishonesty' (1998) 62 J Crim L 580, 581.
55 Griew (n 50) 343.

56 ibid.
57 See K Campbell, 'The Test of Dishonesty in *R v Ghosh*' (1984) 43 CLJ 349; see also *Ivey* (n 41).
58 JR Spencer, 'Dishonesty: What the Jury Thinks the Defendant Thought the Jury Would Have Thought' [1982] CLJ 222, 224.
59 A Samuels, 'Dishonesty' (2003) 67 J Crim L 324, 325.
60 *Ivey* (n 41).
61 *DPP v Patterson* [2017] EWHC 2820 (admin); [2018] ACD 7.
62 *Ivey* (n41) at para 74.
63 G Treverton-Jones, 'In Person: Disciplinary Proceedings: Defining Dishonesty' (2017) 6 LS Gaz 29, 29; cf G Virgo, 'Cheating and Dishonesty' (2018) 77 CLJ 18, 20.
64 Ormerod (n 37) 635.
65 Griew (n 50) 345.
66 J Freedman, 'Tax and Corporate Responsibility' (2003) 695(2) Tax J 1, 3.
67 Campbell (n 57) 358.
68 *R v. Lockwood* (1986) 2 B.C.C. 99333 (CA); only relevant to the second question *R v Hayes* [2015] EWCA Crim 1944; [2016] 1 Cr App R (S) 63; cf J Rogers, 'Case Comment: Dishonesty in the First LIBOR Trial' (2016) 3 Arch Rev 7.
69 *Hayes* (n 68) at [19] cited in N Dent, A Kervick, '*Ghosh*: A Change in Direction?' (2016) 8 Crim LR 553, 555.
70 J Fisher, 'HSBC, Tax Evasion and Criminal Prosecution' (2015) 1253 Tax J 6.
71 See research by Fafinski and Finch, discussed in S Chand, 'Women Judge, But Do They Convict?' (BBC News, 7 September 2009) <http://news.bbc.co.uk/1/hi/sci/tech/8242870.stm> accessed 30 March 2018.
72 Freedman (n 66) 3.
73 ibid.
74 Ormerod (n 37) 638.
75 SP Green, *Lying, Cheating, and Stealing: A Moral Theory of White-Collar Crime* (OUP 2007) 243.
76 MP Devereux, J Freedman, J Vella, 'Tax Avoidance' (Paper No 1, Oxford University Centre for Business Taxation, 3 December 2012) <www.sbs.ox.ac.uk/sites/default/files/Business_Taxation/Docs/Publications/Reports/TA_3_12_12.pdf> accessed 30 March 2018, 15.
77 HMRC, 'Exploring Public Attitudes to Tax Avoidance in 2015' (HMRC Research Report 401, February 2016) <www.gov.uk/government/uploads/system/uploads/attachment_data/file/500203/Exploring_public_attitude_to_tax_avoidance_in_2015.pdf> accessed 30 March 2018.
78 See for instance, *R v Charlton* [1996] STC 1418; discussed in Ormerod (n 37) 638.
79 See generally Devereux, Freedman and Vella (n 76).
80 M Wasik, 'Mens Rea, Motive and the Problem of Dishonesty in the Law of Theft [1979] Crim LR 543, 552; see also Griew (n 50) 341.
81 HMRC (n 8)
82 HMRC have been criticised for prosecuting lower-value cases to meet targets National Audit Office, *Tackling Tax Fraud: How HMRC Responds to Tax Evasion, The Hidden Economy and Criminal Attacks* (HC 2015–16, 610-I) at [16].
83 Kiernan and Scanlon (n 39) 6.
84 Law Commission (n 46) at 7.40.
85 *Feely* (n 43) at 541.
86 R Tur, 'Dishonesty and the Jury' in AP Griffiths (ed), *Philosophy and Practice* (CUP 1985) 83.
87 Law Commission (n 37) 7.52.
88 Law Commission (n 46) 5.13.
89 HM Treasury (n 7).

90 Fraud Lawyers Association, 'Tackling Offshore Tax Evasion: A New Criminal Offence – Response to the HMRC Consultation from the Fraud Lawyers' Association' <http://tinyurl.com/zfnrscx> accessed 30 March 2018; See also McBain (n 40) 76.

91 C Turnbull-Hall, R Thomas, 'Length of Tax Legislation as a Measure of Complexity' (Office of Tax Simplification, April 2012) <http://tinyurl.com/h7ljqlo> accessed 30 March 2018.

92 Wasik (n 80) 550.

93 *Ivey* (n 41).

94 M Dyson, P Jarvis, 'Poison Ivey or Herbal Tea Leaf?' (2018) 134 LQR 198, 202–3.

95 HMRC (n 14) 3.

96 *Sweet v Parsley* [1970] AC 132 (HL) at 163.

97 A Ashworth, 'Should Strict Criminal Liability be Removed from all Imprisonable Offences?' in A Ashworth, *Positive Obligations in Criminal Law* (OUP 2013) 117.

98 J Stanton-Ife, 'Strict Liability: Stigma and Regret' (2007) 27 OJLS 151, 151.

99 A Brudner, 'Imprisonment and Strict Liability' (1990) 40 UTLJ 738, 753.

100 Where the identification principle would apply *Lennard's Carrying Co Ltd v Asiatic Petroleum Co Ltd* [1915] A.C. 705 (HL) at 713; see also *Meridan Global Funds Management Asia Ltd v Securities Commission* [1995] 2 A.C. 500 (HL) at 509; Criminal Finances Act 2017, Part 3.

101 AP Simester, 'Is Strict Liability Always Wrong?' in AP Simester (ed), *Appraising Strict Liability* (OUP 2005) 26.

102 See generally AP Simester (ed), *Appraising Strict Liability* (OUP 2005); G Lamond, 'What is a Crime?' (2007) 27 OJLS 609, 629.

103 Ashworth (n 97) 112.

104 ibid; citing HLA Hart, Punishment and Responsibility: Essays in the Philosophy of Law (2nd edn, OUP 2008) 152; see also *B (A Child) v Director of Public Prosecutions* [2000] 2 AC 428 (HL) at 470.

105 J Horder, 'Strict Liability, Statutory Construction, and the Spirit of Liberty' (2002) 118 LQR 458, 458.

106 Simester (n 101) 34.

107 RA Duff, *Answering for Crime: Responsibility and Liability in the Criminal Law* (Hart 2007) 243.

108 Cost considerations can be seen to influence the policy in HMRC (n 8).

109 See for instance, ICAEW, 'Tackling Offshore Tax Evasion: A New Criminal Offence' (Consultation Response, 6 November 2014) <http://tinyurl.com/zkj5mwj> accessed 30 March 2018; CIOT, 'HMRC Consultation Document – Tackling Offshore Tax Evasion: A New Criminal Offence for Offshore Tax Evaders – Response by the Chartered Institute of Taxation' (9 October 2015) <http://tinyurl.com/h3gkmqv> accessed 30 March 2018.

110 Taxes Management Act 1970, s106B(1)(b), s106C(1)(c), s106D(1)(b); SI 2017/988 (n 19), Reg 3.

111 SI 2017/988 (n 19), Reg 2C.

112 For example, 'asset rich cash poor migrants', Low Incomes Tax Reform Group, 'Tackling Offshore Tax Evasion: A New Criminal Offence for Offshore Tax Evaders – HMRC Consultation Document – Response from the Low Incomes Tax Reform Group' (31 October 2014) <http://tinyurl.com/hvfu2sc> accessed 30 March 2018.

113 Taxes Management Act 1970, s106B(2).

114 s106C(2).

115 s106D(2).

116 HMRC (n 14) 9.

117 *R v Unah* [2011] EWCA Crim 1837

118 A Reed, 'Strict Liability and the Reasonable Excuse Defence' (2012) 76 J Crim L 293, 297.

119 J Horder, 'Whose Values Should Determine When Liability is Strict?' in AP Simester (ed), *Appraising Strict Liability* (OUP 2005) 124.
120 Duff (n 107) 245.
121 HMRC (n 14) 9.
122 Duff (n 107) 246.
123 'A prerequisite of the offence has always been dishonesty. None of the case law indicates that oversight, unintentional error etc, was criminally culpable' McBain (n 40) 76.

Bibliography

Ashworth A, 'Should Strict Criminal Liability be Removed from all Imprisonable Offences?' in A Ashworth, *Positive Obligations in Criminal Law* (OUP 2013)
Brudner A, 'Imprisonment and Strict Liability' (1990) 40 UTLJ 738
Campbell K, 'The Test of Dishonesty in *R v Ghosh*' (1984) 43 CLJ 349
Chand S, 'Women Judge, But Do They Convict?' (BBC News, 7 September 2009) <http://news.bbc.co.uk/1/hi/sci/tech/8242870.stm> accessed 30 March 2018
CIOT, 'HMRC Consultation Document – Tackling Offshore Tax Evasion: A New Criminal Offence for Offshore Tax Evaders – Response by the Chartered Institute of Taxation' (9 October 2015) <http://tinyurl.com/h3gkmqv> accessed 30 March 2018
Dent N and Kervick A, 'Ghosh: A Change in Direction?' (2016) 8 Crim LR 553
Devereux MP, Freedman J, Vella J, 'Tax Avoidance' (Paper No 1, Oxford University Centre for Business Taxation, 3 December 2012) <www.sbs.ox.ac.uk/sites/default/files/Business_Taxation/Docs/Publications/Reports/TA_3_12_12.pdf> accessed 30 March 2018
Duff RA, *Answering for Crime: Responsibility and Liability in the Criminal Law* (Hart 2007)
Dyson M, Jarvis P, 'Poison Ivey or Herbal Tea Leaf?' (2018) 134 LQR 198
Elliott DW, 'Dishonesty in Theft: A Dispensable Concept' [1982] Crim LR 395
Fisher J, 'HSBC, Tax Evasion and Criminal Prosecution' (2015) 1253 Tax J 6
Fraud Lawyers Association, 'Tackling Offshore Tax Evasion: A New Criminal Offence – Response to the HMRC Consultation from the Fraud Lawyers' Association' <http://tinyurl.com/zfnrscx> accessed 30 March 2018
Freedman J, 'Tax and Corporate Responsibility' (2003) 695(2) Tax J 1
Green SP, *Lying, Cheating, and Stealing: A Moral Theory of White-Collar Crime* (OUP 2007)
Griew E, 'Dishonesty: Objections to Feely and Ghosh' [1985] Crim LR 341
Hart HLA, *Punishment and Responsibility: Essays in the Philosophy of Law* (2nd edn, OUP 2008)
HMRC, 'No Safe Havens 2014' (14 April 2014) <www.gov.uk/government/uploads/system/uploads/attachment_data/file/303012/No_safe_havens_2014.pdf> accessed 30 March 2018
HMRC, 'Exploring Public Attitudes to Tax Avoidance in 2015' (HMRC Research Report 401, February 2016) <www.gov.uk/government/uploads/system/uploads/attachment_data/file/500203/Exploring_public_attitude_to_tax_avoidance_in_2015.pdf> accessed 30 March 2018
HMRC, *Tackling Offshore Tax Evasion: A New Criminal Offence for Offshore Evaders* (Summary of Responses and Further Consultation, July 2015)
HMRC, *Tackling Offshore Tax Evasion: A New Criminal Offence for Offshore Evaders* (Summary of Responses, December 2015)

HMRC 'Guidance: HMRC Policy' (December 2015) <www.hmrc.gov.uk/prosecutions/crim-inv-policy.htm> accessed 30 March 2018

HMRC, *Measuring Tax Gaps 2017 Edition: Tax Gap Estimates for 2015–16* (Official Statistics, 26 October 2017)

HM Treasury, *Spending Review 2010* (Cmd 7942, 2010)

HM Treasury, *Summer Budget 2015* (HC 2015–16, 264)

Horder J, 'Strict Liability, Statutory Construction, and the Spirit of Liberty' (2002) 118 LQR 458

Horder J, 'Whose Values Should Determine When Liability is Strict?' in Simester AP (ed), *Appraising Strict Liability* (OUP 2005)

ICAEW, 'Tackling Offshore Tax Evasion: A New Criminal Offence' (Consultation Response, 6 November 2014) <http://tinyurl.com/zkj5mwj> accessed 30 March 2018

Jefferson M, 'Conspiracy to Defraud and Dishonesty' (1998) 62 J Crim L 580

Kiernan P, Scanlon G, 'Fraud and the Law Commission: The Future of Dishonesty' (2003) 24 Comp Law 4

Lamond G, 'What is a Crime?' (2007) 27 OJLS 609

Law Commission, *Fraud* (Law Com No 276, 2002)

Law Commission, *Legislating the Criminal Code: Fraud and Deception: A Consultation Paper* (Law Com No 155, 1999)

Low Incomes Tax Reform Group, 'Tackling Offshore Tax Evasion: A New Criminal Offence for Offshore Tax Evaders – HMRC Consultation Document – Response from the Low Incomes Tax Reform Group' (31 October 2014) <http://tinyurl.com/hvfu2sc> accessed 30 March 2018

McBain G, 'Modernising the Common Law Offence of Cheating the Public Revenue' (2015) 8 *Journal of Politics and Law* 40

National Audit Office, *Tackling Tax Fraud: How HMRC Responds to Tax Evasion, The Hidden Economy and Criminal Attacks* (HC 2015–16, 610-I)

OECD, *Standard for Automatic Exchange of Financial Account Information in Tax Matters* (July 2014, OECD Publishing)

OECD, 'OECD Delivers New Single Global Standard on Automatic Exchange of Information' (OECD, February 2014) <www.oecd.org/g20/topics/taxation/oecd-delivers-new-single-global-standard-on-automatic-exchange-of-information.htm> accessed 30 March 2018

Ormerod D, 'The Fraud Act 2006 – Criminalising Lying?' [2007] Crim LR 193

Ormerod D, 'Summary Evasion of Income Tax' [2002] Crim LR 3

Ormerod D, 'Cheating the Public Revenue' [1998] Crim LR 627

Reed A, 'Strict Liability and the Reasonable Excuse Defence' (2012) 76 J Crim L 293

Rogers J, 'Case Comment: Dishonesty in the First LIBOR Trial' (2016) 3 Arch Rev 7

Samuels A, 'Dishonesty' (2003) 67 J Crim L 324

Simester AP, 'Is Strict Liability Always Wrong?' in Simester AP (ed), *Appraising Strict Liability* (OUP 2005)

Spencer JR, 'Dishonesty: What the Jury Thinks the Defendant Thought the Jury Would Have Thought' [1982] CLJ 222

Stanton-Ife J, 'Strict Liability: Stigma and Regret' (2007) 27 OJLS 151

Steel A, 'The Meanings of Dishonesty in Theft' (2009) 38 CLWR 103

Steel A, 'The Harms and Wrongs of Stealing: The Harm Principle and Dishonesty in Theft' (2008) 31 UNSWLJ 712

Treverton-Jones G, 'In Person: Disciplinary Proceedings: Defining Dishonesty' (2017) 6 LS Gaz 29

Tur R, 'Dishonesty and the Jury' in AP Griffiths (ed), *Philosophy and Practice* (CUP 1985)

Turnbull-Hall C, Thomas R, 'Length of Tax Legislation as a Measure of Complexity' (Office of Tax Simplification, April 2012) <http://tinyurl.com/h7ljqlo> accessed 30 March 2018

Virgo G, 'Cheating and Dishonesty' (2018) 77 CLJ 18

Wasik M, 'Mens Rea, Motive and the Problem of Dishonesty in the Law of Theft [1979] Crim LR 543

9 Brexit and financial crime

Rhonson Salim[1]

9.1 Introduction

The United Kingdom's decision to leave the European Union has revealed a plethora of legal and practical conundrums inherent in the unravelling of a closely bound legal relationship that subsisted for only 45 years. The scale of the complexity involved in untangling the constitutional arrangements between the EU and UK is gradually becoming apparent to policy makers. Additionally, as negotiations proceed on the nature of the post Brexit relationship with the EU, the UK's ambition to create a 'new, deep and special partnership with the European Union' will need to cohabit with the normative underpinnings of the European Union and its legal instruments. This inherently will involve addressing a series of challenges. One of these is judicial cooperation in criminal matters. This chapter seeks to outline some challenges to the maintenance of judicial cooperation in some criminal matters, particularly as it affects countering financial crime in the context of law enforcement activities.

9.2 The pre-Brexit EU landscape in cooperation in criminal matters

European judicial cooperation in criminal matters has its origins under what was then known as the Third Pillar ('JHA') of the Treaty on European Union. This pillar covered areas such as controls on combating terrorism, serious crime, drug trafficking, international fraud; judicial cooperation in criminal and civil matters; creation of a European Police Office ('Europol') with a system for exchanging information between national police forces; and a common asylum policy. It operated at an intergovernmental level and required measures to be adopted by unanimity in the European Council whilst giving the European Parliament a consultative role and the then European Court of Justice (now 'CJEU'), limited jurisdiction. This method of operation severely limited legislative developments, particularly the requirement for unanimity.

Greater judicial and political efforts were made to transfer areas from the third pillar into the then first pillar. The Treaty of Amsterdam started this transference whilst also strengthening cooperation through the usage of new legal instruments such as Framework Decisions. Additionally, at the 1999 Tampere Meeting, the European Council set in motion steps to ultimately abolish obstacles to the free movement of judicial decisions in Member States including those in criminal law.[2] This free movement of judicial decisions meant that Member States were required to recognize a judicial decision taken by a judicial authority in another Member State as if the decision had been taken by a judicial authority in its own jurisdiction. For the European Council, the concept of mutual recognition was to be the cornerstone of judicial cooperation in criminal matters as it was viewed as the most suitable mechanism to overcome inefficiencies in cooperation between states. Judicially, European criminal law was also seen as in need of harmonization to protect the effectiveness of EU law including those falling within the first pillar.[3] Criminal law then, became in need of transference from the intergovernmental to supranational i.e. into the contours of community law.[4]

This conversion of EU criminal law into the supranational culminated in the Treaty of Lisbon. Under the Treaty of Lisbon, a reformation of legislative instruments (including prior EU treaties) occurred. Instead of Framework Decisions, Decisions and Conventions, EU criminal law now took the form of '. . . strong EU legal instruments (such as Directives) and EU institutions such as the Commission, the European Parliament and the Court of Justice assume their full powers of intervention and scrutiny'.[5] Notably, the EU Charter of Fundamental Rights, which contains specific rights and principles relating to criminal law and procedure, was also incorporated into the Treaty of Lisbon.[6] Pursuant to the Lisbon Treaty, The Treaty on the Functioning of the European Union ('TFEU') was amended. Under Art. 82–86 TFEU, mutual recognition of criminal judgments and judicial decisions, as well the approximation of criminal laws and regulations of the Member States, were given greater prominence than before. The European Parliament and the Council were granted powers to establish minimum rules on (a) mutual admissibility of evidence between Member States; (b) the rights of individuals in criminal procedure and (c) the rights of victims of crime.[7] Additionally, the Parliament and Council were also empowered to establish minimum rules concerning the definition of criminal offences and sanctions in the areas of money laundering, corruption, counterfeiting of means of payment, computer crime and organised crime amongst others.[8]

9.3 The UK paradigm of cooperation in criminal matters

The United Kingdom's cooperation with the EU in criminal matters contains an underlying level of complexity inherent to the piecemeal nature of the UK's participation in this area as an EU Member State. Despite the attempts outlined earlier to further harmonise European criminal law through increased integration, the UK's cooperation in this area has been historically centred on reticence. The UK has sought to keep the intergovernmental approach based on an approximation of laws and advocated for 'alternative mechanisms such as mutual recognition . . . as an alternative to harmonization'.[9] With the entry into force of the Treaty of Lisbon, the UK's involvement in the European criminal justice area took on two different dimensions depending upon whether the legal instrument was adopted pre entry into force of the Lisbon Treaty (old instruments) or post entry (new instruments).

9.3.1 Old instruments

In negotiating the Lisbon Treaty, the UK secured unique treatment in the applicability of old instruments in force. Pursuant to Protocol 36[10] on transitional provisions, five years after the entry into force of the Treaty of Lisbon, the CJEU would gain full competence over old instruments still left under the third pillar. What was unique to the United Kingdom's arrangement was the acceptance of a legal 'wait and see strategy'[11] on behalf of the UK towards this transference of competence. The United Kingdom was able to negotiate its ability to 'opt-out' of the applicability of the old instruments before the CJEU acquired full competence.[12] This notice of 'opt out' had to be given at latest six months before the five year date expired. Should such notice be given to the Council, all the old instruments of the third pillar would cease to apply to the United Kingdom upon the expiry of the five year transitional period. Whilst the opt-out is advantageous in itself, the United kingdom was able to 'have its cake and eat it' by additionally securing the option to re 'opt-in' to measures it previously opted out of, if in a future date it decided it was better to take part in some or all of the measures.[13]

In July 2013, the United Kingdom gave its opt-out notification.[14] However, in November 2014, it decided to opt back into 35 instruments.[15] These include the Framework Decision on the European Arrest Warrant,[16] the Framework Decision on the joint investigation teams[17] and Article 54 of the Convention implementing the Schengen agreement enshrining the *ne bis in idem* principle, amongst others.

9.3.2 New instruments

Similar to the approach taken to old instruments, the United Kingdom negotiated a power to opt-out of any new post Lisbon instruments adopted from 1st December 2009[18] as well as the power to opt-in at a future suitable date. What is striking about the opt-in power is the extent to which it can be exercised. The UK secured the option to either opt-in before or after the adoption of an instrument.[19] This allows the UK to influence the creation and scope of the instrument prior to adoption. It also allows it to opt out before it takes effect, wait to see its application in practice after adoption by other Member States and then opt-in if the UK desires.[20] The United Kingdom has opted into some post Lisbon measures. These include the Directive on the European Investigation Order,[21] the Directive on the Right to Interpretation and Translation[22] and the Directive on Suspects' Right to Information.[23]

9.4 Financial crime measures

As the UK Government negotiates its future relationship with the EU, Brexit will affect the fight against financial crime given the United Kingdom's piecemeal approach to cross border cooperation in criminal matters as outlined above. In its position paper, '*Security, law enforcement and criminal justice-A Future Partnership paper*'[24] the United Kingdom declared its wish to 'build on, and where possible enhance, the strong foundation of existing cooperation',[25] and to '. . . continue the facilitation of operational business across borders, avoiding operational gaps . . .'[26] To achieve this, preservation of the benefits of existing measures such as confiscation, the European Arrest Warrant, as well as continued participation with institutions such as Europol and Eurojust will need to be maintained. The effects of Brexit upon some of these measures are examined below.

9.5 Confiscation

Confiscation of the proceeds of crimes remain an invaluable tool in the fight against cross border financial crime. However, whilst important, the success of the current confiscation regimes remain limited. The Asset Forfeiture Division of the Revenue and Customs Prosecution Office ('RCPO') in the United Kingdom estimated in September 2008 that 86% of unenforced confiscation orders relate to assets overseas or hidden overseas.[27] In 2016, it was estimated that 98.9 per cent of criminal profits are not confiscated in EU Member States and these remain at the disposal of criminals.[28] Brexit threatens to exacerbate these poor outcomes.

The current EU legal framework in the area of freezing and confiscation includes two types of measures based on mutual recognition (for procedural law matters) and harmonisation (substantive law measures establishing minimum rules concerning the definition of criminal offences and sanctions).[29] The United Kingdom has not opted into the harmonisation measures but participates in the mutual recognition ones. A key mechanism in the former is Directive 2014/42/EU on the freezing and confiscation of instrumentalities and proceeds of crime in the EU. Despite the Directive being broadly in line with existing UK jurisprudence, the United Kingdom opted out of the application of the Directive on the basis that it might undermine the UK's existing asset recovery regime including provisions on non-conviction based confiscation which are governed by the Proceeds of Crime Act 2002 ('POCA'). The essential fear was that the Directive might provide a basis for asserting that more stringent criminal law standards and safeguards should apply in the UK.[30]

What is notable is that the Directive evidenced the EU's approach towards regulation of this area. The legal basis of the Directive is found under TFEU Art.82(2), which allows the setting of minimum standards *in order to facilitate* greater mutual recognition.[31] The Directive evidences that the relationship between harmonisation and mutual recognition measures are more concrete and fundamentally intertwined than before. This interlinkage is now being further enhanced by a proposed future regulation to replace the mutual recognition Framework Decisions.[32] The proposed regulation seeks to simplify the current procedures and improve the cross-border enforcement of freezing and confiscation orders. It also reduces the scope of national courts to refuse some confiscation orders and aims to improve the speed and efficiency of execution of such orders through tighter timelines reduced recognition and an enforcement procedure. By adopting a regulation measure, the European Commission is seeking greater control, greater legal certainty, and an avoidance of transposition problems that the Framework Decisions facilitated. In the European Commission's view, '. . . whereas the Directive improves the domestic possibilities to freeze and confiscate assets, the proposal aims to improve the cross-border enforcement of freezing and confiscation orders. *Together*, [emphasis added] both instruments should contribute to effective asset recovery in the European Union.'[33] In light of the current ineffectual ability to confiscate the proceeds of crime, the solution of the EU therefore, seems to be to utilise greater consolidation and synchronisation of both procedural and substantive law to improve poor confiscation rates. Even if the United Kingdom adopts the proposed regulation as it intends to do,[34] the reluctance to adopt the Directive's standards will be an obstacle and the UK may end up doing so should it wish to fully benefit from the regulation in the future. It is therefore likely that with the onset of Brexit and the potential divergences to be created by the operation of parallel regulatory regimes, confiscation rates between the UK and EU would not improve unless a greater synchronisation of regimes between the EU and UK is ensured. One solution to this conundrum would be the mirroring of regulatory regimes between the UK and EU, with inbuilt mechanisms for each party to update standards quickly. This mirroring can take place via bilateral treaties between the UK and EU Member States. However, this solution has its own obstacles, which are explored later in this chapter.

As demonstrated by the argument above, potentially higher standards and protections[35] contained in EU mechanisms may exist post Brexit. This will be problematic for the UK, given its reluctance to accept those standards in the past. Secondly, as the United Kingdom does not intend to keep the Charter of Fundamental Rights as part of domestic law on or after exit day,[36] the continued applicability of the Charter towards all existing and future EU laws may either limit the areas covered under any future agreement between the EU and UK or limit the scope of such agreement. This is likely given existing case law from the CJEU.[37] The CJEU jurisprudence has shown that the court will be steadfast in its supervision of how the EU and Member States dealings with third countries comply with human rights under the Charter.[38]

9.6 European Arrest Warrant

The European Arrest Warrant ('EAW') is one instrument used to ensure accountability of perpetrators for financial crimes committed within Member

States of the EU. It allows a Member State to bring an individual, residing in another Member State, to justice before its national courts. The legal basis of the European Arrest Warrant lies within the Framework Decision on the European Arrest Warrant.[39] This Decision facilitates the surrender of individuals for prosecution or the fulfilment of a custodial sentence with little formality.[40] The EAW is an important tool to increase accountability of company directors who may take advantage of the removal of borders within the EU to flee the English and Welsh jurisdiction.

Whilst the EAW (as a mutual recognition mechanism) operates on the basis of mutual trust, this trust is not unconditional and grounds of refusal of EAWs exist. One such ground is where the execution of an EAW would result in breaches of an individual's human rights.[41] Assuming there is agreement between the UK and EU on participation in the EAW, it is this ground which will prove substantively problematic in the post Brexit landscape. There is a high risk that a national court of an EU Member State will take the view that current, or future, UK human rights protections are not adequate, or of sufficient certainty, for that court to give effect to an extradition request from a UK judicial authority. Recent jurisprudence from Member State courts foreshadow this possibility. In *Minister for Justice and Equality v O'Conner*[42] the extradition of a company director charged with conspiracy to cheat the public revenue in the UK was suspended. In the Irish Supreme Court, Mr. O'Connor, the director, successfully advanced the argument that his European Union citizenship rights that he enjoyed as a matter of EU law, would no longer be capable of enforcement upon Brexit. Of particular concern to the Irish Supreme Court was his enjoyment of rights under the Charter of Fundamental Rights. As a subsidiary point, the court also shared O'Connor's concern that his entitlement to have the extent of any such rights definitively determined by the CJEU may be removed upon Brexit. The case demonstrates that Member State courts will look to ensure that EU nationals will be able to enforce in a practical and *equivalent* way, any EU law rights which they may enjoy by virtue of being EU nationals even post Brexit.

In addition to the above, human rights' protections in the operation of the EAW have been reinforced, not only through their consideration by executing authorities in giving effect to an extradition request, but through distinct EU law measures on procedural rights for defendants.[43] At present, the UK has not adopted some of these legislative measures.[44] Post Brexit, this absence of adoption will undermine any effort to participate in the EAW scheme, especially as the UK will be seeking to participate as a non-EU state. The crux of this difficulty is that these legislative measures create a direct causal link under EU constitutional law to the effective operation of mutual recognition in criminal matters.[45] A non-Member State, by virtue of its exclusion from the EU system, would not be subject to EU constitutional law. It will be posing a serious risk to the coherent operation of such law between EU Member States if it fails to implement equivalent measures found in those EU Member States. Accordingly, it is to be expected that unless the UK adopts a variety of legislative measures not currently subscribed to, extradition requests from UK judicial authorities will not be given the same credence in EU Member States as those originating from an EU Member State.

9.7 Double jeopardy

The principle of *ne bis in idem* or prohibition of double jeopardy is a long standing principle found in multiple instruments facilitating judicial cooperation in criminal matters.[46] At its core, the principle operates to prevent repeated exercise of a state's right to punish criminal offences (whether by multiple penalising procedures or excessive punishments). An important question to be solved upon Brexit would be the interaction of specific mechanisms used by UK authorities in combatting financial crimes. Of particular concern are the use of Deferred Prosecution Agreements ('DPAs') by UK authorities and its interaction with the principle of *ne bis in idem* as defined in EU jurisprudence.

DPAs[47] are agreements between a prosecutor and a commercial organisation that are approved by the criminal courts.[48] The agreement suspends prosecution of the organisation for a defined period in exchange for the fulfilment of specific conditions (such as the payment of a financial penalty). DPAs are only available to commercial organisations in respect of specified 'economic crime' offences.[49] These offences include common law and statutory offences such as conspiracy to defraud, cheating the public revenue and fraudulent trading.[50] Crucially, the DPA has the effect of discontinuing any criminal proceedings and fresh criminal proceedings may not be instigated except in certain limited circumstances. DPAs are perceived to be a hybrid that sits between a guilty plea and a civil recovery.[51] Upon Brexit, the question arises as to whether a company who fulfils a DPA can be additionally subjected to criminal proceedings in the EU and reciprocally, whether an EU company previously subjected to administrative penalties of a criminal nature can be subjected to criminal prosecution in the UK?

The *ne bis* principle is an integral part of EU law, appearing in the EU Charter of Fundamental Rights,[52] mutual recognition instruments and secondary EU law such as the Convention Implementing the Schengen Agreement ('CISA').[53] Procedurally, by its inclusion in these instruments, the jurisdictional scope of application is broad and in some instances, the protection provided by the principle extends to third countries.[54] Through its incorporation within EU law, the principle is given a horizontal application as Member States become obliged to recognise and give effect to criminal judgements from other Member States. It therefore means that irrespective of the location of the criminal act, the principle applies as long as the first judgment is issued by a Member State court that had jurisdiction over the case.[55] What is noticeable is that Art. 54 of CISA uses the term 'person' in a general sense and it is arguable that legal persons (such as companies) may be able to avail themselves of the scope of the principle.[56]

In its jurisprudence, the CJEU has used mutual trust and the need for harmonisation to bestow an expansive and purposive interpretation to the principle in EU law. The focus is on the linkage between a set of circumstances rather than the legal classification of those circumstances or the type of legal interest involved.[57] Accordingly, the principle also applies to 'procedures whereby further prosecution is barred . . . once the accused has fulfilled certain obligations and, in particular, has paid a certain sum of money. . .'[58] Within EU law, this particularly applies where the case bears a necessary connection with EU law. In its recent judgments of *Garlsson* and *Menci*,[59] the court took the view that criminal proceedings in an EU Member State can be brought even after the imposition of a final administrative, criminal penalty. What the CJEU found essential was that the national legislation in a Member State creating/facilitating the duplication ensures that any penalties which it authorises does not exceed what is strictly necessary in order to achieve the objective of the legislation. Therefore, both the duplication of proceedings and the penalties must be proportionate in order to achieve the objective of the legislation. The effect of the CJEU's interpretation creates a unique position in EU law regarding judicial cooperation in criminal matters in that it undermines mutual trust through the latitude afforded to national legislation.

The possibility exists that post Brexit, a defendant UK company who fulfils the terms of a DPA can be subjected to a duplication of criminal and administrative penalty proceedings in an EU Member State. This could be the case if the national court in that Member State perceives that the defendant's action giving rise to the UK criminal proceedings also infringes an objective of general interest within EU law. Such objectives include, but are not limited to, the integrity of the financial markets of the European Union and public confidence in financial instruments. This would also be the likely result as the protections that apply horizontally to limit double criminal proceedings would be no longer applicable *vis-á-vis* the UK, that is, the protections available pursuant to the Charter. The CJEU jurisprudence opens the door towards the application of divergent regimes and levels of protection between EU Member States, leaving it very unpredictable for UK companies to gauge both criminal and financial risk.

Unlike the EU principle of *ne bis in idem*, the English rule of *autrefois acquit/convict* is more demanding and restrictive. It requires sameness of offence and facts for the principle to apply.[60] Accordingly, administrative/civil alternatives do not come within the scope of the rule[61] and post Brexit, an EU company subjected to an administrative penalty within the EU may find itself subjected to criminal proceedings in the UK.

One solution to the current overlap could be the conclusion of agreements between judicial authorities in EU Member States and the UK with regard to the division of offences which would be subjected to prosecutions or other administrative penalty agreements. Whilst they would not offer horizontal coherency, they could offer a politically satisfactory outcome.

9.8 Future possibilities?

In order for any post Brexit arrangement to function properly, the UK will need to ensure the desired regulatory and administrative equivalence on a continuous basis as the above discussion of the EAW and confiscation rules demonstrate.[62] Furthermore, these arrangements will need to be supported by a means of resolving any disputes between the UK and the EU. A key stumbling block is the UK's position on the CJEU as shown in *O'Connor*.[63] What seems to have been missed in the UK's position paper on the CJEU is that, in some form or other the UK will be subject to the jurisdiction of the CJEU's jurisprudence albeit indirectly via its interpretation of EU law. Additionally, it will be difficult to replicate in another dispute resolution mechanism, the full breadth of competence currently covered by CJEU. The CJEU covers not only trade disputes, but questions of human rights, immigration, asylum and crime etc.[64]

In its position paper, the UK referenced the Schengen association agreements as examples of the EU's relationships being 'based on overarching legal frameworks that support close and dynamic cooperation with third countries'.[65] Whilst these work, they would be unsuitable for the depth of cooperation that the UK seeks. The inherent deficiency with such type of agreements[66] is the limited participation these third countries are afforded, particularly as it regards voting rights. Furthermore, the context of some of these agreements is, and will be different to the UK. Countries such as Iceland continue to maintain a high degree of equivalence to EU law by virtue of its continued membership to regional agreements such as EFTA.

As mentioned above, an alternative and most likely option will be bilateral agreements between the UK and individual EU Member States. However, by virtue of being concluded with each Member State, these agreements do not guarantee horizontal coherency across all Member States of the EU. Effective cooperation in the fight against financial crime and fraud will not be possible via these individualised mechanisms.

9.9 Conclusion

Judicial cooperation in criminal matters is based upon the concept of mutual trust. At its basic, this principle means that each Member State of the EU can be confident that all other Member States respect and ensure an equivalent level of protection of the values enshrined in Art. 2 TEU. It also creates a presumption as to the levels of application and compliance of EU law. Third States who do not fully and comprehensively subscribe to these principles cannot expect to be given the same level of deference and involvement as a Member State. This will be the state of play that the UK faces upon Brexit day as a Third State. Should the UK wish to maintain meaningful co-operation in criminal matters with the EU post-Brexit, it will no longer be able to continue with the opt-in and 'wait and see' privileges it enjoys. Irrespective of the post-Brexit route it takes, judicial decision and law enforcement cooperation in the fight against financial crime will not be the same between the UK and EU Member States as the present status quo. The UK seems to be hoping for the use of mutual recognition as the basis of cooperation for the future, partly because it politically worked for the UK in the past and partly because it allowed the UK the engage in cooperation á la carte when it suited. The UK was able to have its cake and eat it in this arena and wishes for this to continue even after Brexit. On the other hand, cases such as *O'Conner*[67] shows that EU Member States will insist on 'equivalence', a standard with a higher degree of judicial harmonisation but which additionally allows the EU to set the limits of cooperation. Brexit will negatively affect the fight against financial crime with and within the EU. The question to be determined is to what extent.

Notes

1 Lecturer in law, The Open University, UK. The chapter reflects the law and negotiating positions regarding Brexit up to 30 April 2018.
2 See Tampere European Council: Presidency Conclusions, 15 and 16 October 1999 (Presidency Conclusions, No. 200/1/99). See also 'Programme of measures to implement the principle of mutual recognition of decisions in criminal matters'. OJ 2001/C 12/02.
3 See Case C-176/03 *Commission v Council* [2005] ECR I-7879 where the CJEU took the view that criminal law could be subject to harmonization for the protection of the environment.
4 V Mitsilegas, 'The uneasy relationship between the UK and European criminal law: from opt-outs to Brexit?' (2016) Crim. L.R. 519.
5 V Mitsilegas, 'The uneasy relationship between the UK and European criminal law: from opt-outs to Brexit?' (2016) Crim. L.R. 519.
6 Title VI of the EU Charter of Fundamental Rights.
7 See. Art. 82(2).
8 See. Art. 83.
9 A Weyembergh, 'Consequences of Brexit for European Union criminal law' (2017) 8(3) NJECL 285–286.
10 Art. 10.
11 En. Iv. , V Mitsilegas, 'The uneasy relationship between the UK and European criminal law: from opt-outs to Brexit?' (2016) Crim. L.R. 519, 522 .
12 The instruments totalled 135 in number. Art. 10(4) of Protocol 36. See A Hinarejos, JR Spencer and S Peers, 'Opting out of EU Criminal Law: What is Actually Involved?' CELS Working Paper, New Series, No. 1, September 2012/
13 Art. 10(5) of Protocol 36. The United Kingdom's opt back is effective only after approval by the Council and on condition that the opt in does not '[. . .] seriously [affect] the practical operability of the various parts thereof, while respecting their coherence'.
14 See UK notification according to Article 10 (4) of Protocol No 36 to TEU and TFEU, 24 July 2013, Council doc. 12750/13, 26 July 2013.
15 See Notification of the United Kingdom under Article 10 (5) of Protocol 36 to the EU Treaties, 20 November 2014, Council doc. 15398/14, 27 November 2014 and Commission Decision 2014/858/EU of 1 December 2014 on the notification by the United Kingdom of Great Britain and Northern Ireland of its wish to participate in acts of the Union in the field of police cooperation and judicial cooperation in criminal matters adopted before the entry into force of the Treaty of Lisbon and which are not part of the Schengen acquis (OJ L 345, 1 December 2014, 6).

16 Council Framework Decision 2002/584/JHA of 13 June 2002 on the European Arrest Warrant and the surrender procedures between Member States, OJ L 190, 18 July 2002, 1–20.
17 Council Framework Decision 2002/465/JHA on joint investigation teams, OJ L 162, 20 June 2002, 1–3.
18 See Art. 1 and 2 of Protocol 21, OJ C 326, 26 October 2012, 47–390.
19 See Art. 3 and 4 of Protocol 21.
20 See V Mitsilegas, 'The uneasy relationship between the UK and European criminal law: from opt-outs to Brexit?' (2016) Crim. L.R. 519.
21 Directive 2014/41/EU of the European Parliament and of the Council of 3 April 2014 regarding the European Investigation Order in criminal matters, OJ L 130, 1 May 2014, 1–36.
22 Directive 2010/64/EU of the European Parliament and of the Council of 20 October 2010 on the right to interpretation and translation in criminal proceedings, OJ L 280, 26 October 2010, 1–7.
23 Directive 2012/13/EU of the European Parliament and of the Council of 22 May 2012 on the right to information in criminal proceedings OJ L 142, 1 June 2012, 1–10 (see recital no 4).
24 Available here <www.gov.uk/government/uploads/system/uploads/attachment_ data/file/645416/Security__law_enforcement_and_criminal_justice_-_a_future_ partnership_paper.PDF> accessed 1 May 2018.
25 ibid, 6.
26 ibid.
27 European Union Committee – 19th Report, *Money laundering and the financing of terrorism*, para 68. Found at <https://publications.parliament.uk/pa/ld200809/ ldselect/ldeucom/132/13206.htm#note49> accessed 1 May 2018.
28 Europol, *Does crime still pay? Criminal asset recovery in the EU*. Survey of statistical information, 2016.
29 Council Framework Decision 2003/577/JHA on the execution in the EU of orders freezing property or evidence; Council Framework Decision 2006/783/JHA on the application of the principle of mutual recognition to confiscation orders. The 2003 FD has been partially superseded by Directive 2014/41/EU on the European Investigation Order which establishes procedures for the freezing and transfer of evidence. Council Framework Decision 2001/500/JHA on money laundering, the identification, tracing, freezing, seizing and confiscation of instrumentalities and the proceeds of crime; Council Framework Decision 2005/212/JHA on confiscation of crime-related proceeds, instrumentalities and property
30 House of Commons European Scrutiny Committee – Tenth Report Documents considered by the Committee on 25 November 2015, para. 21.1 <https:// publications.parliament.uk/pa/cm201516/cmselect/cmeuleg/342-x/34225.htm> accessed 1 May 2018.
31 Emphasis added.
32 See 'Proposal for a Regulation of the European Parliament and of the Council on the mutual recognition of freezing and confiscation orders' (SWD (2016) 468 final) Accessed here: <http://europeanmemoranda.cabinetoffice.gov.uk/files/2016/12/ ST-15816–2016-INIT-EN_(1).PDF> accessed 1 May 2018.
33 Regulation proposal, 3–4.
34 House of Lords, 'Proposed Regulation of the European Parliament and of the Council on the Mutual Recognition of Freezing & Confiscation Orders' COM (2016) 819 final: Written statement – HCWS101.
35 The proposed confiscation regulation will encapsulate EU level protections on procedural rights in criminal proceedings, including but not limited to the Directive 2010/64/EU on the Right to Interpretation and Translation in Criminal Proceedings,

Directive 2012/13/EU on the Right to Information about Rights and Charges and Access to the Case File, Directive 2013/48/EU on the Right of Access to a Lawyer and Communication with Relatives when Arrested and Detained, Directive 2016/343 on the Strengthening of Certain Aspects of the Presumption of Innocence and the Right to be Present at One's trial.

36 See s. 5(4) of the EU Withdrawal Bill.

37 See for example, *Schrems v Facebook* EU:C:2015:650; [2016] 2 C.M.L.R. 2.

38 ibid at para. 105.

39 Framework Decision 2002/584/JHA of 13 June 2002 on the European Arrest Warrant [2002] OJ L190/1.

40 For a discussion of the constitutional issues, see, V Mitsilegas, 'The Constitutional Implications of Mutual Recognition in Criminal Matters in the EU' (2006) 43 Common Market Law Review 1277.

41 See for example, CJEU case of *Pál Aranyosi and Robert Căldărar v Generalstaats-anwaltschaft Bremen* (C-404/15) EU:C:2016:198.

42 [2018] IESC 3 (2018).

43 Directive on Access to a Lawyer.

44 ibid.

45 See V Mitsilegas, 'The uneasy relationship between the UK and European criminal law: from opt-outs to Brexit?' (2016) Crim. L.R. 519, 525.

46 See for example, Convention Implementing the Schengen Agreement (CISA), Framework Decision 2002/584/JHA on the European Arrest Warrant and the surrender procedures between Member States [2002] OJ L190/1.

47 Available pursuant to Section 45 and Schedule 17 the Crime and Courts Act 2013 to the CPS and SFO. A lower standard is expected from a prosecutor in order to pursue a DPA. The prosecutor needs a 'reasonable suspicion' that an offence has been committed rather than a 'realistic prospect of conviction' as required to commence criminal proceedings.

48 The Crown Court approves the DPA after determining that it is in the interests of justice and that its terms are 'fair, reasonable and proportionate'.

49 Four DPAs have been entered into at present. This includes a £497.25 million DPA in 2017 with Rolls Royce and a DPA with Tesco Stores Limited in April 2017, in which Tesco agreed to pay a £129 million financial penalty.

50 Specifically, offences under the Fraud Act 2006, Bribery Act 2010, Companies Act 2006 and Theft Act 1968.

51 B Morgan, Joint Head of Bribery and Corruption, SFO speech. found here <www.sfo.gov.uk/2017/03/08/the-future-of-deferred-prosecution-agreements-after-rolls-royce/> accessed 1 May 2018.

52 See Art 50 ff of the Charter.

53 See Art. 54–58 of Convention Implementing the Schengen Agreement (CISA). CISA became part of EU law via the integration of the Schengen acquis into The Treaty of Amsterdam. The UK re-opted pursuant to Art. 10(5) of Protocol No. 36 and Art. 4 of the Schengen Protocol as from Dec 2014.

54 For example, Art. 4(5) of the EAW Framework Decision and Framework Decision on the application of the principle of mutual recognition to financial penalties.

55 C-297/07 *Staatsanwaltschaft Regensburg v Klaus Bourquain* [2008] ECR p I-09425, para. 29–31. This is distinct from the scope of the principle under ECHR (Art. 6 and 4 of protocol 7) which offers protection as it concerns inter-state proceedings.

56 For more discussion on this question, see S. Peers, EU Justice and Home Affairs Law, 3rd edn (Oxford, Oxford University Press, 2011) 842.

57 See *Van Esbroeck C-436/04*, para. 36. The relevant criterion is 'the identity of the material acts, understood in the sense of the existence of a set of concrete circumstances which are inextricably linked'. In *Van Straaten C-150/05*, the CJEU

accepted that the principle is applicable even when the parties in both states are not the same.

58 See joint cases C-187/01 and C-385/01 Hüsein Gözütok and Klaus Brügge [2003] ECR I-01345, para. 48.

59 C-537/16 *Garlsson Real Estate SA and Others v Commissione Nazionale per le Società e la Borsa (Consob)* and C-524/15 Luca Menci.

60 *Connelly v Director of Public Prosecutions* [1964] AC 1254, *R v J (JF)* [2014] QB 561.

61 *R v Lama* [2014] EWCA Crim 1729.

62 This is part of the EU negotiating guidelines for future relationship with the UK. See European Council, 'Art. 50 negotiating guidelines of the EU 27 Member States on the framework for the future relationship between the EU and UK', Art. 7.

63 See Minister for Justice and Equality v O'Conner (n 42).

64 For a discussion of this issue, see the Select Committee on the European Union Justice Sub-Committee, 'Corrected oral evidence on Brexit: enforcement and dispute resolution', Tuesday 27 February 2018. Accessed on 1 May 2018.

65 Para 37.

66 See for example, Agreement Concluded by the Council of the European Union and the Republic of Iceland and the Kingdom of Norway concerning the Latters' Association with the Implementation, Application and Development of the Schengen Acquis (Schengen Association Agreement) 1999.

67 See *Minister for Justice and Equality v O'Conner* (n 42).

Bibliography

Agreement Concluded by the Council of the European Union and the Republic of Iceland and the Kingdom of Norway concerning the Latters' Association with the Implementation, Application and Development of the Schengen Acquis (Schengen Association Agreement) 1999

Case C-617/10 *Åkerberg Fransson EU:C:2013:105*

Case C-176/03 *Commission v Council* [2005] ECR I-7879

Case C-187/01 and C-385/01 *Hüsein Gözütok* and *Klaus Brügge* [2003] ECR I-01345

Case C-537/16 *Garlsson Real Estate SA and Others v Commissione Nazionale per le Società e la Borsa (Consob)*

Case C-524/15 *Luca Menci*

Case C-404/15 *Pál Aranyosi and Robert C_ld_raru v Generalstaatsanwaltschaft Bremen* EU:C:2016:198

C-297/07 *Staatsanwaltschaft Regensburg v Klaus Bourquain* [2008] ECR p I-09425

Charter of Fundamental Rights of the European Union, 2000/C 364/01

Commission Decision 2014/858/EU of 1 December 2014 on the notification by the United Kingdom of Great Britain and Northern Ireland of its wish to participate in acts of the Union in the field of police cooperation and judicial cooperation in criminal matters, OJ L 345

Connelly v Director of Public Prosecutions [1964] AC 1254

Convention implementing the Schengen Agreement of 14 June 1985 between the Governments of the States of the Benelux Economic Union, the Federal Republic of Germany and the French Republic on the gradual abolition of checks at their common borders (CISA), OJ L 239

Council of the European Union, 'Programme of measures to implement the principle of mutual recognition of decisions in criminal matters'. OJ 2001/C 12/02

Council Framework Decision 2005/214/JHA on the application of the principle of mutual recognition to financial penalties, OJ L 76

Council Framework Decision 2005/212/JHA on confiscation of crime-related proceeds, instrumentalities and property, OJ L 68

Council Framework Decision 2002/584/JHA of 13 June 2002 on the European Arrest Warrant and the surrender procedures between Member States, OJ L 190

Council Framework Decision 2003/577/JHA on the execution in the EU of orders freezing property or evidence, OJ L 196

Council Framework Decision 2002/465/JHA on joint investigation teams, OJ L 162

Council Framework Decision 2001/500/JHA on money laundering, the identification, tracing, freezing, seizing and confiscation of instrumentalities and the proceeds of crime, OJ L 182

Crime and Courts Act 2013

Department for Exiting the European Union, 'Security, law Enforcement and criminal justice-A future partnership paper'. 2017

Directive 2014/41/EU of the European Parliament and of the Council of 3 April 2014 regarding the European Investigation Order in criminal matters, OJ L 130

Directive 2010/64/EU of the European Parliament and of the Council of 20 October 2010 on the right to interpretation and translation in criminal proceedings

Directive 2012/13/EU of the European Parliament and of the Council of 22 May 2012 on the right to information in criminal proceedings OJ L 142

European Commission, Proposal for a Regulation of the European Parliament and of the Council on the mutual recognition of freezing and confiscation orders (SWD (2016) 468 final

European Council, Art. 50 negotiating guidelines of the EU 27 Member States on the framework for the future relationship between the EU and UK. 2018

Europol, 'Does crime still pay? Criminal asset recovery in the EU', 2016

European Union Committee, 19th Report, 'Money laundering and the financing of terrorism' 2008–2009

European Union (Withdrawal) Bill 2017–19

Hinarejos, A., Spencer., J.R., and Peers S., 'Opting out of EU Criminal Law: What is Actually Involved?' CELS Working Paper, New Series, No. 1, September 2012

House of Commons European Scrutiny Committee, 10th Report, 'Documents considered by the Committee', 2015

House of Lords, Proposed Regulation of the European Parliament and of the Council on the Mutual Recognition of Freezing & Confiscation Orders COM (2016) 819 final:Written statement – HCWS101

Minister for Justice and Equality v O'Conner [2018] IESC 3 (2018)

Mitsilegas, V., 'The uneasy relationship between the UK and European criminal law: from opt-outs to Brexit?' (2016) Crim. L.R. 519

Notification of the United Kingdom under Article 10 (5) of Protocol 36 to the EU Treaties, 15398/14

Protocol No 36 to TEU and TFEU, Council document 12750/13

R v Lama [2014] EWCA Crim 1729

R v J (JF) [2014] QB 561

Schrems v Facebook C:2015:650; [2016] 2 C.M.L.R. 2

Select Committee on the European Union Justice Sub-Committee, *Corrected oral evidence on Brexit: enforcement and dispute resolution*, Tuesday 27th February 2018

Tampere European Council, Presidency Conclusions, 15 and 16 October 1999 (No. 200/1/99)

Treaty of the Functioning of the European Union, OJ C 326

Treaty of Lisbon amending the Treaty on European Union and the Treaty establishing the European Community, OJ C 306

Weyembergh, A., 'Consequences of Brexit for European Union criminal law' (2017) 8(3) NJECL pg. 285

10 Do we need a failure to prevent fraud offence?

Bill Davies[1]

10.1 Introduction

The failure to prevent mechanism first arrived[2] in the UK legal system in section 7 of the Bribery Act 2010. Although the introduction of the regime was influenced by pressure to honour international commitments[3] and there are similarities in the approach employed elsewhere,[4] it was a new model that imposed strict liability on Commercial Organisations for failing to prevent bribery. A similar provision has now been enacted in the UK for failure to prevent the criminal facilitation of tax evasion.[5]

It is argued here that the failure to prevent offence is an innovative and ground breaking provision that has the clear advantage of sidestepping many of the intractable legal difficulties that beset the imposition of criminal liability on a corporate form. In addition section 7 is an excellent template for a similar, much needed provision which could be either incorporated within the Fraud Act 2006 or within the ambit of a wider failure to prevent economic crime offence elsewhere. The central theme is an analysis of the use under the failure to prevent mechanism of a quasi-code of corporate governance, buttressed by a very real threat of criminal sanctions, to effect systematic and cultural changes in corporate culture in sectors traditionally plagued by bribery and corruption.

The chapter first considers the operation of the failure to prevent offence under the Bribery regime and evaluates how the new provision, operating in tandem with the Deferred Prosecution regime, has addressed the well-known defects in the identification doctrine by reference to recent high profile cases. Secondly it explores the effectiveness of tackling economic crime with Corporate Governance methods, in particular considering the success of the Bribery Act in making demonstrable changes in corporate culture. This theme of cultural change is investigated and comparisons are made with the development of voluntary codes of corporate governance and also the introduction of section 172 of the Companies Act 2006 both of which sought to influence cultural change by different routes.

Finally, this chapter identifies key aspects of the failure to prevent offence bribery regime that have made it a success and concludes that it would work equally well for the offence of fraud under the Fraud Act 2006.

10.2 The failure to prevent offence

Section 7 of the Bribery Act 2010 imposes liability on a Commercial Organisation for failing to prevent bribery, if a person associated with the Commercial Organisation bribes another person. The bribery itself must be intended to either obtain or retain business or advantage in the conduct of business for the Commercial Organisation. This provision is interesting because it represents a sea change by the legislature in the way the law tackles the problem of corporate liability. The new approach eschews the common law identification doctrine that requires the courts to identify human actors as the directing mind and will of the company in order to meet the *mens rea* requirement of the offence in question. Dispensing with *mens rea* entirely, the new offence imposes a strict liability offence on organisations for failing to prevent bribery by an associated person. A notable point here about the terms used is that both 'Commercial Organisations'[6] and 'Associated Persons'[7] are given a very broad definition. Commercial Organisations are not restricted by any legal niceties of personality requirements and those with charitable aims are not exempt. Although the organisations have to be connected with the UK to come within the ambit of the provision, this connection can in fact be very tenuous and this in combination with section 12 (5),[8] means that section 7 has extraterritorial effect. Meanwhile it is clear under section 8 that Associated Persons are not required to fulfil a particular position within the Organisation (employee for example) this immediately broadens the ambit of the offence and means that the actions of individuals far away from the epicentre can therefore implicate an Organisation.

The potentially draconian nature of the offence is ameliorated by two factors. First, a Commercial Organisations has a complete defence if it can demonstrate that it has 'adequate procedures'[9] in place to combat Bribery and second, the offence falls within the Deferred Prosecution Agreement regime,[10] this means that a court can sanction an agreement between the Commercial Organisation and a prosecutor that avoids prosecution. Section 9 of the Bribery Act 2010 also provides for the Ministry of Justice to publish guidance on how to put in place adequate procedures. The bribery regime therefore resembles a bespoke system of corporate governance designed to inculcate a bribery and corruption intolerant culture within the corporate governance of Commercial Organisations and indeed the wider geographical, economic and sectoral arenas in which they operate.

After a quiet start that left some to doubt[11] the effectiveness of the new provision, there have recently been a number of high profile cases brought by the Serious Fraud Office, which have successfully applied section 7 of the Bribery Act 2010 in conjunction with the Deferred Prosecution Regime.[12] These successes appear to be an important influence on the government's call for evidence in January 2017[13] that sought responses on a range of proposals, one of which being the extension of the failure to prevent mechanism to cover other economic crimes.

In the largest case so far, a Deferred Prosecution Agreement in *Serious Fraud Office v Rolls-Royce Plc, Rolls-Royce Energy Systems Inc*[14] sanctioned the payment of a staggering penalty of £239,082,645.00 in addition to £258,170,000 in disgorgement of profits. The case is not just remarkable for the payments agreed but also for the scale and longevity of the potentially criminal activities that were detailed in court and now set out as a matter of public record in the Appendix to the judgment. The extent of this activity combined with the fact that initial investigation by the Serious Fraud Office was not triggered by a self-report from the company, indicate that this case may easily have been one where the corporate behaviour could have been considered so egregious that only criminal prosecution would have sufficed, leading to the inevitable corporate collapse of one of the UK's leading companies. It is clear from the judgment that prosecution was avoided only as a result of 'extraordinary' levels of co-operation by Rolls-Royce.

The sheer amount of damages combined with a fair slice of unfavourable publicity, might make one wonder whether there was any real benefit for Rolls-Royce in deferring prosecution. The answer to this however lies in the nature of much of the business that companies such as Rolls Royce operate involve bidding for government contracts around the world, all bound by various sets of public procurement rules which will ordinarily contain either a permanent or a time restricted ban on companies applying for public contracts.

10.3 Changing the corporate culture – tackling economic crime with corporate governance

Tackling economic crime by means of corporate governance is hardly new as it is viewed as an important reason for having company legislation at all. For example, studies have analysed successive Companies Acts from the Joint Stock Companies Act 1844 within the penumbra of fraud prevention. Similarly, the same could be said of much of the cornucopia of law and regulation that surrounds the regulated sector.[15]

To a large extent the same is true of the various iterations of the voluntary codes of corporate governance from Cadbury onwards much of which were inspired by various corporate scandals, which were often themselves founded ultimately on some form of criminal or potentially criminal activity. The Cadbury report itself made the case that whilst combatting fraud will never be a zero sum game, by affirming principles of openness, integrity and accountability, the risks could be lessened. The report also suggested that had a similar code been in place earlier that a number of corporate scandals would have come to light earlier.[16]

Whilst the failure to prevent mechanism, clearly is part of the legislative framework and therefore can be characterised within the 'legal' mechanisms of corporate governance mentioned above, on closer application it is a hybrid creature that contains many of the same attributes as the codes of governance.

There is clearly a code of governance in the Bribery Guidance that the Act provides for under section 9, relating to the adequate procedures defence and the steps that companies can put in place to avoid prosecution. Like the UK Code of Corporate Governance (the Code), the Guidance itself is not compulsory and although a potentially hazardous course of action, a Commercial Organisation could depart from the suggested procedures and still avoid prosecution. Both the Code and the Bribery Guidance are founded on underlying principles and central to both sets of principles is a focus on the importance of the company's leadership. With the Code this is the role of the board and the importance of its effectiveness,[17] with the Guidance we have Principle 2 and reference to top-level management commitment to preventing bribery and fostering a bribery intolerant culture.[18]

This top-down approach is critical to the operation of the Bribery regime and targets a significant problem with the common law identification doctrine, which acts as a great disincentive for a director to be actively closely involved for fear of being held to be the *alter ego* of the company. The disincentive is further compounded by the complexity and sophistication of many firms where the decision making process is often as horizontal as it is vertical with a large number of decision makers at a number of levels.

This situation creates inevitable complexity within the chain of command and acts an in-built incentive for senior management to distance itself from operational matters.[19] These difficulties highlight one of the major criticisms against the identification theory itself, namely the often impossible and illogical, evidentiary task of identifying the senior manager who is the directing mind of the company in situations where decisions are made by many people at different levels of the organisation. This does not fit easily with the identification doctrine which works better, albeit ineffectually on the whole in a smaller quasi-partnership company where the directors and shareholders are more likely to be involved in the day to day running of the business and it is far easier to visualise how an actor can be deemed to be the *alter ego* of the company itself.

The bribery regime meanwhile, places overall responsibility on the top-level management to foster a culture in which bribery is never acceptable. Although the detail about what procedures organisations develop and implement will depend on the circumstances, and the principles are not prescriptive, the centrality of top-level commitment within the Guidance means there is now a positive incentive for senior management to be closely involved.

This is therefore an approach to confronting bribery that differs from many of the historical examples of statutory corporate governance mechanisms in the various Companies Acts. Whilst it imposes a default responsibility on the Commercial Organisation if bribes have been proffered in its name (indeed this is the visible part of the prohibition on the face of section 7 of the Bribery Act 2010) this is only a small fraction of the reality. The real aim of the provision is not to punish Commercial Organisations for acts of Bribery, it is aimed at ensuring that appropriate standards of corporate governance are implemented and adhered to. If appropriate standards, or rather 'adequate procedures' are in place, then the actual bribery (under section 7 at least) will be irrelevant as the well-run company will not be liable. It remains the case that, ironically, a well-run company could still be potentially liable under the identification doctrine. In these circumstances it is probably just as well that the doctrine is virtually ineffective. The focus on changing culture is implicit throughout much of the guidance and explicit in the academic literature and parliamentary papers which preceded the enactment dating back at least to the Nolan committee report.[20]

This holistic, cultural change approach does not just relate to the Act and the guidance, it is also an aspect of the Deferred Prosecution regime itself. Even where the Commercial Organisation has failed to put in place Adequate Procedures, and even where there has been wrongdoing on an exceptional scale crossing a number of years, prosecution can be avoided by a company demonstrating that it has improved its culture of governance markedly. Deferred Prosecution may well result in an enormous fine and a large amount of negative publicity. It will also not prevent individuals in the organisation being responsible for offences other than section 7 of the Bribery Act 2010. The key benefit for most Commercial Organisations, at least for those that have already been the subject of such deals, is that avoiding criminal sanction means that they will not fall foul of procurement rules when tendering for government contracts. Within the Deferred Prosecution cases this emphasis on cultural change is equally evident, and hence the case law and guidance places great emphasis on self-reporting and co-operation by the Commercial Organisation in the investigation.

The scale of the pay-out by Rolls Royce goes some way to countering any arguments that deferring prosecution is a soft option for a company embroiled in a corruption scandal. The existential risk posed by a potential criminal prosecution on the other hand means that the attraction of the Deferred Prosecution Agreement scheme is compelling. As the availability of the Deferred Prosecution Agreement depends largely on the extent that the company has cooperated with the investigation and also to the extent to which cultural change and practice has been affected, the logical path for a vulnerable company to follow is to engage fully with the cultural change agenda.

10.4 Changing the corporate culture – a previous statutory attempt

This is not the only recent instance of the legislature so deliberately attempting to change corporate culture, another obvious example was section 172 of the Companies Act 2006, the duty to promote the success of the company. This provision, which is centre of stage in the codified directors' duties, was put into law following a long period of parliamentary scrutiny. This length of this legislative consultation was itself underpinned by academic debates that had themselves rumbled on since the 1930s.[21] The question underpinning section 172 was a fundamental one of who is the company run for, for present purposes it can crudely be portrayed as being whether the model should be a shareholder wealth maximisation model or a stakeholder model (or pluralistic[22] approach, to adopt the terminology chosen by the Company Law Review Steering Group.) The outcome was neither, but an enlightened shareholder model that retained the primacy of the shareholder whilst instructing directors to have regard to a number of factors when performing the duty. These factors include the following:

(a) the likely consequences of any decision in the long term,
(b) the interests of the company's employees,
(c) the need to foster the company's business relationships with suppliers, customers and others,
(d) the impact of the company's operations on the community and the environment,
(e) the desirability of the company maintaining a reputation for high standards of business conduct, and
(f) the need to act fairly between members of the company.

As can be gleaned from the content, this is effectively a legislative attempt to inculcate principles of corporate social responsibility into mainstream company law. There is nothing particularly unusual about seeing reference to similar considerations in non-binding codes of governance. What was new, was to see them embedded in an Act of Parliament.

Whether section 172 has actually made any appreciable difference in terms of enhancing standards of corporate social responsibility is very difficult to ascertain as, in contrast to the voluminous academic literature on the provision, the case law considering section 172 is meagre. The absence of litigation involving section 172 and indeed the directors' duties in general following the banking crisis is particularly notable.[23]

The difficulty with section 172 and arguably its greatest failing is its lack of obvious enforceability. As these are only factors which the board must take into consideration when making their decisions, there is no direct duty to fulfil any one of these particular aims. Furthermore, the directors' duties are a corporate governance control mechanism internal to the company, the duties are owed to the company and generally speaking[24] the company only can sue for breach. The other stakeholder groups referred to in (a) – (f) above and any wider constituencies who would have a genuine interest in companies maintaining high standards of business conduct have no *locus standi* to bring an action. This means that the approach contains the exhortation to improve the corporate culture but no real mechanism of any potency to enforce the change. It is in short a right without an obvious remedy.

There may well be a persuasive, non-litigious role that section 172 plays in enhancing Corporate Social Responsibility, as a useful reminder to directors of wider social considerations but it is at best questionable that the effect of the provision has justified the enormous amount of research literature, practitioner and academic and ultimately parliamentary time that preceded its introduction.

The brief discussion above serves only to show the dramatic successes of the failure to prevent mechanism in sharp relief with the major difference being the underpinning of a quite detailed scheme of governance that enables and prompts compliance, with the very real threat of a strict liability offence that brings potential for limitless fines and ultimately commercial ruin if cultural change is not affected.

10.5 Extending failure to prevent to the Fraud Act 2006

The foregoing is an enthusiastic and perhaps over eulogistic endorsement of the failure to prevent offence in the Bribery Act 2010. There will no doubt be amendments over the years to the legislation and the guidance, influenced by judicial scrutiny and academic opinion. It should be emphasised that it also will never root out bribery completely. It is difficult however, not to be positive about the new provision given its recent successes which have been in stark contrast with the position before the Bribery Act 2010 came into force.

The question remains whether the provision would work with the Fraud Act 2006. It does not follow that what is deemed successful in one area will be successful in another and although the mechanism has already been duplicated elsewhere this has been too recent to gauge its effect. Many of the underlying issues are identical. The central problem of establishing corporate liability under the identification problem is ubiquitous to corporate law therefore striving towards a new scheme that actually works seems laudable. Moving towards a system where the corporate culture and procedures of a company are effectively challenged is both rational and achievable, contrasting with the ridiculous pursuit of concepts of directing minds of complex organisations.

This being said, the failure to prevent mechanism is not the only potential way forward and is but one of a number of reform ideas suggested in the Call for Evidence that include: amending the identification doctrine; creating a strict (vicarious) liability offences; making 'failure to prevent' an element of the offence, and; regulatory reform on a sector by sector basis.

There is a distinct impression that amending the identification is not a realistic option and the paper effectively discounts this option in the same breath as it proposes it.[25] Unfortunately this does not mean that a move away from the identification doctrine towards a more rational statutory scheme is inevitable. The chances of future reform in this area will depend on many factors, not least political determination to see reform through, and in the current febrile environment this cannot be taken for granted.

The vicarious liability option seems to owe its inspiration from the *respondeat superiore* liability in the United States. This option has similarities with the failure to prevent offence; its major defect, particularly if a due diligence/adequate procedures defence was included (as suggested) is that introducing vicarious liability into the provision produces another unnecessary layer of complexity.

The assertion made in the paper that vicarious liability 'is generally regarded as an effective and just means of attributing liability' has also been strongly contested elsewhere however and the advantages of this option over the failure to prevent offence are difficult to see.[26]

The option of making 'failure to prevent' part of the offence in effect entails a reversal of the burden of proof as compared with the Bribery Act offence. The obvious inference is that such a provision would be harder and costlier to enforce and more importantly it moves away from the essence of the corporate governance model by taking away a strong incentive for Commercial Organisations to ensure their 'adequate procedures' are fit for purpose.

The 'regulatory reform' option will no doubt attract considerable attention from the responses to the Call for Evidence and whatever the outcome, any new provision clearly needs to be informed by the existing regulatory structure in particular areas. In many ways this aspect of the consultation may prove the most enlightening. Although it is possibly a little premature to say however, a sector by sector approach could create further complexity with a variety of different piecemeal developments.

On this basis it is tempting to view the failure to prevent option as the most promising on offer and there are a number of advantages to adopting it. On a purely practical point there is also a certain logic in extending the offence to fraud given that it is already grouped with bribery and tax evasion in the Deferred Prosecution scheme, meaning that an important part of the corporate governance structure is already in place.[27]

The offence would preserve the focus on only the obtaining of business or a business advantage, therefore targeting criminal activity that is carried out in order to further the aims of the Commercial Organisation. This is significant, as punishing the Commercial Organisation for just these activities rather than extending it to all frauds committed by associated persons will mean that instances where an employee defrauds his or her own employer will not be caught by the provision. Thus, companies who have suffered the fraud will not suffer an additional and potentially unjust burden of a criminal prosecution. This nexus with business advantage raises questions however as to how many fraud offences that fulfil the criteria there are likely to be and it may be that in cases of bribery such a determination may be that much more obvious. The question as to the type of corporate crime that would be caught by a failure to prevent fraud offence is certainly more nuanced, and harder to answer definitively.

The guidance issued by the Ministry of Justice would need to be different. One could argue that the fundamentals would be identical and there is no reason, for example, why the six principles of proportionate procedures, top level commitment, risk assessment, due diligence, communication (including training) and monitoring and review could not feature prominently in any fraud guidance, just as they also currently feature in the draft guidance issued for the Tax offence.

10.6 Conclusion

If the experience with the Bribery Act 2010 is any guide, the development of any new provision that tackles the problem of corporate liability for fraud is likely to take some time. It is optimistically suggested here that the failure to prevent mechanism is already suitable, if not as a ready-made provision, at least in a modified form. Whatever the outcome of the reform process and the eventual direction of travel it is hoped that some of the key features of the failure to prevent model, particularly relating to incentivising cultural change in corporate governance persist.

Notes

1 Principal Lecturer and Head of School of Law, University of Worcester. Email: bill.davies@worc.ac.uk.
2 For an interesting historical analysis of both statutory and common law measures that have for all practical purposes come very close to being 'failure to prevent' offences see: SF Copp and A Cronin, 'New models of corporate criminality: the development and relative effectiveness of "failure to prevent" offences' (2018) 39 *Company Lawyer* 104.
3 Primarily the OECD Convention on Combating Bribery of Foreign Officials in International Business Transactions, Paris, December 7, 1997.
4 Notably the Foreign Corrupt Practices Act 1977 in the USA.
5 Criminal Finances Act 2017 Pt 3, sections 45 and 46.
6 Bribery Act 2010, section 7(5).
7 ibid, section 8.
8 ibid, section 12(5) states: 'An offence is committed under section 7 irrespective of whether the acts or omissions which form part of the offence take place in the United Kingdom or elsewhere'.
9 ibid, section 7(2).
10 Crime and Courts Act 2013, Schedule 17.
11 Apparently the quiet start was an important factor in the earlier decision to shelve proposals to extend the failure to prevent offence to other economic crimes. See Eduardo Reyes, 'MoJ drops "failure to prevent economic crime" offence plans', 29 September 2015, *Law Society Gazette* <www.lawgazette.co.uk/news/government-drops-plan-to-extend-corporate-criminal-liability/5051277.article> accessed 26 April 2018.
12 *Serious Fraud Office v Rolls-Royce Plc* [2017] Lloyd's Rep. F.C. 249 (Crown Ct (Southwark)), *Serious Fraud Office v Standard Bank Plc* (now ICBC Standard Bank Plc) (Final) [2016] Lloyd's Rep. F.C. 102 (Crown Ct (Southwark)), and *Serious Fraud Office v XYZ Ltd* [2016] Lloyd's Rep. F.C. 509 (Crown Ct (Southwark)).
13 Ministry of Justice, Corporate Liability for Economic Crime: Call for Evidence (January 2017) <https://consult.justice.gov.uk/digital-communications/corporate-liability-for-economic-crime/supporting_documents/corporateliabilityforeconomiccrime consultationdocument.pdf> accessed 4 May 2018.
14 *Serious Fraud Office v Rolls-Royce Plc* [2017] Lloyd's Rep. F.C. 249 (Crown Ct (Southwark)).
15 See: SF Copp and A Cronin, 'New models of corporate criminality: the problem of corporate fraud – prevention or cure?' (2018) 39 Company Lawyer 139 and SF Copp, 'Limited Liability and Freedom', in SF. Copp (ed.), *The Legal Foundations of Free Markets* (Institute of Economic Affairs, 2008) 173.

16 For example: 'No system of corporate governance can be totally proof against fraud or incompetence. The test is how far such aberrations can be discouraged and how quickly they can be brought to light. The risks can be reduced by making the participants in the governance process as effectively accountable as possible. The key safeguards are properly constituted boards, separation of the functions of chairman and of chief executive, audit committees, vigilant shareholders and financial reporting and auditing systems which provide full and timely disclosure'. Cadbury Report (1992), *Report of the Committee on the Financial Aspects of Corporate Governance*, Gee, London. Para 7.2.

17 'Every company should be headed by an effective board which is collectively responsible for the long-term success of the company. There should be a clear division of responsibilities at the head of the company between the running of the board and the executive responsibility for the running of the company's business. No one individual should have unfettered powers of decision. The chairman is responsible for leadership of the board and ensuring its effectiveness on all aspects of its role. As part of their role as members of a unitary board, non-executive directors should constructively challenge and help develop proposals on strategy'. *Financial Reporting Council, UK Corporate Governance Code (April 2016) Section A: Leadership.*

18 'The top-level management of a commercial organisation (be it a board of directors, the owners or any other equivalent body or person) are committed to preventing bribery by persons associated with it. They foster a culture within the organisation in which bribery is never acceptable.' The Bribery Act 2010 Guidance about procedures which relevant commercial organisations can put into place to prevent persons associated with them from bribing. *The Ministry of Justice*, 20 March 2011, available at: <www.justice.gov.uk/downloads/legislation/bribery-act-2010-guidance.pdf> accessed 4 May 2018.

19 Thus exacerbating problems of asymmetric information always a concern in a sophisticated organisation anyway, for an example of a detailed analysis of the problems of information asymmetries see SF Copp and A Cronin, 'The failure of criminal law to control the use of off balance sheet finance during the banking crisis' (2015) 36 Company Lawyer 99 (2018) 39.

20 Nolan Committee, Report on Standards in Public Life 1995, Cm.2850–1.

21 For example the Dodd/Berle public debate based on views expressed in: AA Berle, 'Corporate Powers as Powers in Trust' (1931) 44 (7) Harvard L Rev 1049 and E Merrick Dodd, 'For Whom are Corporate Managers Trustees?' (1932) 45(7) Harvard L Rev 114.

22 Company Law Review Steering Group, *Developing the Framework*, 2000, para.2.12.

23 See: J. Loughrey (ed), *Directors' Duties and Shareholder Litigation after the Crisis* (Edward Elgar, 2012)

24 In limited circumstances, shareholders can also bring derivative claims and unfair prejudice petitions, sections 260–263 and sections 994 Companies Act 2006.

25 'Retaining the identification doctrine in any form would perpetuate the notion that a company can commit a criminal offence. It would encourage corporate efforts to limit potential liability through the adoption of evasive internal structures. It would not promote the prevention of economic crime as a component of corporate good governance'. See Ministry of Justice, Corporate Liability for Economic Crime: Call for Evidence (January 2017) (n 13) 17.

26 C Wells, 'Corporate Failure to Prevent Economic Crime – a Proposal' [2017] Crim. L.R. 423, 432.

27 It has also been pointed out that the scheme is 'familiar with compliance officers'. See Wells (n 27) 439.

Bibliography

Berle A, 'Corporate Powers as Powers in Trust' (1931) 44 (7) Harvard L Rev 1049

Bribery Act 2010

Cadbury Report, *Report of the Committee on the Financial Aspects of Corporate Governance,* Gee, London 1992

Companies Act 2006

Convention on Combating Bribery of Foreign Officials in International Business Transactions, Paris, December 7, 1997

Copp SF, 'Limited Liability and Freedom', in SF. Copp (ed.), *The Legal Foundations of Free Markets* (Institute of Economic Affairs, 2008) 173.

Copp SF and Cronin, A 'New models of corporate criminality: the problem of corporate fraud – prevention or cure?' (2018) 39 Company Lawyer 139

Copp SF and Cronin A, 'New models of corporate criminality: the development and relative effectiveness of "failure to prevent" offences' (2018) 39 Company Lawyer 104

Copp SF and Cronin A, 'The failure of criminal law to control the use of off balance sheet finance during the banking crisis' (2015) 36 Company Lawyer 99

Company Law Review Steering Group, *Developing the Framework,* 2000

Crime and Courts Act 2013

Criminal Finances Act 2017

Dodd EM, 'For Whom are Corporate Managers Trustees?' (1932) 45(7) Harvard L Rev 114

Financial Reporting Council, UK Corporate Governance Code (April 2016)

Foreign Corrupt Practices Act of 1977 (FCPA) (15 U.S.C. § 78dd-1, et seq.)

Loughrey J (ed), Directors' Duties and Shareholder Litigation after the Crisis (Edward Elgar, 2012)

Ministry of Justice, *The Bribery Act 2010 Guidance about procedures which relevant commercial organisations can put into place to prevent persons associated with them from bribing (12 March 2011)*

Ministry of Justice, *Corporate Liability for Economic Crime: Call for Evidence* (January 2017) Cm 9370

Nolan Committee, *Report on Standards in Public Life* 1995, Cm 2850–1

OECD *Anti Bribery Convention on Combating Bribery of Foreign Officials in International Business Transactions,* Paris, December 7, 1997

Reyes E, 'MoJ drops 'failure to prevent economic crime' offence plans' *Law Society Gazette,* 29 September 2015

Serious Fraud Office v Rolls-Royce Plc [2017] Lloyd's Rep. F.C. 249 (Crown Ct (Southwark))

Serious Fraud Office v Standard Bank Plc (now ICBC Standard Bank Plc) (Final) [2016] Lloyd's Rep. F.C. 102 (Crown Ct (Southwark))

Serious Fraud Office v XYZ Ltd [2016] Lloyd's Rep. F.C. 509 (Crown Ct (Southwark))

Wells C 'Corporate Failure to Prevent Economic Crime – a Proposal' [2017] Crim. L.R. 423

11 A judge's perspective of the impact of the Fraud Act 2006

His Honour Toby Hooper QC[1]

11.1 Introduction

I set out in this chapter to discuss a judge's perspective of the impact of the Fraud Act 2006, and to illustrate this perspective by reference to the drafting and interpretation of the Act itself, to particular considerations in directing the jury, and to aspects of court procedure, sentencing, and asset recovery applicable to the Act.

When, on 13 January 2017, I delivered at the School of Law of the University of Worcester the keynote on which this chapter is based, I identified reasons, no doubt among others which those present might wish to add, to congratulate the School of Law on the initiative of this Workshop.[2]

First, the Workshop was a worthy marker of the 10th anniversary of this important Act of Parliament which boasts in my judgment two achievements not always encountered in combination, namely addressing serious public mischief while attracting the appreciation of judges and legal professionals for combining succinctness, clarity and precision of expression in doing this. Secondly, this anniversary fell in the School of Law's foundation academic year.

The Act received Royal Assent on 8 November 2006 and came into force on 15 January 2007. When I originally delivered my keynote I did not foresee that 2017 would mark a significant development in the law relating to fraud, namely that on 25 October 2017 the Supreme Court would deliver judgment in *Ivey v Genting Casinos Ltd trading as Crockfords*.[3] I am glad of the opportunity which preparation of this chapter provides to update my paper to take account of the substantial revision of the definition of dishonesty in criminal cases which *Ivey* represents.

11.2 The structure, drafting and interpretation of the Act

11.2.1 Structure

I pay tribute to the drafting of this legislation. Its attraction to judges can best be assessed by analysing certain features of its drafting. In my judgment this is effective parliamentary drafting.

My respect for the Law Commission is such that my starting point is to notice Parliament's commitment to the Law Commission's Fraud Law Report of 2002 which inspired the Act.[4] The Act is a tribute to the public function of the Law Commission, with its precept of comprehensively but concisely identifying the state of current law and making proposals for its reform.

The Law Commission was established in 1965. The work of the Law Commission in investigating and reporting on fraud aptly evokes observations which the founding Chairman of the Commission, Sir Leslie Scarman, then a High Court Judge and later a Law Lord, made in a series of lectures in 1967 collected and published in 1968 as *Law Reform: The New Pattern*.[5] Scarman observed that law reform is not exclusively a legal topic: it is also a social and moral problem,[6] and that the founding Law Commissioners 'laid down as their overall policy that the law should be simple, more readily accessible, more easily understandable and more certain'.[7]

These words had particular resonance in the year 2017 in which a former University law lecturer, and Law Commissioner, Baroness Hale, was appointed President of the Supreme Court.

It is surely no disrespect to the Law Commission that Parliament chose not to adopt its recommendation to abolish the offence of conspiracy to defraud. The majority of those who responded to this point in the Home Office's consultation following the Law Commission Report were opposed to abolition on the basis of serious practical concerns about the ability to prosecute multiple offences in the largest and most serious cases of fraud and a desire to see how the new statutory offences worked in practice before abolishing conspiracy to defraud.[8] There were also concerns that limitations on the scope of statutory conspiracy meant that certain types of secondary participation in fraud might only be caught by the common law offence. It is also noticeable that the common law offence of cheating the public revenue remains in force, as do statutory offences of money laundering, forgery and false accounting, and I shall return to these in the context of sentencing. It was no good reason to revoke the offence of conspiracy to defraud that the statutory offence of fraud is inchoate.

These considerations focus particular attention on the Attorney-General's Guidelines on the use of the common law offence of conspiracy to defraud, setting out issues which the Attorney-General asks prosecuting authorities in England and Wales to consider before charging the common law offence in the light of the Fraud Act 2006. These Guidelines are published on the Crown Prosecution Service website.[9] They may be supplemented by Department-specific guidance which individual Directors of the prosecuting authorities may issue.

11.2.2 Drafting

I turn to what Parliament did enact. I do not intend to repeat other contributions, but there will be overlap, particularly with Maureen Johnson's research which is explored in Chapter 6. I intend only to justify my commitment to the drafting of the Act for the pragmatic purpose of a judge directing a jury in accordance with Parliament's intention. For these purposes, the straightforward structure of the Act signals its straightforward substance in its enactment of, as is well understood, one general offence of fraud, with three ways of committing this offence, namely by false representation (section 1(2)(a) and section 2), by failing to disclose information (section 1(2)(b) and section 3), and by abuse of position (section 1(2)(c) and section 4). Without derogation from my commitment to the drafting of the Act, I shall explain that this structure imposes sentencing challenges. The Act creates new offences of obtaining services dishonestly,[10] and of possessing, making and supplying articles for use in fraud.[11] The Act enacts other offences on which I will not dwell.

The Act achieves the objectives which it sets itself by specifying, in plain English, first a broad target, the offence of fraud, then secondly the precise strike capability which each of the three ways, or gateways, of committing fraud represents. Parliament refrains here from conferring disputably wide powers of executive action, so-called Henry VIII clauses.

11.2.3 Dishonesty: Ghosh and Ivey

The clarity and symmetry of sections 1 to 4 derives from the foundation of the Act in the concept of dishonesty common to each of the three gateways. The use of this term in this context recognises the definition of dishonesty which the Court of Appeal. Criminal Division, established in 1982 in *R v Ghosh*[12] as a two-stage test. Stage 1: whether the behaviour would be regarded as dishonest by the ordinary standards of reasonable and honest people. Stage 2: if so, whether the defendant was aware that his conduct was dishonest and would be regarded as dishonest by reasonable and honest people.

This was the state of the law at the time of the Law Commission Report of 2002 and at the time of the enactment of the Fraud Act 2006, and as it remained until 25 October 2017 when the Supreme Court decided *Ivey*.[13]

The Supreme Court in *Ivey* expressed concern about the subjective nature of the second stage of the *Ghosh* test, that the less a defendant's standards conform to society's expectations, the less likely he is to be held criminally responsible for his behaviour. The Supreme Court was concerned that the law should not excuse those who make a mistake about contemporary standards of honesty. A purpose of the criminal law is to set acceptable standards of behaviour.

The Supreme Court, recognising that in civil actions the law has settled on an objective test of dishonesty, and directing itself that there can be no logical or principled basis for the meaning of dishonesty to differ according to whether the issue arises in a civil action or in a criminal prosecution, declared that the second leg of the *Ghosh* test does not correctly represent the law, and that directions based on it ought no longer to be given.

The Supreme Court declared that the test of dishonesty should be that used in civil actions, namely as set out by Lord Nicholls in the House of Lords in *Royal Brunei Airlines Sch Bhd v Tan*[14] and by Lord Hoffmann in the Privy Council in *Barlow Clowes International Limited v Eurotrust Ltd.*[15] First, the jury must ascertain, subjectively, the actual state of the defendant's knowledge or belief as to the facts. The reasonableness or otherwise of his belief is a matter of evidence, often in practice determinative, going to whether he held that belief, but it is not an additional requirement that his belief must be reasonable. The question is whether it is genuinely held. When once his actual state of mind as to knowledge or belief as to facts is first established, the jury has, secondly, to decide the question whether his conduct was honest or dishonest by applying the standards, to be judged objectively, of ordinary decent people. There is no requirement that the defendant must appreciate that what he has done is, by those standards, dishonest.

I shall say more about the potential complexity of the trial of fraud cases later, but for the time being I observe that I believe that the concept of dishonesty as the Supreme Court has defined it is readily understandable to a jury properly directed, just as I used to believe that the *Ghosh* test was readily understandable. Now, strict adherence to the plain English wording which Lord Hughes uses in his judgment in *Ivey*, which is the judgment of the Court because the four other Justices sitting agreed with it, is in my judgment the necessary basis for proper jury direction. I note as a matter of historical significance that the constitution of the court in *Ivey* was what judges and practitioners call a 'strong court'. Lord Neuberger was President of the Supreme Court when *Ivey* was argued. Lady Hale was then Deputy President and is now President. Lord Kerr was formerly Lord Chief Justice of Northern Ireland. Lord Thomas of Cymgwiedd was Lord Chief Justice of England and Wales when *Ivey* was argued. Lord Hughes was formerly Vice-President of the Court of Appeal, Criminal Division.

11.2.4 Other provisions

I have commended the clarity and symmetry of sections 1 to 4 of the Act. Similar clarity, also via plain English, is to be found in the definition of 'representation' for the purposes of section 2. Thus, as Maureen Johnson shows in Chapter 6, section 2 readily catches 'phishing' and its various emanations, and conduct by use of a device, and averts a defence that a representation cannot be made to a device.

Likewise, the offence of fraud by failing to disclose information, section 3, engages the concept of failure in breach of a legal duty which is in my judgment a straightforward concept as to which it was my practice to direct juries by sticking as closely as the circumstances of the particular case permitted to the definition of 'legal duty' which the Law Commission adopted in paragraph 7.28 of its Report. This definition is: 'duty deriving from statute, or from the fact that the transaction in question is one of utmost good faith, or from the express or implied terms of a contract, or from the custom of a particular trade or market, or from the existence of a fiduciary relationship'.

True it may be that the concept of 'position' for the purposes of the offence (which section 1(2)(c) creates and section 4 describes) of fraud by abuse of position may be a little more elusive than the more accessible concepts which I have just addressed. My solution was to grasp and hold fast to the common sense proposition that the concept of position may properly be regarded as easier to recognise than to define, that is, it is case specific. To justify this approach it is necessary to direct the jury clearly as to what evidence comprises the factual matrix in which the prosecution alleges that the particular position, or relationship, lies, and, to achieve this, to require the prosecution clearly to specify this. I say more below about court case management powers of compelling case clarity on each side of the adversarial fence, prosecution and defence.

As the Law Commission said in paragraph 7.38 of its Report: 'The question of whether the particular facts alleged can properly be described as giving rise to that relationship will be an issue capable of being ruled upon by the judge and, if the case goes to the jury, of being the subject of directions'.[16]

I observe in passing that this pragmatic approach of the Law Commission evidences in my judgment the benefit of judicial and practising professional membership of the Law Commission since its inception, as well, of course, as that of its distinguished legal academic members. This approach vindicates the intention of its founding chairman, Leslie Scarman, that the Commission should 'represent an attempt to introduce into the law-making process the independent thought and technical learning which one expects to find in the courts'.[17]

The practical importance of the concepts of gain and loss which section 5 defined lies in practice in the enactment of the concept of loss in addition to, or as an alternative to, proof of gain. This achieves justice in circumstances where the prosecution can more readily prove loss to victim than gain to perpetrator. This occurs in many cases to which contemporary financial circumstances, and inclination to mischief, give rise.

Sections 6, 7 and 8 enact offences of, in summary, possessing, making or supplying articles for use in fraud. These enactments take effect in four important practical ways. First, the extension of the offence under section 25 of the Theft Act 1968, of going equipped for burglary, theft or cheat to possession otherwise than at 'place of abode'. The restriction to 'place of abode' had proved troublesome to interpret, and potentially unjustly restrictive of a prosecutor's reach. Second, the extension of the offence under section 1 of the Forgery and Counterfeiting Act 1981 so that proof of a general intention to commit fraud will suffice, so the prosecution do not have to prove double intention. Third, the further extension of the offence under 25 of the Theft Act 1968 so that it suffices for the prosecution to prove that the accused had the article with him with the intention that it should be used by someone else. Fourth, the extension of both offences by the specific definition of 'article' in section 8 to include any program or data held in electronic form.

In one Serious Fraud Office case I tried, an 'article' issue was the electronically copied logo of one of the world's three largest banks used to deceive, so the jury found, some very intelligent people. Parliament had to move with the times with the term 'article'.

For the purpose of illustrating how the modern judge can properly regard the Fraud Act 2006 as an adept instrument readily explainable to juries, I do not propose specifically to address the albeit important provisions as to participating in fraudulent business, but I will briefly mention, by way of the same appreciation, the offence which section 11 enacts of obtaining services dishonestly. This neatly extends to such modern-day mischief as dishonestly accessing online services the scope of the offence under section 3 of the Theft Act 1978, left in force, of making off without payment.

11.2.5 Evidential provisions

Before moving on to consider how court procedure has evolved in aid of the objectives of the Act, I briefly address just one other feature of the Act, namely the evidence provisions of section 13. Section 13 enacts a shrewd exception to the privilege against self-incrimination in the public interest of the protection of those whom, in particular, trusteeship or executorship should properly protect. In summary, section 13 provides that a person cannot claim the privilege against self-incrimination to defeat a claim in the civil courts for breach of those duties.

Consider an equivalently shrewd provision in the very different circumstances of the Children Act 1989, section 98. In summary, this provides that in local authority care order application proceedings a person cannot claim the privilege against self-incrimination to defeat the Children Act proceedings, and or to defeat prosecution for perjury. I believe that such cross-jurisdictional reflection is timely in light of the disposition of the Supreme Court in *Ivey* to consistency between the civil and criminal fraud jurisdictions, and the interest which the Judicial College has shown in recent years in training judges in the comparison of the law, practice and procedure of different jurisdictions so as more effectively to discharge their functions in their own.

11.3 Procedure

I now make some observations about Crown Court procedure in aid of the objectives of the Act. These provisions are not confined to cases under the Act, but are particularly useful there. They recognise the potential complexity of criminal fraud litigation.

The current governing instrument is the Criminal Procedure Rules 2015, as amended. By rule 3.2 the court must further the overriding objective of the rules by actively managing the case. The overriding objective is based on its equivalent in the Civil Procedure Rules 1998, and also more recently adopted in family court procedure. The overriding objective is that criminal cases be dealt with justly. This is defined to include acquitting the innocent and convicting the guilty, dealing with the case efficiently and expeditiously, and dealing with the case in ways that take into account the gravity of the offence alleged, the complexity of what is in issue, and the severity of the consequences for the defendant and others affected, for example victims of fraud.

The case management which, as I have introduced, rule 3.2 enjoins the court to apply to further the overriding objective includes early identification of the real issues, early setting of a timetable for the progress of the case, ensuring that evidence, whether disputed or not disputed, is presented in the shortest and clearest way, and making use of technology where appropriate. Rule 3.3 imposes duties on the parties of active co-operation which it is implicit in the court's case management powers that the court may, within reason and always proportionately to the overriding objective, compel. In my experience this power permits, I repeat within reason and always proportionately to the overriding objective, compelling appropriate admissions, or, as a last resort, the judge ruling to that effect. Rule 3.4 provides the court with, among other case management powers, the power to require that issues in the case should be identified in writing. The recent amendment to Rule 25.9 of the Criminal Procedure Rules 2015 by paragraph 10 of the Criminal Procedure Amendment Rules 2016 provides, as to the court's powers at trial that, where there is a jury, in order to help the jurors to understand the case, and to resolve any issues in it, the court may invite the defendant concisely to identify what is in issue, and, if necessary in terms approved by the court, if the defendant declines to do so, direct that the jurors be given a copy of any defence statement, albeit edited if necessary to exclude reference to inappropriate or inadmissible matters. I suggest that this chimes pragmatically with the results of Professor Cheryl Thomas' jury research which Nicola Monaghan explores in Chapter 12.[18] Moreover, I suspect that the risk of revealing inconsistency must be a powerful discouragement to a defendant to withhold co-operation.

Current best practice as to the duration of fraud trials is specified in The Protocol for the Control and Management of Heavy Fraud and Other Complex Criminal Cases which the Lord Chief Justice issued in 2005.[19] Generally a trial of no longer than three months should be the target, but it is recognised that there will be cases where a duration of six months, or, in exceptional cases, even longer may be inevitable. The intention is to reduce trials to the barest essentials of the public interest in proving what is sufficient in proportion to the alleged wrongdoing to enable sentencing to fit the crime, if such is proved, and consequential asset confiscation likewise proportionate. This intention enjoins active prosecutorial discretion, in particular as to avoiding over-loaded indictments.

11.4 Sentencing

11.4.1 Sentencing context

The sentencing of any case under the Fraud Act 2006 is a complex and anxious exercise because the wide scope of the Act addresses a range of behaviours and personal circumstances which fraud offenders present, because of the range of victim impact involved (on occasions none as this is an inchoate offence capable of being constituted by conduct not result), and because judges are conscious that the public perception is that fraud sentencing tends to be unduly lenient. Moreover, some inconsistency between maximum sentences for comparable or similar offences may be detected. The maximum sentence for the offence of fraud under Section 1 of the Fraud Act 2006 is ten years' imprisonment.

These circumstances require particular attention in fraud cases to two sets of Attorney-General's Guidelines. First, 'The Acceptance of Pleas and the Prosecutor's Role in the Sentencing Exercise', published on the Crown Prosecution Service website.[20] Secondly, 'Plea Discussions in Cases of Serious or Complex Fraud'.[21]

I compare some related offences in ascending order of maximum sentence. Theft, section 1 of the Theft Act 1968, and false accounting, section 17 of the Theft Act 1968: seven years. Fraud, section 1 of the Fraud Act 2006: ten years as I have said. Forgery under section 1 of the Forgery Act 1981, which requires proof of a double intention which the 'article' offence under section 7 of the Fraud Act 2006 does not, carries the same maximum sentence of ten years' imprisonment as section 7. Money laundering under sections 327, 328 and 329 of the Proceeds of Crime Act 2002 carries a maximum sentence of fourteen years' imprisonment even though those offences can implicitly involve potentially less culpable secondary parties. The offence of cheating the public revenue, that is tax and VAT, being a common law offence, carries no maximum sentence, even though, but for the public revenue, the offence is identical to the offence under section 1 of the Fraud Act 2006. Similarly, conspiracy to defraud, even though that offence can implicitly involve secondary parties.

11.4.2 Sentencing principles

I would like to encourage confidence in the sentencing process, now as in my sentencing remarks when a judge. To this end, I briefly summarise the purposes of sentencing in any case. I suggest that the application of rational statutory sentencing purpose overrides such inconsistency as I have identified, but that the sentencing judge must strictly apply the reasoning required.

The purposes of sentencing are currently set out in section 142 of the Criminal Justice Act 2003 in the following terms: 'Any court dealing with an offender in respect of an offence must have regard to the following purposes of sentencing – (a) the punishment of offenders, (b) the reduction of crime (including its reduction by deterrence), (c) the reform and rehabilitation of offenders, (d) the protection of the public, and (e) the making of reparation by offenders to persons affected by their offences'. Note the absence of any word such as 'vengeance' or 'revenge'. Section 143 provides that in considering the seriousness of any offence the court must consider the offender's culpability in committing the offence, and any harm which the offence caused, was intended to cause, or might foreseeably have caused. Section 152 provides that the court must not pass a custodial sentence unless it is of the opinion that the offending was so serious that neither a fine alone nor a community sentence can be justified for it. Section 153 provides that a custodial sentence must be for the shortest term that in the opinion of the court is commensurate with the seriousness of the offending. Section 244 provides that an offender serving a sentence of imprisonment is to be released at the half-way point of the term.

11.4.3 Sentencing Guidelines

By section 125 of the Coroners and Justice Act 2009 judges are bound to follow Sentencing Guidelines, no longer merely to have regard to them. The Sentencing Council and its predecessor the Sentencing Guidelines Council has, as its objective in devising Guidelines, the promotion of consistent and predictable sentencing, surely a worthy precept of the rule of law. The only exception to the duty to follow Sentencing Guidelines is if the court is satisfied that to follow the Guideline would be contrary to the interests of justice in the particular case.

Each Sentencing Guideline identifies a number of categories for each offence which it addresses. Each category specifies a sentencing range and starting point in accordance with the statutory definition of seriousness in section 143 of the Criminal Justice Act 2003, above, as harm and culpability. The court is then required to adjust the sentence from the starting point, but only within the range, to recognise any aggravating and mitigating factors, but without double-counting of factors already taken into account in the earlier part of the exercise. The court should only take into account credit to reduce sentence for a plea of guilty after it has identified the appropriate sentence in accordance with the process described. This credit may be as great as one-third.[22]

The Sentencing Guideline for Fraud was published in 2014 and applies to sentences passed on or after 1 October 2014 in respect of offences, whenever committed, by persons aged 18 or over and corporate bodies.[23] The Guideline sets out sentencing ranges for a number of offences of fraud (including conspiracy to defraud), money-laundering, and bribery. The sentencing judge keeps in mind that the context of fraud is not only harm in terms of gain or loss, or both, but also that it is in the nature of the statutory offence of fraud which the Fraud Act 2006 enacts that the offence is inchoate: there may be culpability without harm.

11.4.4 Sentencing comparisons: introduction

In order to provide some perspective on sentencing in fraud cases, I shall briefly attempt some sentencing comparisons as between fraud cases and cases of, to provide a broad spread of comparison, violence, drug dealing, and causing death by dangerous driving.

I give the following illustrations, based on applicable Guidelines, of what offending might attract a sentence of five years imprisonment and of what offending may attract a sentence of two years imprisonment in each such case. In choosing these terms, I call to mind that two years is the term at or below which the Court has power to suspend a sentence of imprisonment. I say more below about suspending a sentence.

Each illustration is based on the assumption of an offender convicted at trial, so not entitled to a reduction in sentence for pleading guilty.

11.4.5 Sentencing comparisons: fraud other than benefit fraud

Under the Fraud Act 2006 the maximum sentence for an offence of fraud is ten years imprisonment. For the purposes of my illustrations I distinguish between benefit fraud and fraud other than benefit fraud.

A sentence of five years imprisonment may be expected in the former case in either of the following two circumstances. First, where there is fraud involving about £300,000 with high culpability, defined as, for example, any one of the following factors: leading a group activity, abuse of a position of trust, sophisticated planning or perpetration, sustained period of offending, a large number of victims or any vulnerable victim. Secondly, where there is fraud involving a higher value of about £1 million but lesser culpability (that is falling short of high culpability, defined as above) and involving circumstances such as coercion, the absence of motivation of personal gain, or a peripheral role.

A sentence of two years' imprisonment may be expected in a case of fraud (other than benefit fraud) in either of the following two circumstances: first, fraud involving about £300,000 with lesser culpability as above defined; secondly, fraud involving about £50,000 in a significant role, for example where the offending is part of a group activity, but in the absence of any high culpability factor, as above defined.

11.4.6 Sentencing comparisons: benefit fraud

A sentence of five years' imprisonment may be expected in the case of benefit fraud involving about £500,000 with the higher culpability characteristics as for other fraud in so far as they are applicable. Such high amount is rarely encountered, as official intervention tends to occur sooner.

A sentence of two years' imprisonment may be expected in a case of benefit fraud in either of the following circumstances: first, fraud involving about £300,000 where the claim was not fraudulent from the outset; secondly, fraud involving about £75,000 with high culpability, defined as, for example, abuse of a position of trust.

Sentencing for lower-level frauds is undoubtedly controversial. A benefit fraud involving as much as £1,000 may attract a fine of half-a-week's earnings (or benefits).

11.4.7 Sentencing comparisons: violence

The offence of causing grievous bodily harm with intent to cause grievous bodily harm under section 18 of the Offences against the Person Act 1861 carries a maximum sentence of life imprisonment. Grievous bodily harm is defined as really serious injury. A sentence of five years' imprisonment may be expected in a case of a vulnerable victim or a sustained attack, or in a case of significant premeditation or the use of a weapon.

A sentence of two years' imprisonment falls below the lowest guideline category range for a section 18 offence but may conceivably be imposed in a case of a stab wound of least severity in circumstances of extreme provocation where the offender is of otherwise exemplary good character and where the court is satisfied that compliance with the guideline would be contrary to the interests of justice.

11.4.8 Sentencing comparisons: drugs

The offence of supply or possession with intent to supply under sections 4 and 5 of the Misuse of Drugs Act 1971, of either Class A, that is heroin or cocaine and other similar drugs carries a maximum sentence of life imprisonment, and Class B, that is cannabis or other similar drugs, a maximum sentence of fourteen years' imprisonment. A sentence of five years' imprisonment may be expected in a Class A case of street dealing in street dealing quantities, and in a Class B case for wholesaling of, for example, about 200 kg of cannabis in a role short of controlling or directing the operation.

A sentence of two years' imprisonment may be expected in a Class A case involving small quantities in circumstances of such lesser culpability as the offender becoming involved by coercion or intimidation, and in a Class B case of the higher culpability of controlling or directing an operation albeit involving similar small quantities.

11.4.9 Sentencing comparisons: causing death by dangerous driving

The offence of causing death by dangerous driving under section 1 of the Road Traffic Act 1988 carries a maximum sentence of fourteen years' imprisonment. A sentence of five years' imprisonment may be expected in a case where the driving created a substantial risk of danger by, for example, driving at a greatly excessive speed, or racing, or gross avoidable distraction such as reading or texting, or driving while impaired by drink or drugs.

A sentence of two years' imprisonment may be expected in a case where the driving is judged markedly less culpable than the creation of a significant risk of danger, but is dangerous driving within the statutory definition because it falls far below what would be expected of a competent and careful driver, and where it would be obvious to a competent and careful driver that driving in that way would be dangerous.

11.4.10 Sentencing comparisons: an overview

At first glance the common perception that sentencing for fraud tends to undue leniency may be explained by the headline comparisons which I have made. I suggest, however, that studied comparison shows that the Sentencing Council works successfully to maintain proportionality between the ranges of appropriate sentence for different kinds of offences while facilitating predictability and consistency of sentencing within each.

Moreover, section 143 of the Criminal Justice Act 2003 underpins the Sentencing Council's work across the range of offences which it addresses. As I have observed, section 143 provides that the seriousness of any offence is to be judged by reference to culpability and to harm which the offended caused, intended to cause or might foreseeably have caused.

I suggest, therefore, that joined-up understanding of criminal justice legislation, and of its emanations in Sentencing Guidelines, assists judges in the sentencing process and should foster public confidence in the process. I further suggest that these considerations should encourage prosecutors more readily to charge inchoate offending as Parliament intended in the Fraud Act 2006, with the consequential public benefits of earlier intervention and prevention of harm.

11.4.11 Suspending a sentence

A current concern in sentencing in many less serious offences of fraud is the issue of whether to suspend a sentence of imprisonment. A sentence may be suspended if, but for the power to suspend, the Court would have imposed a sentence of two years' imprisonment or less. The power to suspend arises under section 189 of the Criminal Justice Act 2003 as amended. Exercise of that power is itself the subject of a Sentencing Council Guideline on the Imposition of Community and Custodial Sentences, applicable to offenders aged eighteen or over sentenced on or after 1 February 2017 regardless of the date of the offence.

It is well known that the exercise of the power to suspend a sentence of imprisonment is often controversial, public perception of the avoidance of immediate imprisonment tending to overlook the sentencing judge's engagement of statutory purposes of punishment or rehabilitation by alternative means.

No judge wants the public to view the power to suspend sentences as either an easy option for the judge, or a soft option for the offender. In practice, the imposition of a suspended sentence is not an easy option for the judge because the exercise requires the judge expressly to justify suspending, and expressly to specify the particular community requirements forming part of the suspended sentence order, which, to fulfil the statutory purposes of sentencing which I have summarised above, may be complex.

The recent Guideline specifies as factors indicating that it would not be appropriate to suspend a sentence that the offender presents a risk or danger to the public, that appropriate punishment can only be achieved by immediate custody, or a history of poor compliance with court orders.

Factors indicating that it may be appropriate to suspend are a realistic prospect of rehabilitation, strong personal mitigation, and that immediate custody will result in significant harmful impact on others, particularly dependants, particularly if impairing rehabilitation. Current law continues to apply to the effect that the court retains the power to activate a suspended sentence in case of breach of community requirements imposed as part of the suspended sentence, for example unpaid work, or further offending in the course of the period of suspension.

11.5 Asset confiscation

I have referred in passing to asset confiscation under the Proceeds of Crime Act 2002 after conviction. This legislation has in my experience an under-estimatedly long reach, including as to assumptions that hidden assets exist, albeit unidentifiably, and as to default terms of imprisonment which, even if served, do not extinguish liability. I have known cases where the justice of the case can, I believe, fairly be said to have been achieved by an appropriate prison sentence and a substantial Proceeds of Crime Order, only for the convicted person to fail to pay some or all of the order and serve the default prison term, or the appropriate proportion of it in a case of partial payment (albeit that serving any part of the default term does not extinguish any part of the liability to pay), all that on the back of an order based on hidden assets, never identified, but which are the statutorily required inference to be drawn from lifestyle assumptions in particular cases, including fraud and drugs.

In one fraud case I sentenced I imposed a prison sentence of three years and a confiscation order of £3 million. This attracted national publicity. *R v Keith Owen*, Worcester Crown Court, 11 March 2010: The Times, 12 March 2010. The case came back two years later when the offender had paid only about £1 million of the confiscation order. The prosecution proved to the required standard of proof that failure of repayment evidenced hidden assets. I was bound to impose the tariff default prison sentence in the order of about a further three years' imprisonment. This did not even receive local publicity, so the public were unaware of that significant sequel evidencing the long reach of the law of asset confiscation.

Mention of asset confiscation is incomplete without mentioning the power of the National Crime Agency to issue civil recovery orders which allow a judge even in the absence of a criminal conviction to order seizure of property and other assets where there is no legitimate explanation for ownership. The lower standard of proof in such quasi-civil proceedings renders this course attractive, particularly where a prosecution has failed. Moreover, this course engages the resources of public authority, not of the implicitly already beleaguered victim or victims. Again, these orders are not confined to fraud cases.

11.6 Conclusion

My perspective of the impact of the Fraud Act 2006 is that it has been a successful, pragmatic piece of legislation, adept to the modern commercial circumstances which it is called on to address. Its practical application has been enhanced by the range of procedural and evidential tools available to the modern judge. The public can have confidence in its efficacy as to process, as to sentencing and as to asset confiscation.

Notes

1 Hon. Fellow, University of Worcester, formerly a Circuit Judge and Honorary Recorder of the City of Hereford.
2 'The Fraud Act 2006: Ten Years On', which took place on 13 January 2017 at the School of Law, University of Worcester.
3 [2017] UKSC 47.
4 Law Commission, *Fraud* (Law Com No 276, 2002).
5 L Scarman, *Law Reform: The New Pattern* (Routledge & Kegan Paul, 1968).
6 ibid 7.
7 ibid 16.
8 Home Office, *Fraud Law Reform, Consultation on proposals for legislation* (2004), <http://webarchive.nationalarchives.gov.uk/+/http://www.homeoffice.gov.uk/documents/cons-fraud-law-reform/> accessed 6 March 2018.
9 Attorney General's Office, *Guidance: Use of the common law offence of conspiracy to defraud* (2007, revised 2012) <https://www.gov.uk/guidance/use-of-the-common-law-offence-of-conspiracy-to-defraud—6> accessed 6 March 2018.
10 Section 11 of the Fraud Act 2006.
11 Sections 6 and 7 of the Fraud Act 2006.
12 [1982] QB 1053.
13 *Ivey* (n 3) and Law Commission, *Fraud* (n 4).
14 [1995] 2 AC 378.
15 [2005] UKPC 37.
16 Law Commission, *Fraud* (n 4).
17 Scarman (n 5) 15.
18 C Thomas, *Are Juries Fair?* (Ministry of Justice Research Series 1/10, 2010) <www.justice.gov.uk/downloads/publications/research-and-analysis/moj-research/are-juries-fair-research.pdf> accessed 17 April 2018.
19 [2005] 2 All ER 42.
20 Attorney General's Office, *Guidance: The acceptance of pleas and the prosecutor's role in the sentencing exercise* (2009, revised 2012).
21 This is published on the Serious Fraud Office website <www.sfo.gov.uk> accessed 6 March 2018.
22 Sentencing Council 'Reduction in Sentence for a Guilty Plea' 2007, <www.sentencingcouncil.org.uk> accessed 17 April 2018.

23 Sentencing Council, 'Fraud Bribery and Money Laundering Offences: Definitive Guidelines' <https://www.sentencingcouncil.org.uk/wp-content/uploads/Fraud_bribery_and_money_laundering_offences_-_Definitive_guideline.pdf> accessed 17 April 2018.

Bibliography

Attorney General's Office, *Guidance: The acceptance of pleas and the prosecutor's role in the sentencing exercise* (2009, revised 2012)

Attorney General's Office, *Guidance: Use of the common law offence of conspiracy to defraud* (2007, revised 2012)

Barlow Clowes *International Limited v Eurotrust Ltd* [2005] UKPC 37

Coroners and Justice Act 2009

Criminal Justice Act 2003

Criminal Procedure Rules 2015

Criminal Procedure Amendment Rules 2016

Fraud Act 2006

Fraud and Counterfeiting Act 1981

Home Office, Fraud Law Reform, Consultation on proposals for legislation (2004)

Ivey v Genting Casinos Ltd trading as Crockfords [2017] UKSC 47

Law Commission, Fraud (Law Com No 276, 2002)

Misuse of Drugs Act 1971

Offences against the Person Act 1861

Proceeds of Crime Act 2002

R v Ghosh [1982] QB 1053

Road Traffic Act 1988

Royal Brunei Airlines Sch Bhd v Tan [1995] 2 AC 378

Scarman, L. *Law Reform: The New Pattern* (Routledge & Kegan Paul, 1968)

Sentencing Council, 'Fraud Bribery and Money Laundering Offences: Definitive Guidelines'

Sentencing Council, 'Guideline on the Imposition of Community and Custodial Sentences'

Sentencing Council 'Reduction in Sentence for a Guilty Plea' 2007

Theft Act 1968

The Protocol for the Control and Management of Heavy Fraud and Other Complex Criminal Cases [2005] 2 All ER 42

Thomas, C. *Are Juries Fair?* (Ministry of Justice Research Series 1/10, 2010)

12 The fraudster at work

The interaction of the criminal justice process with the operation of an employer's disciplinary procedures

Stephen Hurley[1]

12.1 Introduction

The Fraud Act 2006 created a number of criminal offences which naturally trigger an investigative and criminal justice process. However, where the alleged fraudster is currently employed, the interaction between this process and the employer's own disciplinary process is often one fraught with tensions and ambiguities. In this chapter, we shall consider how the processes interact in fact, the legal principles involved drawn from statute, case law and official guidance and the factors which employers and employees might consider when deciding how best to deal with these issues.

Common problems areas for employers include: whether an employer still needs to investigate at all if an employee is charged with a criminal offence; whether any employer investigation would be allowed or appropriate before any criminal proceedings are completed; whether there are risks attached to delaying; whether an employer can use evidence collected by the police in their criminal investigation as part of its own procedures; and, to what extent an employer should be able to rely on the fact an employee is convicted when deciding whether to dismiss.

Investigations of allegations of fraud committed by employees may often be more problematic than for other types of allegation. For an employer, at one extreme, the fraud may involve many parties, perhaps operating in different countries and legal jurisdictions with voluminous documentary evidence to be considered.

The legal tensions arise in particular from the employer's need to avoid any dismissal of an employee breaching the right of any qualifying employee not to be unfairly dismissed under the Employment Rights Act 1996.[2]

12.2 The need for the employer to investigate

Given the seriousness of any allegation of fraud and the implicit element of dishonesty involved, it may be tempting for an employer to consider that any investigation is unnecessary. This may be especially the case if the employee is not simply suspected by the employer of misconduct, but actually charged by the police with a relevant criminal offence.

However, as explained below, a mere suspicion or even charging are not enough: an investigation is almost always required.

The ACAS[3] Code of Practice on Disciplinary and Grievance Procedures[4] states that: '. . . whenever a disciplinary . . . process is being followed it is important to deal with issues fairly. There are a number of elements to this: . . . Employers should carry out any necessary investigations, to establish the facts of the case.'[5] The Code later explains that: 'If an employee is charged with, or convicted of a criminal offence this is not normally in itself reason for disciplinary action.'[6]

Only in the most extreme circumstances would an employer be able to dispense with the need for its own investigation. An example of such a case is that of *Carr v Alexander Russell Ltd.*[7] Mr Carr worked as a labourer and was off work as a result of an industrial accident. However, on being informed that he had been charged with theft of property belonging to the company, his employer wrote to him to tell him that: 'in view of the fact that you have been formally charged by the police for the theft of property . . . belonging to Alexander Russell Ltd, we regret we must terminate your contract of employment . . . forthwith.'[8] In rejecting his appeal against an Employment Tribunal's rejection of his unfair dismissal claim, Lord McDonald in the Court of Session was not prepared to accept that an employee should always, in all circumstances, be allowed to state their case. While stressing that each case depended upon its own facts, Lord McDonald was mindful that here the employee had been, according to the police's report to the employer, caught red handed at the quarry where the missing property was found. Further, the Employment Tribunal found that Mr Carr had never protested his innocence to his employer or raised a grievance.[9]

However, it is probably going too far as a matter of law to require the employee to take the initiative in suggesting a defence to the misconduct allegation.

The need for a separate investigation by the employer is partly due to the different issues raised by suspected employee criminality and the differing legal standards involved. Mr Justice Phillips explained this in the case of *Harris (Ipswich) Ltd v Harrison:*[10]

> Where an employee is charged with a criminal offence alleged to have been committed in the course of his employment, and consequently dismissed, it does not follow that because he is later acquitted the dismissal by the employers was unfair.[11] The function of the [Employment] Tribunal is not to determine the employee's guilt or innocence of the crime alleged, but to consider the behaviour of the employers . . . ; that is to say whether . . . having regard to equity and the substantial merits of the case, they acted reasonably in treating the employee's involvement in the alleged offence as a sufficient reason for dismissing him.[12]

Phillips J succinctly cited Lord Denning MR's remarks in *Taylor v Alidair Ltd*: 'If a man is dismissed for stealing, so long as the employer honestly believes it on reasonable grounds, that is enough to justify dismissal. It is not in fact necessary for the employer to prove that he was in fact stealing.'[13]

The current statutory test for deciding if a dismissal is unfair is set out in section 98(4) of the Employment Rights Act 1996.[14] This test was explained in the context of misconduct issues in the cases of *British Home Stores Ltd v Burchell*[15] and *Boys and Girls Welfare Society v McDonald*.[16] In summary, the Employment Tribunal must be satisfied that the employer genuinely believed that the employee had been guilty of the misconduct alleged, based upon reasonable grounds following a reasonable investigation.[17]

A secondary reason why it is sensible to keep distinct the need for an employer investigation is that it is not simply criminal offences with which the employee may have been charged that may be of concern to the employer. Other matters of misconduct may be in issue. As Phillips J explained:

> [I]nvolvement in the alleged criminal offence often involves a serious breach of duty or discipline. The cashier charged with a till offence, guilty or not, is often undoubtedly in breach of company rules in the way in which the till has been operated. The employee who removes goods from the premises is often in breach of company rules in taking his employer's goods from the premises without express permission; and it is irrelevant to that matter that a jury may be in doubt whether he intended to steal them.[18]

In the case itself, the police had searched Mr Harrison's deep freeze at his home and found 'various articles of meat, most of which were undoubtedly the products of the employers'.[19] In terms of fraud in the financial sector, regulatory rules may also be relevant. See for example the Conduct Rules set for Senior Managers in the banking sector by the Financial Conduct Authority in the UK.[20]

12.3 Whether any employer investigation should be delayed until the conclusion of criminal proceedings

An employer may feel duty bound to delay any internal disciplinary investigation until any criminal proceedings are dealt with. There may be a fear on the employer's part that any such internal process may in some way be unfair to the employee or prejudice him or her.

In Scotland at least, such a concern appeared a factor in the thinking of Lord McDonald in the case of *Carr*.[21] While not laying down any firm rule for all cases, he noted that the Employment Tribunal had held that:

> [I]t would have been improper for the respondents to carry out any form of enquiry into the circumstances of the theft while a criminal prosecution was pending. I am in no doubt that this is correct. If he had been asked

for an explanation and had denied his implication matters would not have been advanced in any way; had he admitted implication not only would his dismissal then be warranted but his subsequent trial might be prejudiced.[22]

However, this concern was soon rejected by the EAT sitting in England in the case of *Harris (Ipswich) Ltd.*[23] Mr Justice Phillips observed that in the *Carr* case:[24]

[I]t is suggested to be improper after an employee has been arrested and charged with a criminal offence, alleged to have been committed in the course of his employment, for the employer to seek to question him when the matter of dismissal is under consideration. While we can see that there are practical difficulties, and care is necessary to do nothing to prejudice the subsequent trial, we do not think that there is anything in the law of England and Wales to prevent an employer in such circumstances . . . from discussing the matter with the employee or his representative; indeed, it seems to us that it is proper to do so.[25]

This more relaxed view was further recognised by the Employment Appeal Tribunal sitting in Edinburgh in the more recent case of *Lovie Ltd v Anderson*.[26] Lord Johnston noted that after criminal charges are brought:

it goes too far to say that the employer is precluded from carrying out any investigation . . . but equally he must be careful not to trap the employee into making any sort of admission against his interests, which the criminal law does not require him to do, and indeed protects him in that respect.[27]

Indeed, in the *Lovie Ltd* case, the Employment Appeal Tribunal indicated that not only would a carefully handled employer investigation be allowed in such circumstances, a failure to carry one out may contribute to a later dismissal being unfair.[28] The case itself concerned a lorry driver who had been suspected of exposing himself to a number of different women while his lorry was parked in a layby. Before any criminal charges were brought against him, the employer did briefly ask Mr Anderson about the alleged incidents. Mr Anderson denied any wrongdoing and was suspended by his employer. Subsequently, after Mr Anderson had been charged with two offences of indecent exposure, the employers wrote to him and informed him that his employment was terminated with immediate effect.

Mr Anderson succeeded in his claim for unfair dismissal on the basis of the employer's investigation being inadequate and the Employment Appeal Tribunal upheld that decision. Lord Johnston laid particular emphasis on the significance of the act of criminal charges being brought. Commenting on the less than compelling explanation provided by the employee before being suspended, Lord Johnston explained that:

[W]hile the circumstances were highly suspicious, and the explanation already proffered as to why the employee was at that particular layby unsatisfactory, the fact that the charges were brought crystallised the issue. Reaction by the employer was understandable, but against an obligation of having to act reasonably, we consider the tribunal was entitled to conclude that one further step should have been taken.[29]

This permissive approach is also endorsed in the ACAS Guide to Discipline and Grievances at Work. It is accepted that 'where the [alleged] conduct requires prompt attention the employer need not await the outcome of the prosecution before taking fair and reasonable action'.[30]

Whether or not to wait for any police investigation and/or criminal prosecution to finish is a vexed issue. As Mr Justice Phillips observed in *Harris (Ipswich) Ltd*:[31]

It is often difficult for an employer to know what is best to do in a case of this kind, particularly where the employee [if charged] elects to go for trial. Unfortunately, it may be many months before the trial takes place, and it is often impractical for the employer to wait until the trial takes place before making some decision as to the future of the employee so far as his employment is concerned.[32]

Much will depend on the facts of each case. As Mr Justice Phillips went on to explain:

What it is right to do will depend on the exact circumstances, including the employer's disciplinary code. Sometimes it may be right to dismiss the employee, sometimes to retain him, sometimes to suspend him on full pay, and sometimes to suspend him without pay.[33] The size of the employer, the nature of the business, and the number of employees are also relevant factors. It is impossible to lay down any hard and fast rule. It is all a matter for the judgment of the [Employment] Tribunal.[34]

If an employer does decide to investigate alleged misconduct even while the criminal process is ongoing, the official guidance does point to sensible steps an employer should take in such a situation. In the ACAS Guide to Discipline and Grievances at Work it is suggested that:

[W]here an employee, charged with . . . a criminal offence, refuses or is unable to co-operate with the employer's disciplinary investigations and proceedings, this should not deter an employer from taking action. The employee should be advised in writing that unless further information is provided, a disciplinary decision will be taken on the basis of the information available and could result in dismissal.[35]

That dismissal may be a legitimate option in such circumstances was confirmed by the Court of Appeal in *Harris and Shepherd v Courage (Eastern) Ltd*.[36] While accepting that no hard and fast rule could be adopted and all the circumstances of the case have to be looked at, Lord Justice Waller agreed with the Employment Appeal Tribunal's view that the strength of the evidence against the employee may be a particular factor to consider. He entirely agreed with Mr Justice Slynn's comments in the Employment Appeal Tribunal that: 'If the employee chooses not to give a statement at that stage [i.e. pre-trial] . . . the reasonable employer is entitled to consider whether the material which he has is strong enough to justify his dismissal without waiting.'[37]

12.4 The possible risks if any employer investigation is delayed

However, if an employer decides not to investigate itself immediately and instead to await the conclusion of any related criminal proceedings, the issue arises as to whether the act of delaying itself poses any legal risks to the lawfulness of the employer's actions or later decisions. The ACAS Code of Practice on Disciplinary and Grievance Procedures makes clear that delay is an issue that employers should be alive to. In paragraph five of the Code it warns that: 'It is important to carry out necessary investigations of potential disciplinary matters without unreasonable delay to establish the facts of the case.'[38] Further, it notes that 'in cases where a period of suspension with pay is considered necessary, this period should be as brief as possible . . .'.[39] Case law also supports the importance of this factor. In the case of *RSPCA v Cruden*[40] it was held that a lengthy period of unjustified delay (seven months in the case in question between the alleged incident and the disciplinary hearing) itself may result in a dismissal being unfair, even if there was no prejudice to the employee due to the delay.[41]

This view was endorsed in the more recent decision of the Employment Appeal Tribunal in *A v B*.[42] There, Mr Justice Elias, in upholding an employee's appeal against the initial rejection of their unfair dismissal claim, noted that: 'the question whether an employer has carried out such investigations as is reasonable in all the circumstances necessarily involves a consideration of any delays. In certain circumstances a delay in the conduct of the investigation might of itself render an otherwise fair dismissal unfair.'[43] In this case there had been a delay of two and half years between the date of the allegations against the claimant (a residential social worker) and the disciplinary hearing during twelve months of which the police had been investigating the possibility of criminal charges being brought (though ultimately they were not).

However, it would seem that at least the portion of any delay caused by the employer's decision to await the conclusion of a police investigation is unlikely to be the subject of judicial criticism, at least in the context of any later unfair dismissal proceedings. In the case of *Secretary of State for Justice v Mansfield*[44] the Employment Appeal Tribunal had to consider whether a lengthy delay of almost two years in dealing with disciplinary allegations against a prison officer accused of planting drugs on a prisoner had caused his later dismissal to be unfair. On the facts of the case they held it had not. Mr Justice Bean noted that:

> a decision maker forming a view on whether disciplinary proceedings should be continued alongside a criminal investigation has a wide discretion. It is unusual for a decision to postpone the disciplinary proceedings while continuing to pay the employee to be criticised on the grounds of delay.[45]

The Employment Appeal Tribunal in *Mansfield* observed that in the previous case of *A v B*:[46]

> it is not without significance in our view that counsel for the employee in *A v B* . . . made no complaint about the suspension of investigations for the duration of the police investigation. This is not to say that a concession by counsel makes law, but we note that this Appeal Tribunal did not comment adversely about it, nor express surprise about it.[47]

As seen above, a long delay which prejudices the employee's ability to defend him or herself is itself another possible ground of challenge to the fairness of a dismissal. However, such prejudice was not apparent on the facts of *Mansfield* itself. As the Employment Appeal Tribunal noted:

> There was no basis on which the Employment Tribunal could hold that [the delay] rendered Mr Mansfield's dismissal unfair, particularly when they were unable to point to any prejudice caused by it . . . This was not a case where the postponement of the disciplinary proceedings and the subsequent discontinuance of the criminal prosecution meant that witnesses were being asked for the first time two years after the incident what their recollection of the matter has been. The main witnesses were interviewed in 2006.[48]

12.5 The involvement of the police or use of evidence collected by the police in the employer's own investigation

In general, police involvement in the employer's internal disciplinary proceedings are not seen as appropriate. The case of *Read v Phoenix Preservation Ltd*[49] is instructive here. The employee was called to a meeting by his manager to answer an allegation that he had struck his supervisor. However, present at the meeting were two police officers. There were conflicting versions subsequently of what exactly happened at the meeting. The employee alleged that his subsequent dismissal was unfair but his complaint was dismissed by the Employment Tribunal.

The Employment Appeal Tribunal subsequently remitted his case to a new Tribunal having found that the original Tribunal had erred. Mr Justice Popplewell declined to make any findings of fact which might prejudice the new hearing. However, he noted that it was accepted that 'if the police officers were present during this enquiry without the consent of the appellant and without his foreknowledge, that was a wholly improper course to have been taken and one which should not have taken place'.[50] Further, contrary to the Tribunal's finding on the point, the Employment Appeal Tribunal noted that 'it is simply not possible to support that contention that he had every opportunity to put forward matters in his own defence if the police were there conducting a criminal enquiry and had administered a caution to him'.[51]

Direct police involvement in disciplinary proceedings is frowned upon in the ACAS Guide as well. The non-binding advice given is that 'where the police are called in they should not be asked to conduct any investigation on behalf of the employer, nor should they be present at any meeting or disciplinary meeting'.[52]

A more lenient approach is taken in the case law towards the issue of an employer making use of police statements in internal disciplinary proceedings. Mr Justice Elias (President) giving judgment in the case of *Rhondda Cyon Taf County Borough Council v Close*[53] cited with approval the earlier unreported EAT decision in *Harding v Hampshire County Council*.[54] In that case, 'the EAT observed that whether and when it will be reasonable to rely on such investigations [ie those of the police rather than the employer] is a matter of fact depending on the particular circumstances. Sometimes the police investigation will have been very detailed, sometimes much less so. . . .'[55]

On the facts of the *Close* case itself, Mrs Close was held at first instance to have been unfairly dismissed. She was a care worker. One night, after she had finished her night duty, a patient under her care was found to have stopped breathing. Sadly, he died a week later in hospital due to a heart attack. The matter was investigated by the police in respect of possible manslaughter charges for over two and half years and they took witness statements. A decision was made not to prosecute Mrs Close but her employer did then begin disciplinary proceedings on the basis of alleged misconduct, in particular sleeping on duty and swearing at patients. These allegations had been included in the police witness statements.

Mrs Close's employer relied upon witness statements taken by the police at the time of their initial investigation. No new statements were taken for the purposes of the disciplinary proceedings, however, the witnesses were asked if they had anything to add to the statements they had given – none did. Following her subsequent dismissal for gross misconduct, Mrs Close succeeded at first instance in her claim of unfair dismissal. In particular, the Employment Tribunal held that the employer did not have reasonable grounds for believing that Mrs Close had been guilty of the misconduct alleged as, *inter alia*, they had relied upon police witness statements which, in the Tribunal's view, related to a totally different matter ie the death of the patient.

However, the Employment Appeal Tribunal allowed the employer's appeal and substituted a finding of a fair dismissal. They concluded that:

> in our judgment, it could not be said that any reasonable employer would have started the investigation again from scratch. Indeed, in a case such as this where the police witness statements were made much closer to the time of the alleged misconduct, there was every reason to suppose that they would have been more reliable than statements taken almost three years later.[56]

Even further flexibility was allowed to an employer in the earlier case of *Dhaliwal & ors v British Airways Board*.[57] Here, a number of baggage handlers at Heathrow Airport were dismissed for carrying out or abetting theft from passengers' luggage. While two of the employees had pleaded guilty at Crown Court, a number of others had maintained their innocence. At the trial of a number of the remaining employees, the trial judge ruled that the oral and written statements that had been taken by the police containing admissions of guilt by the employees were inadmissible either having been obtained unfairly or only with duress. The trials collapsed.

Despite this development, the employers decided to begin a disciplinary investigation and used summaries of the discredited police statements as the main evidence against the employees. Despite maintaining their innocence, all the employees were dismissed. A number brought Employment Tribunal claims unsuccessfully. The Employment Appeal Tribunal upheld the Tribunal's decisions in respect of the appellants. They noted that allowing evidence ruled inadmissible in criminal proceedings as the main basis of disciplinary proceedings:

> [M]ight well in the eyes of many people offend that basic instinct of fair play which is said to lie deep within the British character. But Parliament has based the statutory criteria of fairness upon reasonableness, not sportsmanship; and has based it moreover upon a standard of reasonableness which is to be judged by the yardstick of the response appropriate to the particular circumstances confronting the employer in each case.[58]

The Employment Appeal Tribunal continued that in its opinion:

> the Tribunal were therefore entirely correct . . . in their decision to deal with each case individually upon its merits . . . and to refuse to be drawn into a sweeping condemnation out of hand of any particular category of evidence as being so inherently objectionable as to render it automatically inconsistent with fairness for an employer to place any reliance upon it at all.[59]

However, the Employment Appeal Tribunal noted that they were not suggesting by their decision on the facts that the approach used by the by employers here in any way represented an ideal procedure. On the contrary, the Employment Appeal Tribunal commented that the employers had been 'sailing dangerously close to the wind of unfairness'.[60]

12.6 The employer's ability to rely upon criminal convictions or confessions

If an employer does await the outcome of criminal proceedings, the issue arises as to the extent to which they can then rely on the fact of a conviction as incontrovertible proof that the employee did actually commit the offence.

In the case of *P v Nottinghamshire County Council*[61] an assistant groundsman at a girls' school pleaded guilty at court to a charge of indecent assault against his daughter, and asked for two other offences to be taken into consideration by the court. At a later disciplinary hearing, the employee had explained that he had pleaded guilty simply to avoid his daughter having to attend court. An Employment Tribunal found his dismissal unfair on the ground that his employer had not sufficiently investigated the circumstances of the offences and so could not have made a proper assessment of the risk involved in keeping him employed.

In the Court of Appeal, counsel for the employee (while defending the original Tribunal finding of unfairness on other grounds) conceded that the employer in this case did have reasonable grounds to believe that the offences in question had been committed. As noted *obiter* by Lord Justice Balcombe:

> when an employee has pleaded guilty to an offence, or has been found guilty by a decision of a court or the verdict of a jury, it is reasonable for an employer to believe that the offence has been committed by the employee. Any other conclusion would be ridiculous.[62]

Significantly, Lord Justice Balcombe also suggested that 'all the considerable learning on this point – see eg *British Homes Stores v Burchell* [1978] IRLR 379 – is directed to the case where there has been no plea of guilty or a finding of guilt by a competent court of law'.[63]

The *Burchell* case had involved an employee who had been dismissed for her involvement in dishonest staff purchases. The employer appealed the Employment Tribunal's decision that she had been unfairly dismissed. In allowing the appeal, the Employment Appeal Tribunal provided a three stage test (subsequently often referred to as 'the *Burchell* test') for a Tribunal to adopt when dealing with misconduct dismissals.

In the Employment Appeal Tribunal's view in *Burchell*:

> What the Tribunal have to decide every time is, broadly expressed, whether the employer who discharged the employee on the ground of the misconduct in question (usually, though not necessarily, dishonest conduct) entertained a reasonable suspicion amounting to a belief in the guilt of the

employee of that misconduct at that time. . . . First of all, there must be established by the employer the fact of that belief; that the employer did believe it. Secondly, that the employer had in his mind reasonable grounds upon which to sustain that belief. And thirdly . . . that the employer, at the stage at which he formed that belief on those grounds, at any rate at the final stage at which he formed that belief on those grounds, had carried out as much investigation into the matter as was reasonable in all the circumstances of the case.[64]

In the later case of *Boys and Girls Welfare Society v McDonald*,[65] a residential social worker at a children's home was found at first instance to have been unfairly dismissed following an altercation with a 15-year-old boy at the home. The employee had admitted in a disciplinary hearing that he had spat at (or at least in the direction of) the boy but said he had been spat at first. He also admitted having caught the boy in his face with his hand when trying to defend himself. The employee won his unfair dismissal claim. The Tribunal concluded, amongst other things, that the employer, while genuinely believing that the employee was guilty of misconduct, nevertheless did not have reasonable grounds for that belief and also had not carried a reasonable investigation in all the circumstances.[66]

However, in overturning that decision, the Employment Appeal Tribunal found that the Tribunal had failed to take account of the fact that, since the decision in *Burchell*, the burden of proving reasonableness had been removed from an employer and replaced with a neutral burden. However, it also noted that 'the threefold Burchell test is appropriate where the employer has to decide a factual contest. The position may be otherwise where there is no real conflict on the facts'.[67]

The Employment Appeal Tribunal went on to quote with approval the comments of Waite J in *Royal Society for the Protection of Birds v Croucher*[68] when overturning a finding of unfair dismissal against an employee who had admitted dishonesty in relation to false petrol expense claims:

> Here there was no question of suspicion or of questioned belief: . . . the dishonest conduct was admitted. There was very little scope, therefore, for the kind of investigation to which this appeal tribunal was referring in Burchell's case: investigation, that is to say, designed to confirm suspicion or clear up doubt as to whether or not a particular act of misconduct has occurred.[69]

Applying this principle to the facts of Mr McDonald's case, and concluding that the Employment Tribunal's criticism of the adequacy of the employer's investigation was flawed, the Employment Appeal Tribunal noted in particular that 'this was a case in which the employer proceeded on the basis of the employee's own evidence'.[70]

However, in some cases, an employee pleads guilty to an allegation at court but later denies he actually was guilty at the employer's disciplinary hearing. In the case of *British Gas v McCarrick*[71] the employee was found with 20 plastic cans of his employer's petrol in his van. After a first disciplinary hearing had found him not guilty of stealing the petrol, Mr McCarrick was subsequently charged with theft of the petrol and pleaded not guilty. The case was listed for trial at Liverpool Crown Court.

On the day of the trial, he was advised by his counsel to plead guilty as he faced a 95 per cent chance of a prison sentence if he was convicted after trial. As recounted later by the Vice Chancellor, Sir Nicholas Browne-Wilkinson, in the Court of Appeal:

> at the very last moment, Mr McCarrick decided to plead guilty, so he said, because of his concern that his wife and children would be adversely affected if he were to be sent to prison. He accordingly pleaded guilty and was convicted and fined for the theft.[72]

On hearing of the conviction, British Gas started fresh disciplinary proceedings. Following the new disciplinary hearing at which Mr McCarrick and his witnesses gave evidence, the employers concluded that, while it accepted that pressure had been brought to bear on him by his barrister, nevertheless he was (in the employer's view) guilty of the charge of stealing petrol which amounted to gross misconduct justifying dismissal. Pointedly in the dismissal letter itself, the disciplinary panel commented: 'If a Crown Court accepts that a guilty plea means he stole the petrol is it unreasonable for us to agree and take the same view? We feel that the only reasonable response we can make to a guilty plea is to believe it.'[73]

An Employment Tribunal found the dismissal unfair noting that 'whilst the respondents honestly believed that the applicant committed the offence there were no reasonable grounds to support that belief and no full investigation'.[74] The Employment Appeal Tribunal overturned the Tribunal decision and Mr McCarrick appealed. In rejecting his appeal against the Employment Appeal Tribunal's decision, the Court of Appeal found that the Employment Tribunal had erred in their original decision. The Vice-Chancellor explained that;

> [T]he decision for the [Employment] Tribunal was whether, on the facts which were known or should have been known to the employers, they genuinely believed, on reasonable grounds, that the employee was guilty of the conduct of which he was charged [having summarised the evidence before the employers, he then continued] . . . It was for those internal domestic tribunals to reach a conclusion on that evidence as to whether or not the plea was a genuine plea in the sense of being a truthful admission of guilt. That was a decision for the internal disciplinary body to take.[75]

Therefore, whether an employer is dealing with a conviction after trial, a guilty plea or simply an internal admission in a disciplinary hearing, the *Burchell* principles still apply. However, their application is perhaps modified in two ways.

First, a conviction or admission will normally be strong evidence upon which an employer may found a genuine belief in guilt based on reasonable grounds. However, it will not necessarily be conclusive evidence in all cases. There is still a need for an employer to be at least willing to look behind a conviction or admission if they are later disputed by an employee as not providing a true reflection of their guilt or rather their innocence. Ultimately though, the employer is allowed to reach its own conclusion having considered all the evidence on whether or not they genuinely believe the employee is guilty of the misconduct in question.

Second, there is still a need for an investigation by the employer upon which to found its reasonable belief in guilt. However, especially in the case of a criminal court conviction (whether following a not guilty or guilty plea), it is likely that the level of investigation required of an employer will be fairly limited in its nature at least as regards an investigation of the question of whether or not the employee did commit the act of misconduct. Note though that, perhaps contrary to the implication of the *obiter* comments of Lord Justice Balcombe referred to in the case of *P v Nottinghamshire County Council*,[76] an employer cannot simply point to the fact of conviction and refuse to even consider further (perhaps after being challenged by the employee) whether its belief in the employee's guilt remains a reasonable one. However, given the policy arguments in favour of criminal court convictions carrying weight and also the need (outside of a criminal appeal process) for legal certainty, it will be a rare case where an employer is unable successfully to rest its decision to believe the employee was guilty of the misconduct in question largely upon the fact of a criminal conviction.[77]

In any event though, even if an employee has been convicted of an offence, a separate employer investigation may be necessary in order for the employer to be able to properly take a view on what disciplinary sanction (if any) is appropriate to apply, including taking matters such as mitigation into account.[78]

12.7 The decision whether to dismiss the employee

This chapter has focussed on the issue of some of the procedural interactions between police investigations, criminal prosecutions and the operation of the employer's internal disciplinary proceedings. However, the issue of the substantive decision of whether a particular employee should be dismissed following a particular criminal conviction would deserve a chapter to itself to fully do justice to the case law.

However, it may be sufficient to note here the official guidance of ACAS that:

> An employee should not be dismissed . . . solely because he or she has been
> . . . convicted of a criminal offence. The question to be asked in such cases

is whether the employee's conduct or conviction merits action because of its employment implications.[79]

As the separate ACAS Code explains: 'Consideration needs to be given to what effect the . . . conviction has on the employee's suitability to do the job and their relationship with their employer, work colleagues and customers.'[80]

12.8 Conclusion

The complexity of dealing with the issue of fraud and other economic crimes is well recognised. As noted by Edmonds:

> Corporate economic crime is a complex subject on many levels, and efforts at strict definitional exactitude rapidly become self-defeating. Most obviously, companies cannot do anything – people commit criminal acts. The problem at the heart of this subject is how, and when, to separate the company from the individual and, very often, whether it is actually possible to decide who, amongst the management or board, was responsible for the act or acts complained of.[81]

However, while such complexity may make the employer's internal disciplinary process more difficult to use, it is nevertheless possible. Both the relevant case law discussed above and the official guidance set out some useful parameters for employers to take account of.

Notes

1 Senior Lecturer in Employment and Equality Law, Solicitor, School of Law, University of Worcester.
2 Section 94 of the Employment Rights Act 1996. The section gives the right to every employee who meets the eligibility criteria in the Act not to be unfairly dismissed. The main criterion is that the employee must (unless an exception applies) have two years' continuous employment (section 108).
3 Advisory, Conciliation and Arbitration Service.
4 ACAS Code of Practice No 1 Disciplinary and Grievance Procedures (revised 2015) <www.acas.org.uk/media/pdf/f/m/Acas-Code-of-Practice-1-on-disciplinary-and-grievance-procedures.pdf> accessed 1 May 2018. The Code is not legally binding but will be taken into account by Employment Tribunals when deciding the issue of the fairness of a dismissal. See *Lock v Cardiff Railway Co Ltd* [1998] IRLR 358.
5 ACAS (n 4) [4].
6 ibid [31].
7 [1976] IRLR 220.
8 ibid [2].
9 ibid [4].
10 [1978] IRLR 382.
11 But equally, the mere fact of a conviction (without any further consideration by the employer) does not mean that any later dismissal was necessarily fair. The decision whether or not to dismiss cannot in any sense be 'contracted out' to the criminal courts. See *McLaren v National Coal Board* [1988] IRLR 215.

12 *Harris (Ipswich) Ltd v Harrison* (n 10) [2].
13 [1978] IRLR 82, 85.
14 This states that: 'the determination of the question whether the dismissal is fair or unfair having regard to the reason shown by the employer – (a) depends on whether in the circumstances (including the size and administrative resources of the employer's undertaking) the employer acted reasonably or unreasonably in treating it as a sufficient reason for dismissing the employee, and (b) shall be determined in accordance with equity and the substantial merits of the case.'
15 [1978] IRLR 379.
16 [1996] IRLR 129.
17 [1978] IRLR 379, [2].
18 [1978] IRLR 384, [4].
19 ibid [1].
20 See <www.handbook.fca.org.uk/handbook/COCON/2/?view=chapter> accessed 8 May 2018.
21 [1976] IRLR 220.
22 ibid [6].
23 *Harris (Ipswich) Ltd v Harrison* (n 10).
24 [1976] IRLR 220.
25 ibid [3].
26 [1999] IRLR 164.
27 ibid [8].
28 ibid [9].
29 ibid.
30 Discipline and Grievances at Work: the ACAS Guide (revised August 2017) 36.
31 *Harris (Ipswich) Ltd v Harrison* (n 10).
32 ibid [4].
33 Though such a suspension (i.e. without pay) would need power in the employee's contract to avoid being a breach of contract.
34 *Harris (Ipswich) Ltd v Harrison* (n 10) [4].
35 Discipline and Grievances at Work: the ACAS Guide (revised August 2017) 37. <www.acas.org.uk/media/pdf/9/g/Discipline-and-grievances-Acas-guide.pdf> accessed 4 May 2018.
36 [1982] IRLR 509.
37 ibid [7].
38 ACAS (n 4) [5].
39 ibid [8].
40 [1986] IRLR 83
41 ibid [26].
42 [2003] IRLR 405
43 ibid [66].
44 EAT 0539/09.
45 ibid [25].
46 *A v B* (n 42).
47 *Mansfield* (n 44) [15].
48 ibid [27] and [29].
49 [1985] IRLR 93.
50 ibid [6].
51 ibid [7].
52 ACAS (n 35) 36.
53 [2008] IRLR 868
54 (EAT/10 May 2005).
55 Rhondda Cyon Taf County Borough Council v Close (n 53) [12].

56 ibid [23].
57 [1985] ICR 513.
58 ibid 518 F.
59 ibid 519 B.
60 ibid 521 G.
61 [1992] IRLR 362.
62 ibid [15].
63 ibid [15].
64 ibid [2].
65 *Boys and Girls Welfare Society v McDonalds* (n 16).
66 ibid. Cited at para 15 of the EAT's decision.
67 ibid [29].
68 [1984] IRLR 425, [36]-[38].
69 ibid [29].
70 ibid [33].
71 [1991] IRLR 305.
72 ibid [5].
73 ibid [7].
74 ibid [12].
75 ibid [21].
76 *P v Nottinghamshire County Council* (n 61) [15].
77 For a more typical case, see for example *Secretary of State for Scotland v Campbell* [1992] IRLR 263 (prison officer fairly dismissed after conviction for embezzlement).
78 See for example the Court of Appeal decision in *Whitbread plc (t/a Whitbread Medway Inns) v Hall* [2001] IRLR 275.
79 ACAS (n 35) 36.
80 ACAS (n 4) [31].
81 T Edmonds, 'Corporate Economic Crime: Bribery and Corruption' (Briefing Paper No 7359 House of Commons Library 2017) 3.

Bibliography

A v B [2003] IRLR 405

ACAS, Code of Practice No 1 Disciplinary and Grievance Procedures (revised 2015) <www.acas.org.uk/media/pdf/f/m/Acas-Code-of-Practice-1-on-disciplinary-and-grievance-procedures.pdf> accessed 1 May 2018.

ACAS, Discipline and Grievances at Work: the ACAS Guide (revised August 2017) <www.acas.org.uk/media/pdf/9/g/Discipline-and-grievances-Acas-guide.pdf> accessed> 4 May 2018

Boys and Girls Welfare Society v McDonald [1996] IRLR 129

British Gas v McCarrick [1991] IRLR 305

British Home Stores Ltd v Burchell [1978] IRLR 379

Carr v Alexander Russell Ltd [1976] IRLR 220

Dhaliwal & ors v British Airways Board [1985] ICR 513

Edmonds, T 'Corporate Economic Crime: Bribery and Corruption' (Briefing Paper No 7359 House of Commons Library 2017) 3

Employment Rights Act 1996

Financial Conduct Authority, FCA Handbook <www.handbook.fca.org.uk/handbook/COCON/2/?view=chapter> accessed> 8 May 2018

Halsbury's Laws of England (5th edition, 2014) vol 41

Harding v Hampshire County Council (EAT/10 May 2005)

Harris and Shepherd v Courage (Eastern) Ltd [1982] IRLR 509
Harris (Ipswich) Ltd v Harrison [1978] IRLR 382
Harvey on Industrial Relations and Employment Law Div DI
IDS Employment Law Handbook vol 12
Lock v Cardiff Railway Co Ltd [1998] IRLR 358
Lovie Ltd v Anderson [1999] IRLR 164
McLaren v National Coal Board [1988] IRLR 215
P v Nottinghamshire County Council [1992] IRLR 362
Read v Phoenix Preservation Ltd [1985] IRLR 93
Rhondda Cyon Taf County Borough Council v Close [2008] IRLR 868
Royal Society for the Protection of Birds v Croucher [1984] IRLR 425
RSPCA v Cruden [1986] IRLR 83
Secretary of State for Scotland v Campbell [1992] IRLR 263
Secretary of State for Justice v Mansfield EAT 0539/09
Taylor v Alidair Ltd [1978] IRLR 82
Whitbread plc (t/a Whitbread Medway Inns) v Hall [2001] IRLR 275

13 Who should try 'complex fraud trials'?

Reconsidering the composition of the tribunal of fact 30 years after Roskill

Nicola Monaghan[1]

13.1 Introduction

In 1986, the Fraud Trials Committee (Roskill Committee) published a report recommending that complex fraud trials should be tried by a Fraud Trials Tribunal instead of a jury.[2] While the recommendations of the Roskill Committee are over 30 years old, the issue of the mode of trial for complex fraud trials is still a controversial one and has yet to be settled. In 2009 and 2014, the former Lord Chief Justice, Lord Thomas, delivered speeches in which he drew attention to the Roskill proposals on removing the jury in complex fraud trials and called for the issue to be re-examined,[3] highlighting the 'very serious problems'[4] in prosecuting market crime and stating that '[f]raud trials are still far too slow and immensely expensive; not enough prosecutions are brought'.[5] Lord Thomas called for the question of who should try fraud trials to be reconsidered.[6] This chapter seeks to reignite the debate about the composition of the tribunal of fact in complex fraud cases. While this is a controversial and complicated issue that cannot be finally resolved in this chapter, it does indeed need the careful consideration called for by Lord Thomas. It is submitted that the issue should be subject to a full and comprehensive analysis involving discussion grounded in principles and substantiated by empirical research. This chapter raises three issues that need to be addressed as part of any reconsideration of the composition of the tribunal of fact in relation to any criminal offence. The first of these issues is how we might establish the parameters for determining which cases would be tried without a jury (i.e., what does the term 'complex fraud trials' mean?). The second issue is whether there are clear, principled justifications supported by empirical evidence in favour of removing the jury in such cases, and what the possible alternative tribunal of fact should be. For instance, trial by judge alone, by a panel of judges, or by a mixed panel of a judge and two lay assessors. The third and final issue is whether there are any other measures which might alleviate the main concerns relating to fraud trials without resorting to the abolition of the jury in such cases; such as by providing increased support for jurors and by making changes to the way in which evidence is presented to the jury in court.

Before moving on, it is prudent to briefly mention the two main criticisms of the jury as a tribunal of fact in complex fraud cases, as these will necessarily inform the first issue of defining the parameters for deciding which cases should not be tried by a jury. The first criticism of trial by jury in such cases is a concern about a lack of jury comprehension, especially in complex fraud cases which involve a large quantity of complicated evidence.[7] The second criticism involves the length of complex fraud trials, which can run on for weeks, months, or even years.[8] As we will see, these criticisms are inevitably linked; the extent to which these concerns can justifiably be levelled at the jury to substantiate the argument that the jury should be removed from such cases will be considered at paragraph 13.4 below.

The principal argument advanced in this chapter is that as the removal of the jury in fraud trials would change the nature of the trial in such a significant way, there must be justifications grounded in principle and substantiated by clear evidence before any action to remove the jury is taken. While this issue has been considered previously by the Roskill Committee, by Auld LJ in his *Review of the Criminal Courts*, and by commentators both pre- and post-Roskill,[9] valuable research with juries and judges has been undertaken in the past few decades which must now also be taken into account.[10]

13.2 Background

The majority of the Roskill Committee took the view that 'certain types of fraud case are of such complexity that a different type of tribunal is needed'[11] and recommended that such cases should instead be tried by a specially constituted Fraud Trials Tribunal, consisting of a judge and two lay members.[12] However, this recommendation was never introduced. The issue of who should try complex fraud cases has been raised frequently since the Roskill Committee's Report, particularly after high profile cases of fraud, such as in 1996 after the acquittal of brothers, Kevin and Ian Maxwell, for charges relating to fraudulent misuse of company pension funds,[13] and after the collapse of the Jubilee Line case in 2005, a corruption trial which involved allegations that London Underground officials had been bribed over contracts for the extension to the Jubilee line.[14]

In Auld LJ's *Review of the Criminal Courts in England and Wales* he proposed that a judge should have the option to try serious and complex fraud cases, either sitting with lay members or alone.[15] This led to section 43 of the Criminal Justice Act 2003, which aimed to allow prosecutors to make an application for serious or complex fraud cases to be tried without a jury. This provision was highly controversial and was never actually brought into force. It was finally repealed by section 113 of the Protection of Freedoms Act 2012. In speeches delivered in 2009[16] and 2014,[17] Lord Thomas CJ highlighted the fact that despite all that had been done since the Roskill Report, there were still 'very serious problems' prosecuting such crimes.[18] His Lordship stated that fraud trials 'are still far too slow and immensely expensive; not enough prosecutions are brought', and asked, '[i]s it not time that *Justice* looked at these issues again?'[19] Lord Thomas called for a 'carefully considered report' on the issue.[20] Any potential further erosion of jury trial is controversial and highly significant in terms of the confidence that we place in our jury trial system and in terms of the message that it sends to the public about their role in the criminal justice process. The issue of whether the jury should be removed from trying fraud cases is an important one requiring detailed research and evidence which substantiates the conclusions drawn.

13.3 Establishing the parameters

This section deals with the question of how we determine which types of cases should be tried without a jury. Both the Roskill Committee and Auld referred to 'complex fraud trials' in the context of proposals to remove the jury as tribunal of fact. However, the problem with the term 'complex fraud trials' is that it fails to identify with any precision the cases to which it applies. There are many fraud-related or financial offences which may be complicated in nature, therefore any proposal to remove the jury could not be limited to the offence of fraud. When used in relation to the discussion of removal of the jury, the term 'complex fraud' has been an umbrella term to encompass a whole range of offences which are complicated in nature. However, there have been no clear parameters as to how such cases should be identified.

On the face of it, the term 'complex fraud trials' suggests that trial without a jury would apply in cases where a defendant is charged with 'fraud' and only in cases of fraud that were 'complex'. However, this term was coined before the creation of the offence of fraud under section 1 of the Fraud Act 2006, so it must have been intended to apply to a range of other offences. The term is now out-dated and a new description of the type of trials that might be tried without a jury is required. It is clear that there are many fraud-related and financial offences scattered throughout a range of different statutes, thus it is important to identify the types of cases to which any proposal to remove the jury would apply, and how we define these. The parameters could be set solely by the type of offence with which the defendant has been charged, or by the characteristics of the trial, such as its predicted length and complexity, or by a combination of these.

It is submitted that both the type of the offence charged and the circumstances of the case must be taken into account in determining whether the case could be tried without a jury. It would not be sufficient to rely solely on the title of the offence charged to determine mode of trial. The nature of criminal offences, such as fraud contrary to section 1 of the Fraud Act 2006, can vary dramatically in terms of complexity, from a simple case of a defendant lying on an application for a credit card, to a complicated company pension fund fraud or property fraud. Thus, the title of the offence cannot be the sole factor for determining mode of trial. A comprehensive list of eligible offences that could be tried without a jury should be compiled, but being charged with an offence on the list would not automatically lead to a trial without a jury as the nature of the offences charged would also need to be assessed. The main arguments in favour of trial without a jury are concerned with a lack of jury comprehension of the issues and evidence in the case, and the length of trials. Consequently, the key characteristics for determining which cases should be tried without a jury are the complexity of the case and the predicted length of the trial.

13.4 Substantiating the case for abolition

This section considers whether there is a justifiable reason for the removal of the jury as the tribunal of fact in 'complex fraud trials'. The two main arguments for abolition have already been mentioned: the first is that juries do not have sufficient expertise to be able to fully understand complex fraud trials, and the second relates to the length of such trials. Each of these arguments will be considered below.

13.4.1 Jury comprehension

Lack of jury comprehension of the issues and evidence in a complex fraud trial has been used to justify the removal of the jury in complex fraud cases. The Roskill Committee reported that 'many jurors are almost certainly out of their depth in complex fraud cases'.[21] The Committee relied upon the results of a research project which it commissioned and which was carried out at the University of Cambridge. The project did not involve actual jurors, but was instead conducted with individual volunteers acting as mock jurors. The reason given for this was that direct research of real jurors' comprehension of actual fraud cases would amount to a contempt of court.[22] However, research into the comprehension of actual jurors has been carried out: Professor Cheryl Thomas conducted research with actual jurors for the Ministry of Justice.[23] One of the issues explored by Professor Thomas was the comprehension of actual jurors in criminal trials. In an article in the *Criminal Law Review*, Professor Thomas addressed the 'myth' that section 8 of the Contempt of Court Act 1981 prevented research with real jurors:

> [C]ommentators have routinely and incorrectly claimed that s.8 makes research with actual jurors impossible if not illegal in this country. It is now a well-entrenched and unfounded myth . . . This myth is compounded by a misunderstanding about what s.8 does and does not allow.[24]

In fact, Professor Thomas' research looked in part at juror comprehension and the difference between jurors' perceptions of what they understand and their actual understanding of judicial directions. While this research did not specifically tackle the issue of complex fraud trials, it does clearly demonstrate the type of research that can be undertaken with actual jurors and that must be undertaken prior to any potential reforms to remove the jury from complex fraud trials.

The Roskill Committee relied upon the findings of the Cambridge research unit to support its case for the removal of the jury in complex fraud cases. The Committee felt that only a broad summary of the findings of the research was necessary in its report and it referred to the findings in the following way:

> The research posed the question, when complex information is communicated to individuals in a manner designed to resemble court-room procedure, how much of it is retained? And the answer is, very little indeed. By definition, the research cannot be conclusive, since it cannot be conducted on actual jurors. Nevertheless, the research findings strongly support the view of experienced observers and the promptings of commonsense, that the most complex of fraud cases will exceed the limits of comprehension of members of a jury.[25]

While acknowledging the limits of the research carried out by the Cambridge research unit, the Roskill Committee nevertheless relied upon this and 'commonsense' as its main evidence to substantiate its conclusion that jurors lack the necessary intellectual capabilities to try complex fraud cases. The Committee's reliance on this research has been criticised as 'superficially attractive [but] poor evidence on which to abolish a constitutional right' because '[t]he results do not tell us much more than we already know – that people have difficulty in absorbing complex information'.[26]

In further seeking to justify the removal of the jury in such cases, the Committee also relied upon the results of enquiries that it made of prosecuting authorities, stating that sometimes such authorities refrained from prosecuting cases or opted for less serious charges because of the difficulty in presenting a complex case to a jury.[27] However, one member of the Committee, Walter Merricks, wrote a dissenting opinion in which he stated that out of 179 cases referred to the DPP for the year 1983, only one case was not prosecuted due to complexity.[28]

The jury are partly blamed for the length of complex fraud trials, as they are said to be insufficiently intellectually equipped to deal with both the complicated nature of the evidence adduced in complex fraud trials and the vast quantity of such evidence. The Roskill Committee reported that '[o]ne reason why these trials take so long is that it is necessary to explain complex matters over and over again to the jury to ensure that they have some chance of understanding what it is they are being asked to decide'.[29] This is an argument that was also relied upon by Auld LJ in his Review of the Criminal Courts,[30] and one which failed to impress Professor Michael Zander who wrote a response to Auld LJ's review. In his response, Professor Zander commented that:

[G]radually, as these long cases continue, [the jurors] probably get the hang of the jargon and the concepts and by the end of the case they are likely to be *au fait* with the subject matter.[31]

The suggestion that jurors do not understand the evidence in complex fraud trials is not borne out in the research that has been undertaken with actual jurors. After the collapse of the Jubilee Line trial, Professor Sally Lloyd-Bostock conducted interviews with the actual jurors from the case. She reported that, '[a]ll the jurors were adamant that the jury had a very good understanding of the evidence' and that this claim was 'borne out by their performance in the group discussion'.[32] She noted that jurors 'displayed quite impressive familiarity with the charges, issues and evidence and were able to engage in detailed discussion of the prosecution case nearly a year after it had closed . . . without their notes or access to documents, and without time to think back and refresh their memories'.[33] Professor Lloyd-Bostock found that '[n]ot every juror either claimed or appeared to have equally good comprehension of the case', and the jurors reported that some jurors had a very good understanding and took copious notes, whereas other jurors found the case more difficult to understand and relied on others' understanding of the case. Professor Lloyd-Bostock concludes that these different levels of ability are to be expected and that '[p]rovided the jurors engage co-operatively in their task as a group, the jury as a whole may be able to decide competently even though, individually, some jurors would have difficulty'.[34] While this study is limited in that it only provides us with information relating to one trial, it is the most relevant evidence that we have as it does in fact deal with actual jurors who sat on a lengthy complex fraud trial. The research with actual jurors carried out by both Professor Thomas and Professor Lloyd-Bostock has more value than the research with mock jurors relied upon by the Roskill Committee.

In an article published in the *Criminal Law Review* in 2007, Robert F Julian explored the opinions of nine judges about juries trying serious fraud trials. The judges generally expressed a 'strong belief . . . that trial by jury was entirely appropriate in serious fraud cases and that trial by judges should not replace trial by jury'.[35] They took the view that 'juries were usually able to understand a complex fraud case upon the completion of the trial, explaining that usually the complexity of a serious fraud case gradually evaporates as the trial progresses . . . a longer trial can sometimes give jurors a greater understanding of the facts'.[36] While this study was carried out with a small number of judges, it provides some valuable information into the insights of judge and a further study featuring interviews with a larger sample of judges would be welcomed.

It is not argued here that the jury is the perfect tribunal to try complex fraud trials, rather that it is crucial that more research is carried out with a wider range of real jurors who sat on complex fraud trials and other lengthy and complex cases in order to ascertain the degree to which jurors understand the evidence and legal directions before them.[37]

13.4.2 Length of fraud trials

The second main argument for removing the jury in complex fraud trials arises out of a concern about the length of such trials. It is accepted that complex fraud trials are both long and expensive, and as we have already seen the jury is often blamed for the length of the trial. However, some evidence suggests that jurors are keen for the trial to progress more quickly. In Professor Zander's response to Auld LJ's review, he makes passing reference to a case in which the jury were frustrated by the slow progress of the trial:

> I recall that the foreman of the jury in one of these interminable cases told the Runciman Committee that by the end of the case she passed a note to the judge asking him not to patronise the jury by going so slowly for their benefit and inviting him to move things along more briskly.[38]

In the research carried out by Professor Lloyd-Bostock, jurors also complained about the slow progress of the trial: '[t]he chief difficulty expressed by the jurors was not in finding evidence too technical or complex, but in finding the pace of the trial extremely slow'.[39] She also notes that the jurors wrote to the judge setting out their feelings of despondency at the slow progress and length of the trial'.[40] Further research on actual jurors' views about the length and rate of progress of long trials also needs to be undertaken.

It is clear that a number of factors affect the length of such trials. Professor Lloyd-Bostock's research explored the reasons for the slow progress of the Jubilee Line trial; these were identified as including extended breaks for legal argument due to poor preparation of the case, periods of illness of defence counsel, defendants and jurors, breaks for holidays, and periods of paternity leave for jurors and defence counsel.[41] Therefore, further work to improve case management in complex fraud trials may well be necessary.[42] While case management has been promoted as a priority since the introduction of the Criminal Procedure Rules in 2005, research undertaken by Professor Penny Darbyshire reveals that 'statistics do not provide a qualitative understanding of pre-trial management, which . . . apparently differs greatly between courts and judges and does not depend much on the Criminal Procedure Rules'.[43]

A further issue relating to the length of complex fraud trials is the significant burden placed upon jurors who try these cases. The Roskill Committee was less concerned about this issue (referring to it as 'serious', but 'not . . . the major issue'), but more concerned about jurors' abilities to concentrate for extended periods of time and to remember all the essential facts and figures.[44] However, Professor Lloyd-Bostock's research gives an insight into the impact that such a long trial can have on the lives of jurors who reported needing practical help with matters such as working out what allowances they were entitled to claim, dealing with unsympathetic employers, and not being kept informed of the progress of the trial.[45] Jurors also reported struggling to return to their usual lives after the trial and some jurors' employment and careers had been damaged by the length of their jury service.[46]

Recent news stories have also reported that jurors serving on a 20-month property fraud trial at the High Court in Glasgow have needed counselling and have struggled to return to their usual lives.[47] Jurors have reportedly claimed that after such a long trial, they have needed emotional and psychological support. One juror reported struggling with communicating and joining in with conversations as a result of spending such a long time sitting in a room listening to evidence; others reported needing retraining for jobs that they were familiar with prior to jury service.[48] Research with actual jurors is required in order to further explore the effect that long trials have on jurors' lives and whether measures could be put into place in order to mitigate these.

13.5 Alternative tribunals

This paragraph looks at the alternative tribunals which might try complex fraud trials if the jury were removed from such cases. The options include trial by judge alone, by a panel of judges, or by a mixed panel of judge and lay assessors.

In judge alone trials, the same tribunal decides matters of law and matters of fact. The Roskill Committee observed that trials by judge alone are not without precedent. In the criminal justice system, magistrates, including District Judges, hear summary cases,[49] and civil trials are generally heard by a judge sitting alone.[50] In 1972, the Diplock Commission proposed that the jury be removed from criminal trials relating to terrorist activities in Northern Ireland and that a judge alone should try such cases.[51] These judge-alone trials are known as 'Diplock courts', after Lord Diplock who chaired the Commission.[52] A further example of the use of judge alone trials in the criminal justice system arises where there is evidence of jury tampering. Under section 44 of the Criminal Justice Act 2003, a trial may take place without a jury where there is a real and present danger of jury tampering and such a trial would be necessary in the interests of justice. However, within the criminal justice system, the trial of serious offences without a jury is generally exceptional.

While the Roskill Committee observed that judge alone trials would be 'the most economical way of trying a complex case', this type of tribunal was not the preferred choice of the Committee. It was thought that it would place a 'considerable burden' on the judge who would not have available 'the assistance of those who are skilled in the subject matters of the case to help him to interpret them and to arrive at a balanced conclusion'.[53] Surprisingly, a concern here appears to have been whether judges had the knowledge and experience of the business world to try such cases.[54] Neither trial by a single judge nor trial by a panel of judges were very well supported by witnesses who submitted evidence to the Committee.[55] Robert F Julian's judicial interviews also 'yielded no support for judge-only trials as a replacement for juries'.[56] One judge commented that he or she would be wary of trying a fraud case alone, 'I would be concerned in judge only trials that judges would become hardened by their experience generally. I sit uneasily with the idea that I am the sole judge of fact in these circumstances (Serious Fraud cases)'.[57] Other judges were concerned that judge alone trials would last just as long as jury trials because the prosecution case and indictment would not be 'pruned' as it would for a jury.[58] These interviews provide a valuable insight into judicial perspectives and a further research exercise with a larger sample of judges would make a valuable contribution to this issue.

An alternative option is a mixed panel of a judge sitting with lay assessors. The Roskill Committee recommended that complex fraud trials should be tried by a specially constituted Fraud Trials Tribunal, consisting of a judge and two 'lay members' who are chosen from a panel of experts.[59] The Roskill Committee recommended that there should be a register of 150–200 'lay members' who could be called upon to sit on complex fraud cases and that these should be people with 'skill and expertise in business generally and experience of complex business transactions'.[60] Under this proposal, the judge should be the sole arbiter on questions of law and the exercise of judicial discretion, but the lay members would in all other respects be able to address witnesses and counsel.[61] The Roskill Committee felt that a simple majority verdict would be sufficient and that reasons should be given for the decision, but no dissenting opinion should be disclosed.[62] The Committee took the view that the Fraud Trials Tribunal would 'reduce the length and cost of trials' and increase 'the prospects of a sound verdict being reached', enabling more complex fraud prosecutions to be brought and generally providing a deterrent to fraudsters.[63] However, while these are admirable objectives, the reasoning of the Committee is not substantiated by evidence.

There are also other issues which require consideration if the Fraud Trials Tribunal model were to be adopted. Lord Devlin stated that trying complex fraud trials without a jury was not democratic:

> There is no room in the criminal law for the idea that a case could be too complicated for a jury to understand. To refer a case for decision to a body of experts or even to men and women of superior mental powers would mean that the person accused might be imprisoned for ten of fifteen years or for life, for reasons which could not be made clear to the average citizen. This is not democracy. This is what trial by jury prevents.[64]

One advantage of the current jury system is that counsel and witnesses are required to keep the indictment to the point and clearly explain any complex issues to a lay panel of 12 members of the public. If the prosecution cannot satisfy the jury that the defendant is guilty, then the prosecution fails. This prevents the prosecution from overwhelming the court with unnecessary charges on the indictment and unnecessary case theories. However, there is a danger that the substitution of expert assessors for jurors could turn the trial into something that is incomprehensible to the general public, and which violates principles of open justice.

A further issue to consider is the risk of members of the Fraud Trials Tribunal using extraneous information in reaching its decision. In trials involving a jury, jurors may be excused if they have knowledge about the trial they are sitting on. Jurors who know the defendant or witnesses would usually be discharged in order to avoid the juror from relying on extraneous information in reaching his or her verdict and from communicating any such information to the other jurors. The main reason for this is that the defendant has not had the opportunity to challenge extraneous evidence in open court. The lay members of the Fraud Trials Tribunal would be chosen specifically for their expert knowledge and experience of complex business transactions which may be very similar in nature to those involved in the case. As such, the lay members would need to be careful not to act as expert witnesses giving evidence in the case. They would be permitted to ask questions in court, which would go some way towards safeguarding against their knowledge being unchallenged by the defence, but this does risk turning the lay members into expert witnesses. The presence of the judge on the panel should provide some safeguard against this, as the judge would direct the lay members on their role and to decide their verdict on the evidence heard in open court, but this issue deserves some further consideration.

The issues surrounding the Fraud Trials Tribunal delivering majority decisions and reasoned verdicts were very briefly dealt with by the Roskill Committee, but there is value in a more comprehensive examination of these issues. Very little academic consideration has been given to the use of majority verdicts. It has been argued that majority verdicts weaken the principles of the burden and standard of proof because the dissenting jurors represent a reasonable doubt within the collective body of the jury.[65] Gerry Maher argues that the need for unanimity becomes greater the smaller the jury, but has less weight the larger the jury; this is based on the assumption that a larger group is more representative of society.[66] This is a logical conclusion; it seems an unjustifiable approach to permit a tribunal of three to deliver a majority verdict on a serious criminal offence where the defendant could be sentenced to a lengthy period in prison. Where there are 12 people on the jury, a majority verdict requires the agreement of at least 10 of the jurors. However, where the tribunal of fact consists of only three people, one dissenting view equates to a third of the panel and must surely constitute a reasonable doubt. The use of reasoned verdicts has been more widely debated. Where a tribunal provides reasons for its verdict, this impacts upon the finality of the verdict by opening up the decision to the possibility of an appeal. The Roskill Committee was confident that reasoned judgments would discourage 'hopeless' appeals, but that in any event, the number of appeals resulting from such decisions would be small.[67] Mark Coen and Jonathan Doak have recently argued that explained verdicts should be given by juries in the interests of transparency and that trained, independent lay facilitators should chair the deliberation process and draft the explained verdict.[68] This idea carries merit and is certainly worth further consideration.

13.6 Supporting measures

This section highlights other measures that might be considered in order to support and assist jurors serving on complex fraud trials. Mention has already been made of the efforts that have already been made to the case management of complex fraud trials. Some research shows that there is still work be done here in improving case management[69] and ensuring that only relevant evidence is put before the jury in the most comprehensible format possible. A greater emphasis might be placed upon the delivery and presentation of evidence at trial, including expert evidence, such as through the use of more visual aids, agreed summary documents, glossaries, written directions, etc. Research has shown that these types of materials improve jury comprehension,[70] but it is not clear how often these materials are used. Both the advocacy employed in the courtroom and the judge's summing up are crucial to engaging the jury and ensuring their understanding of any case. As Lord Devlin stated, '[i]f the prosecution cannot make its case comprehensible, the jury is bound to acquit'.[71] To this end, specialised advocacy training and judicial training focusing on complex fraud trials might potentially be developed with the assistance of mock jurors to simulate trials.

It is argued that a greater effort should be made to promote active jury participation. Jurors are permitted to take notes in court and to ask questions via notes to the judge; however, anecdotal evidence suggests that jurors see their role as more of a passive one: '[y]ou were sitting in a room listening to evidence but you didn't communicate'.[72] Further interviews with actual jurors could be carried out to assess the extent to which jurors view their role as a passive one and research could be carried out into the frequency with which jurors ask questions and the number of jurors who take notes during the trial. The idea that jurors take a more active role in the trial process has received some consideration in the United States.[73] While there is some concern about active jury participation leading to the diminution of adversarialism, the approach would also reinforce the jury as an independent decision-maker.[74]

Finally, there must be more practical measures put into place to support jurors through long trials and to reduce the burden on them. Jurors in long trials have complained about the lack of assistance that they had with dealing with administrative matters, such as claiming allowances and dealing with their employers, as well as the effect that a lengthy period of jury service had on their lives. During the trial, jurors in long trials should be allocated a jury officer whose sole responsibility is to assist and support jurors with such issues. Similarly, more emotional and psychological support should be made available to, and promoted to, jurors after the trial, in order that they can transition back into their usual lives and jobs more easily.

13.7 Conclusion

The aim of this chapter was to reignite the debate about removing the jury from complex fraud trials and call for a full and comprehensive analysis of the many issues that such a reform would cause. It is not suggested that trial by jury is without fault, but the concern expressed here is that we should not act rashly to propose removing the jury without further empirical research and discussion. If the jury is to be removed from complex fraud trials, such a move must be grounded in principle and substantiated by evidence. The Roskill Committee's conclusions about jury comprehension were not substantiated and the proposals for a Fraud Trials Tribunal required more detailed consideration. According to the Fraud Advisory Panel which responded to Auld LJ's proposal that the jury be removed in cases of serious and complex fraud, 'no compelling case for change has been made out'.[75] More research is needed in order to explore the issue of who should try complex fraud trials. Such research could take the form of interviews with a larger sample of judges, interviews with a wider range of actual jurors in relation to issues such as comprehension, and surveys of or interviews with actual jurors to find out their views on the length and progress of trials and the effect that such trials have on their lives. It is also argued that alternative measures should be looked at before we are prepared to further erode the right to jury trial, and these include measures such as offering support to jurors to reduce the burden of a lengthy trial, further case management measures, and the promotion of active jury participation.

Notes

1 Senior Lecturer in Law, University of Worcester.
2 Roskill Committee, *Fraud Trials Committee Report* (HMSO, London, 1986) Chapter 8.
3 Thomas LCJ, *The Financial Crisis: The Role of Law and Regulation*, The Lord Merlyn-Rees Lecture delivered at the University of Glamorgan, 5 March 2009, <http://news.glam.ac.uk/media/files/documents/2009-03-09/Lord_Merlyn-Rees_Lecture_2009.pdf> accessed 23 April 2018 and Thomas LCJ, *Reshaping Justice*, speech delivered to *Justice*, 3 March 2014, <www.judiciary.gov.uk/wp-content/uploads/JCO/Documents/Speeches/lcj-speech-reshaping-justice.pdf> accessed 23 April 2018.
4 Thomas LCJ, *Reshaping Justice* (n 3) [37].
5 ibid [38].
6 ibid [39].
7 Roskill Committee (n 2) [8.25] to [8.30] and [8.33] to [8.34].
8 ibid [8.31] to [8.32].
9 Lord Devlin, 'Trial by jury for fraud' (1986) 6(3) OJLS 311, Roskill Committee (n 2), M Levi, 'The future of fraud prosecutions and trials: reviewing Roskill' (1986) 7(4) *Company Lawyer* 139, M Levi, *Investigation, prosecution, and trial of serious fraud*, The Royal Commission on Criminal Justice Research Study No. 14 (1993), M Levi, 'Frauds on trial: what is to be done?' (2000) 21(2) *Company Lawyer* 54, Auld LJ, *Review of the Criminal Courts of England and Wales* (2001) <http://webarchive.nationalarchives.gov.uk/+/http://www.criminal-courts-review.org.uk/ccr-00.htm> accessed 23 April 2018, D Corker, 'Trying fraud cases without juries' [2002] Crim LR 283, S Lloyd-Bostock, 'The Jubilee Line jurors: does their experience strengthen the argument for judge-only trial in long and complex fraud cases?' [2007] Crim LR 255, and RF Julian, 'Judicial perspectives in serious fraud cases – the present status of and problems posed by case management practices, jury selection rules, juror expertise, plea bargaining and choice of mode of trial' [2008] Crim LR 764.

10 C Thomas, *Are Juries Fair?* (Ministry of Justice Research Series, 2010) <www. justice.gov.uk/downloads/publications/research-and-analysis/moj-research/are-juries-fair-research.pdf> accessed 23 April 2018, RF Julian, 'Judicial perspectives on the conduct of serious fraud trials' [2007] Crim LR 751, Julian (n 9) and Lloyd-Bostock (n 9).

11 Roskill Committee (n 2) [8.1].

12 ibid [8.51].

13 The trial of the Maxwell brothers lasted 8 months and was reported to have cost £25 million. See 'Fraud office faces crisis as Maxwell brothers go free', *The Independent*, 20 January 1996 <www.independent.co.uk/news/fraud-office-faces-crisis-as-maxwell-brothers-go-free-1324834.html> accessed 23 April 2018 and 'Trial by jury in fraud cases could end', *BBC News*, 16 February 1998 <http://news.bbc.co.uk/1/hi/uk/57271.stm> accessed 23 April 2018.

14 The Jubilee Line trial lasted 8 months and was reported to have cost £60 million. See '£60m fraud case collapse probed', *BBC News*, 23 March 2005 <http://news.bbc.co.uk/1/hi/england/london/4373461.stm> accessed 23 April 2018 and 'Significant lessons need to be learnt', *BBC News*, 22 March 2005 <http://news.bbc.co.uk/1/hi/uk/4373851.stm> accessed 23 April 2018.

15 Auld LJ (n 9).

16 Thomas LCJ, *The Financial Crisis: The Role of Law and Regulation* (n 3).

17 Thomas LCJ, *Reshaping Justice* (n 3).

18 ibid [37].

19 ibid [38].

20 ibid [39].

21 Roskill Committee (n 2) [8.29].

22 ibid [8.33]. Section 74 of the Criminal Justice and Courts Act 2015 repealed section 8 of the Contempt of Court Act 1981 (for England and Wales only) and replaced it with a criminal offence of disclosing jury's deliberations (now found under section 20D of the Juries Act 1974).

23 C Thomas (n 10).

24 C Thomas, 'Avoiding the perfect storm of juror contempt' [2013] Crim LR 483, 502.

25 Roskill Committee (n 2) [8.34].

26 S Enright and J Morton, *Taking Liberties: The Criminal Jury in the 1990s* (Weidenfeld and Nicolson 1990) 106.

27 Roskill Committee (n 2) [8.36].

28 Roskill Committee (n 2), Note of Dissent by Mr Merricks C9 and Enright and Morton (n 26) 106.

29 Roskill Committee (n 2) [8.31].

30 Auld (n 9) 213.

31 M Zander QC, 'Lord Justice Auld's Review of the Criminal Courts: A response' (November 2001) 23–24 <www.lse.ac.uk/collections/law/staff%20publications%20full%20text/zander/auld_response_web.pdf> accessed on 23 April 2018.

32 Lloyd-Bostock (n 9) 259. The group discussion took place with 8 of the 10 jurors who were still serving at the time that the trial collapsed. The latter part of the discussion explored the jury's understanding of the case and this was led by Stephen Myers who was seconded to the review team from the Serious Fraud Office.

33 ibid 259–260.

34 ibid 260.

35 Julian (n 10) 754.

36 ibid.

37 This point was also made by Walter Merricks in his dissent, see Roskill Committee (n 2), Note of Dissent by Mr Merricks, C18.

38 Zander (n 31) 24.

39 Lloyd-Bostock (n 9) 262.

40 ibid 269.

41 ibid fn 58.

42 See J McEwan, 'From adversarialism to managerialism: criminal justice in transition' [2011] 31(4) *Legal Studies* 519, A Jordanoska, 'Case management in complex fraud trials: actors and strategies in achieving procedural efficiency' [2017] 13(3) *International Journal of Law in Context* 336 and Julian (n 9).

43 P Darbyshire, 'Judicial case management in ten Crown courts' [2014] Crim LR 30, 30.

44 Roskill Committee (n 2) [8.32].

45 Lloyd-Bostock (n 9) 263-270.

46 ibid 268.

47 See 'Jurors tell how longest trial has left them struggling to return to normal life', *The Telegraph*, 27 August 2017 <www.telegraph.co.uk/news/2017/08/27/jurors-tell-longest-trial-has-left-struggling-return-normal/> accessed 23 April 2018, 'Britain's longest-serving jurors reveal they needed counselling after life-changing two-year trial', *The Independent*, 28 August 2017 <www.independent.co.uk/news/uk/crime/longest-serving-jurors-britain-two-year-fraud-trial-edwin-mclaren-lauren-mclaren-glasgow-high-court-a7916416.html> accessed 23 April 2018, and 'We spent almost two years sitting on a jury', *BBC News*, 27 August 2017 <www.bbc.co.uk/news/uk-scotland-40946653> accessed 23 April 2018.

48 'We spent almost two years sitting on a jury', *BBC News* (n 47).

49 Only a small minority of criminal cases ever reach the jury; at least 95 per cent of criminal cases are dealt with in the Magistrates' Court (A Ashworth and M Redmayne, *The Criminal Process* (4th edn, OUP, 2010) 323).

50 Roskill Committee (n 2) [8.45].

51 Diplock Commission, *Report of the Commission to consider legal procedures to deal with terrorist activities in Northern Ireland* (HMSO, 1972).

52 While Diplock Courts were prevalent in the 1970s, they are infrequently held today. One recent example is the trial of two defendants for the murder of two British soldiers which took place in 2012: see 'Brian Shrivers found guilty of Massereene murders', *The Guardian*, 20 January 2012 <www.theguardian.com/uk/2012/jan/20/brian-shivers-guilty-massereene-murders> accessed on 23 April 2018. For further detail about Diplock Courts, see J Jackson and S Doran, *Judge Without Jury* (Clarendon Press, 1995).

53 Roskill Committee (n 2) [8.46].

54 ibid [8.47].

55 ibid [8.46] and [8.47].

56 Julian (n 10) 759.

57 ibid 760.

58 ibid.

59 Roskill Committee (n 2) [8.51].

60 ibid [8.53] and [8.62].

61 ibid [8.66].

62 ibid [8.68] and [8.69].

63 ibid [8.51].

64 Devlin (n 9) 313-314.

65 M Freeman, 'The jury on trial' (1981) *Current Legal Problems* 65, 69.

66 G Maher, 'The verdict of the jury' in M Findlay and P Duff (eds), *The Jury Under Attack* (Butterworths, 1988) 47.

67 Roskill Committee (n 2) [8.72].

68 M Coen and J Doak, 'Embedding explained jury verdicts in the English criminal trial' (2017) 37(4) *Legal Studies* 786.

69 See the research conducted by Darbyshire (n 43).
70 C Thomas (n 10) vi.
71 Devlin (n 9) 313.
72 'We spent almost two years sitting on a jury', *BBC News* (n 47).
73 See V Hans, 'US Jury Reform: The Active Jury and the Adversarial Ideal' (2002) 21(1) *Saint Louis University Public Law Review* 85 and B Michael Dann, '"Learning Lessons" and "Speaking Rights": Creating Educated and Democratic Juries' (1993) 68 *Indiana Law Journal* 1229.
74 Hans (n 73) 97.
75 Fraud Advisory Panel, *Response to the Lord Justice Auld's Review of the Criminal Courts*, 16 January 2002 [1.5(i)].

Bibliography

Ashworth A and Redmayne M, *The Criminal Process* (4th edn, OUP, 2010)
Auld LJ, *Review of the Criminal Courts of England and Wales* (2001)
BBC News, '£60m fraud case collapse probed', 23 March 2005
BBC News, 'Significant lessons need to be learnt', 22 March 2005
BBC News, 'Trial by jury in fraud cases could end', 16 February 1998
BBC News, 'We spent almost two years sitting on a jury', 27 August 2017
Coen M and Doak J, 'Embedding explained jury verdicts in the English criminal trial' (2017) 37(4) *Legal Studies* 786
Contempt of Court Act 1981
Corker D, 'Trying fraud cases without juries' [2002] Crim LR 283
Criminal Justice Act 2003
Criminal Justice and Courts Act 2015
Dann B M, '"Learning Lessons" and "Speaking Rights": Creating Educated and Democratic Juries' (1993) 68 *Indiana Law Journal* 1229
Darbyshire P, 'Judicial case management in ten Crown courts' [2014] Crim LR 30
Devlin, Lord, 'Trial by jury for fraud' (1986) 6(3) OJLS 311
Diplock Commission, *Report of the Commission to consider legal procedures to deal with terrorist activities in Northern Ireland* (HMSO, 1972)
Enright S and Morton J, *Taking Liberties: The Criminal Jury in the 1990s* (Weidenfeld and Nicolson 1990)
Fraud Act 2006
Fraud Advisory Panel, *Response to the Lord Justice Auld's Review of the Criminal Courts*, 16 January 2002
Freeman M, 'The jury on trial' (1981) *Current Legal Problems* 65
The Guardian, 'Brian Shrivers found guilty of Massereene murders', 20 January 2012
Hans V, 'US Jury Reform: The Active Jury and the Adversarial Ideal' (2002) 21(1) *Saint Louis University Public Law Review* 85
The Independent, 'Fraud office faces crisis as Maxwell brothers go free', 20 January 1996
The Independent, 'Britain's longest-serving jurors reveal they needed counselling after life-changing two-year trial', 28 August 2017
Jackson J and Doran S, *Judge Without Jury* (Clarendon Press, 1995)
Julian RF, 'Judicial perspectives on the conduct of serious fraud trials' [2007] Crim LR 751
Julian RF, 'Judicial perspectives in serious fraud cases – the present status of and problems posed by case management practices, jury selection rules, juror expertise, plea bargaining and choice of mode of trial' [2008] Crim LR 764

Juries Act 1974

Levi M, 'The future of fraud prosecutions and trials: reviewing Roskill' (1986) 7(4) *Company Lawyer* 139

Levi M, *Investigation, prosecution, and trial of serious fraud*, The Royal Commission on Criminal Justice Research Study No. 14 (1993)

Levi M, 'Frauds on trial: what is to be done?' (2000) 21(2) *Company Lawyer* 54

Lloyd-Bostock S, 'The Jubilee Line jurors: does their experience strengthen the argument for judge-only trial in long and complex fraud cases?' [2007] Crim LR 255

Maher G, 'The verdict of the jury' in Findlay M and Duff P (eds), *The Jury Under Attack* (Butterworths, 1988)

Protection of Freedoms Act 2012

Roskill Committee, *Fraud Trials Committee Report* (HMSO, London, 1986)

The Telegraph, 'Jurors tell how longest trial has left them struggling to return to normal life', 27 August 2017

Thomas C, *Are Juries Fair?* (Ministry of Justice Research Series, 2010)

Thomas LCJ, *The Financial Crisis: The Role of Law and Regulation*, The Lord Merlyn-Rees Lecture delivered at the University of Glamorgan, 5 March 2009

Thomas LCJ, *Reshaping Justice*, speech delivered to *Justice*, 3 March 2014

Zander M, 'Lord Justice Auld's Review of the Criminal Courts: A response', November 2001

14 Good character directions
Some implications of *Hunter* for Fraud Act 2006 prosecutions

Richard Glover[1]

14.1 Introduction

The Court of Appeal's judgment in *Hunter*[2] was concerned with the provision of good character directions to the jury and was of particular weight because the court was composed of five senior judges including the Lord Chief Justice.[3] This chapter examines the court's analysis of the law and the implications this has for prosecutions under the Fraud Act 2006. In a cogent article published at the time of its enactment, Ormerod was strongly critical of the Fraud Act for the uncertainty in the law caused by the element of dishonesty being 'the principal determinant of criminal liability'[4] in all three forms of fraud.[5] Ten years on from enactment, there seems little reason to revise that opinion.

It is contended here, however, that there is a further aspect to this problem, which has developed more recently as a result of changes to the law on good character evidence. Following *Hunter*, it will be much less common for judges to direct juries on a defendant's good character, which is often an important element in the jury's deliberations on dishonesty. It is well-known that if juries do not hear of the defendant's good character, they tend to assume the worst[6] and, accordingly, before *Hunter*, failures in directing the jury were taken very seriously by the appellate courts.[7] The Court of Appeal's decision in *Hunter* and its interpretation of the leading case of *Aziz*,[8] is examined critically below, but before so doing it is, first, necessary to address the alleged uncertainty in the law caused by the emphasis on dishonesty in Fraud Act 2006 offences.

14.2 Dishonesty in the Fraud Act 2006

Why should dishonesty lead to uncertainty in Fraud Act offences? First, we should be aware that the origins of this element lie in the Theft Act 1968 where, as the Law Commission noted in its *Fraud and Deception* Consultation Paper, it also has a pivotal role.[9] In its final report, although it echoed concerns from the Consultation Paper about dishonesty creating 'undue uncertainty and inconsistency',[10] the Law Commission accepted that the dishonesty element in theft was 'in practice, unproblematic'.[11] Therefore, it was content to rely on dishonesty as the central *mens rea* for fraud offences, despite it not being defined in the Theft Act.

The reason for this absence of definition is that the Criminal Law Revision Committee, which laid the foundations for the Theft Act 1968 in its Eighth Report, believed it was something that 'laymen can easily recognise when they see it'.[12] Accordingly, as dishonesty is considered to be an ordinary word 'in common use, and has no special legal meaning'[13] the jury are not normally directed on it.[14] However, where the defendant contends that he did not believe that his actions were dishonest, the jury must be directed on dishonesty. Until recently, this would have led to a *Ghosh* direction in the following terms:

1 Was what was done dishonest according to the ordinary standards of reasonable and honest people? If no, the defendant is not guilty. If yes:
2 Did the defendant realise that reasonable and honest people regard what he did as dishonest? If yes, he is guilty; if no, he is not.[15]

This direction has been strongly criticised in the extensive literature on *Ghosh*. For example, Campbell argued that the second, subjective limb appears redundant if the jury is directed to take into account all the possible circumstances, including the accused's beliefs about dishonesty.[16] Recently, the Supreme Court reached the same conclusion in *Ivey* v *Genting Casinos (UK) Ltd t/a Crockfords* and, in effect, overruled the *Ghosh* test,[17] setting out an updated test without the second limb:

When dishonesty is in question the fact-finding tribunal must first ascertain (subjectively) the actual state of the individual's knowledge or belief as to the facts. The reasonableness or otherwise of his belief is a matter of evidence (often in practice determinative) going to whether he held the belief, but it is not an additional requirement that his belief must be reasonable; the question is whether it is genuinely held. When once his actual state of mind as to knowledge or belief as to facts is established, the question whether his conduct was honest or dishonest is to be determined by the fact-finder by applying the (objective) standards of ordinary decent people. There is no requirement that the defendant must appreciate that what he has done is, by those standards, dishonest.[18]

That is, although dishonesty is a subjective state of mind, the standard by which that is judged is objective. However, even if we accept that the deficiencies of *Ghosh* are reduced by elimination of its second limb, it is contended that the problem remains that there can be very different views as to what 'ordinary decent people' would decide, which leads to potential uncertainty. Accordingly, it is evident that if deciding what amounts to dishonesty is left to jurors, so that they are required to set a moral standard for honesty and to calculate whether a defendant's conduct falls short of it, there is a danger of 'endemic inconsistency' in application of the standard – different juries will reach different decisions on essentially the same facts.[19]

Due to statutory restrictions,[20] we can only speculate as to quite how juries reach a view on a defendant's dishonesty. However, it is likely that an important factor will be, as the Law Commission observed, whether the defendant is of good character.[21] Therefore, as dishonesty has become the principal determinant of criminal liability for the most important Fraud Act 2006 offences, it follows that the defendant's character is also now central to deciding guilt. However, as is well-known, the Court of Appeal is reluctant to interfere with questions, such as dishonesty, that are matters for the jury.[22] When this deference to the jury is coupled with the Court of Appeal's recent assertion in *Hunter* that it will be 'very slow' to interfere where judges have exercised their discretion not to provide good character directions,[23] the position for Fraud Act defendants appears particularly precarious.

The Fraud Act 2006 spans a range of criminal behaviour from low value welfare benefit frauds to high value 'white-collar' crime. It may be that the latter defendants, in particular, will have no serious previous convictions.[24] It is possible that they may have what might be regarded as old, minor matters, for example, a caution for criminal damage when they were a teenager. They may also have stains on their character as a result of disciplinary matters or earlier regulatory investigations, which did not result in prosecutions. As a result of *Hunter*, any one of these matters may lead to a judge declining to treat the defendant as being of 'good character' and directing the jury accordingly. There is a now much more restricted set of circumstances in which good character directions will be given to the jury and, consequently, this is of importance in relation to Fraud Act 2006 proceedings.

14.3 *Hunter* and good character directions

Following an extensive review of the law, the Court of Appeal sought to provide express guidance on when good character directions should be given in a criminal trial. It is argued here that, notwithstanding the undoubted eminence of this five-judge Court of Appeal, their Lordships fell into error in a number of respects but, in particular, in their understanding of the leading House of Lords decision in *Aziz* by which, of course, they recognised they were bound.[25] However, before we consider this, it is first necessary to address what is meant by 'good character' which, somewhat surprisingly, was not considered in *Hunter* and may, in part, explain some of the difficulties with that judgment.

At common law, as a consequence of the procedural and evidential incapacities from which the accused suffered at that time, the rule emerged that the accused was entitled to prove his general good character, as an exception to the rule that character evidence was generally inadmissible. An accused's 'character' was understood to mean his 'general reputation', although this was not finally settled until the judgment in *Rowton*,[26] where there was a vigorous attempt to dislodge this definition.[27] A thirteen-strong Court of Crown Cases Reserved held that character witnesses were permitted to testify as to the accused's 'general reputation in the neighbourhood in which he lives' in order to show 'the tendency and disposition of the man's mind towards committing or abstaining from committing the class of crime with which he stands charged'.[28] However, importantly, evidence of specific good acts and individuals' opinions were inadmissible.

This rule continues to be criticised, and it is said that the rule is 'more honoured in the breach than in the observance'.[29] However, it is evident, nevertheless, that *Rowton* remains good law.[30] Put simply, the purpose of good character evidence is to help the jury decide whether the accused's reputation meant that 'he was the kind of man who was likely to have behaved in the way that the prosecution alleged'.[31] Accordingly if, as a matter of law, it is the defendant's general reputation that is in issue, it follows that it is only the character the defendant 'brings to the court when charged with the offence'[32] which is relevant, and not matters discovered after the event.[33] However, the Court of Appeal in *Hunter* rejected this analysis as 'a wrong turn in the law'.[34]

It is contended here that, with respect, the error was their Lordships', who seem to have overlooked *Rowton*. The Court of Appeal appeared to regard 'good character' as simply the reverse of 'bad character', which it noted was defined by ss.98 and 112 of the Criminal Justice Act 2003 as 'evidence of or a disposition towards misconduct' and consisting of a criminal offence or 'other reprehensible behaviour', except where this was concerned with the alleged facts of the offence or misconduct in 'connection with the investigation or prosecution of that offence'.[35] That is, contrary to *Rowton*, the Court of Appeal treated the defendant's disposition, rather than general reputation, as admissible good character evidence.

It is, perhaps, understandable why the Court of Appeal should come to this conclusion, given that the Criminal Justice Act 2003 refers to 'character' in the context of a statutory definition of 'bad character'. However, it is submitted that it cannot have been Parliament's intention to overrule *Rowton*, or change the law on good character, as a consequence of its codification of the law on bad character in the 2003 Act. There was no specific reference to the law on good character in the Act and it is evident that this was because the Law Commission Consultation Paper[36] that preceded the Criminal Justice Act 2003 did not recommend changing the law. Indeed, in view of the vigorous debates in Parliament,[37] it seems likely that any changes to the law on good character would have been met with determined opposition. As Monaghan suggests, with hindsight, it might have been helpful if good and bad character had been dealt with comprehensively by the Act but, ultimately, that was not Parliament's intention.[38] Notwithstanding this, the Court of Appeal in *Hunter* proceeded on the basis that the bad character reforms were intended to have an impact on the law on 'good character'.[39] Accordingly, their Lordships were emboldened to re-examine the law on when good character directions should be provided.

14.4 Good character directions following *Hunter*

The Court of Appeal contended that the circumstances in which good character directions were given had 'been extended too far' to include unmeritorious defendants.[40] In addition, their Lordships asserted that the definition of 'bad character' had been broadened by the Criminal Justice Act 2003 well beyond the mere absence of previous convictions, which it considered to have been the prevailing definition before the Act. Accordingly, this broader definition had concomitantly narrowed 'good character', so that the circumstances in which directions were given should be restricted.

In a very clearly structured judgment the Court of Appeal, acknowledging that it was bound by *Aziz* and *Vye*,[41] set out how it interpreted those judgments before providing guidance on the provision of good character directions, which largely replicated the *Vye* directions on credibility and propensity:

> 77 We use the term "absolute good character" to mean a defendant who has no previous convictions or cautions recorded against them and no other reprehensible conduct alleged, admitted or proven . . . This category of defendant is entitled to both limbs of the good character direction. The law is settled.
>
> 78 The first credibility limb of good character is a positive feature which should be taken into account. The second propensity limb means that good character may make it less likely that the defendant acted as alleged and so particular attention should be paid to the fact . . .
>
> 79 Where a defendant has previous convictions or cautions recorded which are old, minor and have no relevance to the charge, the judge must make a judgment as to whether or not to treat the defendant as a person of effective good character. It does not follow from the fact that a defendant has previous convictions which are old or irrelevant to the offence charged that a judge is obliged to treat him as a person of good character. In fairness to all, the trial judge should be vigilant to ensure that only those defendants who merit an "effective good character" are afforded one. It is for the judge to make a judgment, by assessing all the circumstances of the offence(s) and the offender, to the extent known, and then deciding what fairness to all dictates. The judge should not leave it to the jury to decide whether or not the defendant is to be treated as of good character.

In addition, it was held that the judge has a residual, broad discretion to provide a direction in a range of other circumstances where the accused has previous convictions or cautions, or other bad character. For example, where the accused has no previous convictions but admits other 'reprehensible behaviour' under s.101(1)(b) of the Criminal Justice Act 2003. However, with the greatest of respect, it is contended here that the Court of Appeal's interpretation of the law left something to be desired.

First, it is not clear that the law on 'bad character' has been significantly broadened by the Criminal Justice Act 2003 to the extent that the provision of good character directions required revising. The expression 'reprehensible behaviour' is novel but its scope is 'not at all clear',[42] and it is not apparent that it is wider than previous conceptions of what would be sufficient misconduct to constitute bad character. For example, Evans LJ stated in *Durbin*: 'The words "or is of bad character" emphasise that the restriction is not limited to previous convictions . . . but to character generally'.[43] It has also been wrongly assumed that in *Aziz* Lord Steyn had a restricted view of bad character because he referred to the 'usual case of a defendant with no previous convictions'[44] as having good character.[45] However, this seems to have been merely a repudiation of the suggestion that 'positive' good character was required for a good character direction.[46] Accordingly, the premise on which the Court of Appeal in *Hunter* justified its revision of the law appears doubtful.

Secondly, it is clear that the Court of Appeal sought to alter the primary meaning of 'good character' for the purposes of good character directions. The Court of Appeal conceded that a defendant with 'bad character' (which may consist of previous convictions, cautions or other 'reprehensible behaviour') might qualify as being of 'effective good character', but the default position following *Hunter* is that the defendant is not of good character 'in the proper sense'[47] and, therefore, not entitled to any direction. As Hallett LJ stated in the later case of *Morgans*:

> A defendant with convictions is not entitled as of right to any part of the good character direction, for the simple reason he does not have a good character.[48]

Therefore, for example, a defendant charged with a substantial financial fraud under the Fraud Act 2006, who has a minor motoring conviction from thirty years ago, is not regarded as being of good character and, accordingly, no good character direction should be given. The likelihood is that the trial judge will direct the jury that the defendant may be treated as being of 'effective good character', provided the bad character is 'old, minor and irrelevant', which Hallett LJ has insisted must be read conjunctively.[49] However, that is a matter entirely for the judge's discretion and the Court of Appeal has emphasised that it will be 'very slow' to interfere with the exercise of that discretion.[50]

This contrasts markedly with the position before *Hunter*. If the defendant's 'bad character' was 'old, minor and irrelevant' (utilising the terminology from *Hunter*, but read disjunctively) the defendant could still be regarded 'as if he had never been in trouble in the past at all' and a good character direction given.[51] It might be that this would be qualified to reflect that the defendant's character was not without blemishes, but the defendant was still treated as being of good character. For example, Glidewell LJ, who was head of the Judicial Studies Board at the time, held in *Liacopoulous* that a defendant with a 'very minor' previous conviction was of 'positive good character'[52] and Lord Steyn approved the opinion of Glidewell LJ (sitting in the Court of Appeal in *Aziz*) that the appellant was of good character because his convictions were not of 'any relevance or significance'.[53] Accordingly, it is evident that the threshold for the giving of good character directions has increased significantly and even the slightest infraction is liable to lead to a good character direction not being given.

Thirdly, unfortunately, it appears that the Court of Appeal in *Hunter* made an important factual error. It overlooked that the appellant in *Aziz* was not of completely good character, which may have led their Lordships to misconstrue the nature of the judgment in *Aziz*.[54] With respect, the Court of Appeal also appears to have misconstrued Taylor LJ's judgment in *Vye*.[55] This was concerned with appellants with no previous convictions, but a few months later in *Horrex*[56] Taylor LJ clarified that a defendant with a previous conviction could also be treated as being of good character. It made no difference to when a direction could be given. In *Hunter*, Hallett LJ regarded it as an 'important distinction' with later case law, in which the accused had previous convictions,[57] that both *Aziz* and *Vye* were concerned with appellants with no previous convictions but appears to have fallen into error, as is plain from her criticism of the judgment in *Gray*:[58]

> That is not a correct understanding of *R v Vye* or *R v Aziz*. Both were concerned with defendants who had no previous convictions.[59]

The Court of Appeal in *Hunter* stated that it was bound by *Vye* and *Aziz*[60] but it is trite law that the doctrine of *stare decisis* required the Court of Appeal, in the final instance, to follow the House of Lords judgment in *Aziz*, in which the *Vye* directions were approved. It is, therefore, a puzzling feature of *Hunter* that, in apparent justification for recasting the law on good character directions, so much of the judgment is concerned with criticism and discussion of cases such as *Durbin*[61] and *Teasdale*,[62] all of which preceded *Aziz*. However, as Lord Mance observed, more than a decade before *Hunter*, such cases are of 'only historical interest' and the whole subject should:

> . . . now be approached in the first instance by reference to Lord Steyn's speech in [*Aziz*] . . . It is not to be qualified or applied by making exhaustive attempts to fit in all previous authority into a coherent mould.[63]

That old case law may have amounted to, as Lord Steyn opined, a 'veritable sea-change in judicial thinking',[64] but it is submitted that, with respect, the Court of Appeal in *Hunter* was distracted unnecessarily by it and that their Lordships' primary focus should have been the unanimous judgment in *Aziz*. However, it is contended that the Court of Appeal also misunderstood the nature and significance of the judgment in *Aziz* that it purported to follow.

14.5 The House of Lords' judgment in *Aziz*

The Court of Appeal's analysis of the House of Lords' judgment in *Aziz* may be criticised on two main grounds – first, that their Lordships misconstrued the essence of the judgment and second, misunderstood the defeasible nature of the good character rule that was set out therein.

The Court of Appeal examined the provision of good character directions in terms of whether the defendants were *entitled* 'as of right' to such a direction. This, understandably, followed from the grounds of appeal for all five appellants, which were that they were *entitled* to good character directions in one form or another. However, this appears to have distorted the court's assessment of the main issue of when directions should be given to the jury, as it did not recognise the breadth of the *ratio* in *Aziz*. Arguments regarding the defendant's entitlement were referred to by Lord Steyn, but that was not the principal basis for his opinion in *Aziz*.

It is submitted that the essence of the judgment in *Aziz* was not that defendants enjoyed a right to a good character direction but, rather, the principle that the judge has an obligation to put the defendant's character to the jury in a 'fair and balanced way'.[65] The requirement to provide a good character direction appears to flow not from a defendant's rights but, rather, from the obligation to sum up fairly to the jury.[66]

The object of the judge's summing up is, of course, to help the jury reach their verdict and, it follows, this is also the purpose of the good character direction. That being the case, the issue of a defendant's 'entitlement' to a direction ought not to arise. Instead, the key question is whether a direction would help the jury. Therefore, although the jury must not be misled, as was stressed in *Hunter*,[67] there may be occasions where it will simply not assist the jury in weighing up evidence and reaching their verdict not to be given a good character direction where the defendant's bad character is 'old, minor or irrelevant' (utilising the terminology from *Hunter*, but read disjunctively). As juries tend to assume that defendants have bad character if they do not hear a good character direction, it is contended that omitting to direct on good character in these circumstances does not assist the jury and may unfairly prejudice them against the accused. Indeed, arguably, omitting to direct the jury on good character in sufficient detail[68] or sum up in a 'fair, balanced and accurate' way[69] both violate the accused's right to a fair trial under art. 6 of the European Convention on Human Rights. It should, in particular, be borne in mind that specific importance is attached to the provision of judicial directions in England and Wales because juries do not provide reasons for their verdicts. Without a direction as part of a 'framework of fairness', the defendant (and the public) cannot be reassured that good character was taken into account by the jury.[70]

If this principle was the essence of the judgment in *Aziz*, it still remains to be considered how that principle was to be put into practice. The House of Lords' aim was to further clarify the circumstances in which *Vye* directions would be given. Lord Steyn's solution was to lay down a strict rule that a direction should be provided, but also to allow for a very limited 'residual discretion' not to direct the jury in exceptional cases. That is, his Lordship confirmed that what had been a question of discretion for the trial judge[71] had crystallised into an obligation to direct the jury on good character as a matter of law.[72]

When the law is understood in these terms, it appears clear. Nevertheless, the Court of Appeal in *Hunter* found that some trial judges believed they were called upon to provide meaningless and over-generous directions and that attempts to achieve consistency in the law had failed.[73] However, the picture was perhaps more mixed than their Lordships suggested. In *Teeluck* v *Trinidad & Tobago*, Lord Carswell considered the law to be 'much more clearly settled' after *Aziz* and clearly a matter of law rather than a question of discretion[74] but, perhaps, Moses LJ put it best in *Stiedel*.[75] His Lordship referred to the House of Lords' unanimity in holding that there were 'bright line rules' on providing good character directions and that there was only a residual discretion not to do so. This captured the mandatory nature of the rule and the 'fringe' nature of the discretion to omit to provide a direction. With respect, the Court of Appeal in *Hunter* appear to have misunderstood the nature and significance of the House of Lords' judgment in *Aziz*, as it is submitted that the key to understanding Lord Steyn's approach is an appreciation that his Lordship was putting forward a rule on good character with an awareness that it was 'defeasible'.

The philosopher of legal positivism, HLA Hart, has been credited with introducing the idea of 'defeasibility' into legal analysis.[76] 'Defeasibility' may be described as the notion that a legal concept or rule is open to implied exceptions, which cannot be known *ex ante* and, accordingly, only provides *prima facie* and not conclusive obligations.[77] That is, a rule that appears certain may, nevertheless, be contradicted or defeated by the discovery of further facts, as exceptions to rules are 'incapable of exhaustive statement'.[78] This recognises that however well it is constructed, a general rule, such as that a good character direction should normally be given, will rarely be constructed so clearly and precisely that it leaves no room for doubt and no loopholes,[79] or no uncertainty at the borderline.[80] This may be regarded as unattainable because, as Tur observes in his Goldilocks thesis:

> Rules are either too wide and hard or too narrow and soft, frequently both and never, like the porridge or the bed in the fairy tale, 'just right'.[81]

Lord Steyn was a confirmed critic of 'formalism' in statutory interpretation and acknowledged his debt to legal positivism,[82] so it should be no surprise that his Lordship would accept a degree of flexibility in the provision of a legal rule on good character directions. However, this flexibility was of a strictly limited nature. What Lord Steyn outlined in *Aziz* was that there was a mandatory rule in relation to good character directions – that '*prima facie* the directions must be given' where a person was of good character.[83] As we have seen, 'good character' is understood to mean that the defendant's 'general reputation' was good, encompassing no previous convictions (or none that were relevant) and no other relevant 'bad character'. However, his Lordship also accepted that there should, in exceptional circumstances, be a residual discretion for a direction not to be given where it would be an 'absurdity' to do so. The form that any direction should take was left to the 'good sense of trial judges'.[84]

Lord Steyn held that a direction would not be necessary, exceptionally, where this would be an 'insult to common sense'.[85] It is evident that these are very 'strong words'[86] and that, accordingly, Lord Steyn only meant for the discretion to omit a good character direction to be exercised in exceptional circumstances.[87] The discretion to do so was 'narrowly circumscribed', by which his Lordship meant 'heavily constrained by established principles',[88] namely, here, the expectation that a good character direction would, as a rule, normally be provided as a matter of fairness. The narrowness of this discretion is also evident from the facts of *Aziz* itself, which indicate that making false mortgage applications and tax declarations in the context of defrauding the Inland Revenue were insufficient for a good character direction to be dispensed with.

With respect, the defeasible nature of this 'simple and moderate rule'[89] in *Aziz* does not appear to have been appreciated by the Court of Appeal in *Hunter*. Thus, in holding that there was no 'fixed rule' that failing to direct the jury would render a conviction unfair,[90] despite its assertions to the contrary, the court did not follow *Aziz*. However, there are also indications that the court had further deeper differences of opinion with the House of Lords. As Munday has observed, whilst setting out new guidance on the appropriate directions in *Hunter*, the Court of Appeal betrayed its scepticism about the value of good character evidence.[91]

This scepticism fed into the question of whether the jury should be directed on good character at all. Their Lordships doubted whether the jury needed a direction, preferring to assume that they should be trusted to weigh up the evidence appropriately.[92] However if, as with Fraud Act 2006 offences, a defendant's character is central to the offence in question, it does seem appropriate that a mandatory direction should be given in all such cases. It is a commonplace of the criminal law that certain jury directions are standard and due to all accused and it is unclear why, if 'good character', broadly understood, is relevant evidence, that it should be treated differently. After all, just because something accords with common sense or common knowledge does not necessarily mean that it is not the fit subject of a standard direction and for Fraud Act defendants, in particular, it is a form of final safeguard against miscarriages of justice. The need for such a safeguard is especially apparent in light of recent revelations about failings in prosecution disclosure in the Liam Allan case, which have led to a number of successful appeals and aborted trials.[93]

14.6 Conclusion

The effect of *Hunter* is clear. The legal rule on the provision of good character directions has become, in effect, largely a matter of discretion for the trial judge because a defendant with previous convictions or other reprehensible behaviour will no longer be treated as being of 'good character'. There remains the potential for the jury to be directed on good character but, in contrast to the simple rule in *Aziz* that '*prima facie* the direction must be given', the new law appears, to say the least, 'somewhat complex'.[94] The Court of Appeal hoped that its judgment would lead to greater consistency in the way that courts approached the issue but, by placing the trial judge's discretion at the very centre of things, this seems a vain hope and, unfortunately, a recipe for a return to pre-*Vye* days when the provision of good character directions were regarded as something of 'a lottery'.[95] The House of Lords in *Aziz* clarified the law but it appears, with respect, that the nature of the judgment was misinterpreted by the Court of Appeal in *Hunter*. The consequences for Fraud Act 2006 defendants are potentially serious.

Notes

1 Senior Lecturer, School of Law, University of Wolverhampton.
2 *Hunter* [2015] EWCA Crim 631.
3 The court also included Lady Hallett, the Vice-President of the Court of Appeal (Criminal Division), who gave the lead judgment, and Sir Brian Leveson, the President of the Queen's Bench Division.
4 D. Ormerod, 'Criminalising Lying' [2007] *Crim LR* 193, 200.
5 Dishonesty is an element in a number of Fraud Act 2006 offences, see ss. 2–4 and 11.
6 Law Commission, *Evidence of Bad Character in Criminal Proceedings* (Law Com No 273, 2001), paras 6.18–19; S. Lloyd-Bostock, 'The effects on juries of hearing about the defendant's previous criminal record: a simulation study' [2000] *Crim LR* 734.
7 M. Redmayne, *Character in the Criminal Trial* (Oxford University Press, 2015), 217
8 *Aziz* [1996] AC 41.
9 Law Commission, *Fraud and Deception* (Law Com CP No 155, 1999), paras 3.17 and 3.20.
10 n 9, p.120 and para 7.47.
11 Law Commission, *Fraud* (Law Com No 276, 2002), paras 5.14 and 5.18.
12 Criminal Law Revision Committee, Theft and Related Offences (1966) Cmnd 2977, paras 35 and 39.
13 Judicial College, Crown Court Compendium – Part 1: Jury and Trial Management and Summing Up (November 2017), para 8–19.
14 *Roberts* (1987) 84 Cr App R 117.
15 *Ghosh* [1982] QB 1053, 1064. This is how the test is described in D. Ormerod & K. Laird, *Smith & Hogan Criminal Law*, 14th edn (Oxford University Press, 2015), 944 and it accurately replicates Lord Lane CJ's test but in a more accessible way.
16 K. Campbell, 'The test of dishonesty in *R v Ghosh*' [1984] *CLJ* 349, 354–356.
17 As *Ivey* is a civil case and the discussion of dishonesty in the Supreme Court was strictly obiter, there has been some uncertainty as to the authority of the judgment. However, this was largely dispelled in *DPP* v *Patterson* [2017] EWHC 2820 (Admin) by the President of the Queen's Bench Division, Sir Brian Leveson, who held that the second limb of *Ghosh* did not apply. The Court of Appeal (Criminal Division) in *Pabon*

[2018] EWCA Crim 420 has also recently referred to *Ivey* with approval. For criticism of Ivey, see Dyson & Jarvis, 'Poison Ivey or herbal tea leaf?' [2018] 134(Apr) *LQR* 198.

18 *Ivey v Genting Casinos (UK) Ltd t/a Crockfords* [2017] UKSC 67, [74].
19 E Griew, 'Dishonesty: the objections to Feely and Ghosh' [1985] *Crim LR* 341, 344.
20 Contempt of Court 1981, s. 8.
21 n 9, para 5.18.
22 H. Quirk, Identifying miscarriages of justice: why innocence in the UK is not the answer (2007) 70(5) *MLR* 759, 765.
23 n 2, [89]–[98].
24 As mentioned in the Government's *Fraud Review Final Report* (25 July 2006), para 10.41.
25 n 2, [68].
26 *Rowton* (1865) Le & Ca 520.
27 As noted by Lord Devlin in *Jones* v *DPP* [1962] AC 635, 698–699.
28 *Rowton*, n 26, 529–530.
29 D Ormerod & D Perry (eds), *Blackstone's Criminal Practice 2018* (Oxford University Press, 2017), para F14.30.
30 It was specifically endorsed by Lord Goddard CJ in *Butterwasser* [1948] 1 KB 4 and by Lawton LJ in *Redgrave* (1982) 74 Cr App R 10. See also *Gunewardene* [1951] 2 KB 600, 606 to similar effect. Recent approval includes *Grimes* [2017] NICA 19 and *Rowton* also remains authoritative in other Commonwealth jurisdictions, e.g. Australia: *Attwood* v *R* (1960) 102 CLR 353.
31 *Berrada* (1990) 91 Cr App R 131, 134.
32 *Durbin* [1995] 2 Cr App R 84, 91.
33 JC Smith, *Buzalek and Schiffer* [1991] *Crim LR* 116, 117.
34 n 2, [20].
35 n 2, [29].
36 Law Commission, Evidence in Criminal Proceedings: Previous Misconduct of a Defendant (Law Com CP No 141, 1996), Pt. VIII.
37 HC Standing Committee B, *Criminal Justice Bill*, 23 January 2003, cols 532 and 546.
38 N Monaghan, 'Reconceptualising good character' [2015] 19(3) *E & P* 190, 194.
39 n 2, [30]-[31].
40 n 2.
41 *Vye* [1993] 1 WLR 471.
42 HM Malek et al, *Phipson on Evidence* 19th edn (Sweet & Maxwell, 2017), para 19–65.
43 *Durbin*, n 32, 87.
44 n 8, 51C.
45 n 2, [74].
46 Which the Court of Appeal itself accepted: n 2, [77].
47 n 2, [70].
48 *Morgans* [2015] EWCA Crim 1997, [13].
49 *Morgans*, n 48, [14].
50 n 2, [89]-[98]. E.g. *Nankani* [2016] EWCA Crim 888, where directions were not given because of an old caution.
51 *Teeluck* v *Trinidad & Tobago* [2005] UKPC 14, [33] per Lord Carswell; *Thompson* v *R* [1998] AC 811, 844 per Lord Hutton; *M (CP)* [2009] EWCA Crim 158, [10]; *Gray* [2004] EWCA Crim 1074, [57].
52 *Liacopoulous* [1994] Lexis Citation 2279.
53 n 8, 47F; *Aziz* (Court of Appeal) unreported 4 March 1994, 15–16.
54 E Freer, [2015] *Arch Rev* 4.
55 *Vye*, n 41.
56 *Horrex*, 5 October 1993, unreported; [1994] *Crim LR* 205.

57 n 2, [58].
58 *Gray*, n 51.
59 n 2, [27].
60 n 2, [68].
61 *Durbin*, n 32.
62 *Teasdale* (1994) 90 Cr App R 80.
63 *Howell* [2001] EWCA Crim 2862, [17]; see also *Krishna* v *Trinidad & Tobago* [2011] UKPC 18, [37].
64 n 8, 50G.
65 n 8, 53E.
66 HM Malek, *Phipson on Evidence* 19th edn, n 42, para 18–08.
67 n 2, [80].
68 *Condron v United Kingdom* (2001) 31 EHRR 1.
69 *X* v *United Kingdom* (1973) 45 CD 1; 3 DR 10.
70 *Taxquet* v *Belgium* (2012) 54 EHRR 24.
71 E.g. *Aberg* [1948] KB 173.
72 n 8, 51A; see also *Teeluck* v *Trinidad & Tobago*, n 51, [33].
73 n 2, [65]-[66].
74 *Teeluck v Trinidad & Tobago*, n 51, [33].
75 *Stiedl (Bjorn)* [2005] EWCA Crim 3278, [51].
76 In HLA Hart, 'The Ascription of Responsibility and Rights' (1948–49) 49 *Proceedings of the Aristotelian Society* 175. He later repudiated this article in *Punishment and Responsibility* (Clarendon Press, 1968), but others have further developed his ideas, e.g. RHS Tur, 'Defeasibilism' (2001) 21(2) *Oxford Journal of Legal Studies* 355
77 JF Beltran & GB Ratti, 'Legal Defeasibility: An Introduction' in JF Beltran & GB Ratti (eds), *The Logic of Legal Requirements: Essays on Defeasibility* (Oxford University Press, 2012), 1.
78 HLA Hart, *The Concept of Law* (Clarendon Press, 1961), 136.
79 Twining and Miers, 'How to do Things with Rules' 4th edn (Butterworths, 1999), 181.
80 n 78, 128.
81 RHS Tur, 'Legislative technique and human rights: the sad case of assisted suicide' [2003] *Crim LR* 3, 6.
82 J. Steyn, 'Does legal formalism hold sway in England?' (1996) 49(1) *Current Legal Problems* 43, 44.
83 n 8, 53E.
84 n 8, 53F.
85 n 8, 53C.
86 As observed in *Tang Siu Man* v *HKSAR* [1998] 1 HKC 371, 388.
87 This is further underlined by reference to *Horrex*, n 56, in which, notwithstanding that the defendant lied in the witness-box about a previous conviction for possession of an offensive weapon, Taylor LJ held that a good character direction ought to have been given; see also *Gray*, n 51, [45] and [61]; *Doncaster* [2008] EWCA Crim 5, [43]; *Hoyte* [2013] EWCA Crim 1002, [38] to the same effect.
88 It seems clear that Lord Steyn had in mind the same type of distinction that he drew in *Bey* [1994] 1 WLR 39, 45 when considering the discretion to direct on a defendant's lies – between a 'completely open-textured discretion' and one 'heavily constrained by established principles'. The law on lies was later clarified in *Burge* [1996] 1 Cr App R 163.
89 *Tang Siu Man* v *HKSAR*, n 86, 403.
90 n 2, [89].
91 R. Munday, 'Good character directions in criminal trials: an exercise in containment' (2015) *CLJ* 388, 391. See *Hunter* n 2, [67].

92 n 2, [91].
93 D. Brown & A. Mostrous, 'Rape case scandal is just "tip of the iceberg"', *The Times* 16 December 2017.
94 As is noted in the 19th edition of HM Malek, *Phipson on Evidence*, n 42, para 18–16.
95 *Vye*, n 41, 474.

Bibliography

Beltran, JF & Ratti, GB, *The Logic of Legal Requirements: Essays on Defeasibility* (Oxford University Press, 2012)

Brown, D & Mostrous, A, 'Rape case scandal is just "tip of the iceberg"', *The Times* 16 December 2017

Campbell, K, 'The test of dishonesty in *R v Ghosh*' [1984] *Cambridge Law Journal* 349

Dyson, M & Jarvis, P, 'Poison Ivey or herbal tea leaf?' [2018] 134(Apr) *Law Quarterly Review* 198

Freer, E, *Hunter* Case Comment [2015] *Archbold Review* 4

Griew, E, 'Dishonesty: the objections to Feely and Ghosh' [1985] *Criminal Law Review* 341

Hart, HLA, *Punishment and Responsibility* (Clarendon Press, 1968)

Hart, HLA, *The Concept of Law* (Clarendon Press, 1961)

Hart, HLA, 'The Ascription of Responsibility and Rights' (1948–49) 49 *Proceedings of the Aristotelian Society* 175

Judicial College, *Crown Court Compendium – Part 1: Jury and Trial Management and Summing Up* (November 2017)

Law Commission Report No. 276 *Fraud* Cm 5560 (2002)

Law Commission Report No. 273 *Evidence of Bad Character in Criminal Proceedings* Cm 5257 (2001)

Law Commission Consultation Paper No. 155, *Fraud and Deception* (1999)

Law Commission Consultation Paper No. 141, *Evidence in Criminal Proceedings: Previous Misconduct of a Defendant* (1996)

Lloyd-Bostock, S, 'The effects on juries of hearing about the defendant's previous criminal record: a simulation study' [2000] *Criminal Law Review* 734

Malek, HM, *Phipson on Evidence*, 19th edn (Sweet & Maxwell, 2017)

Monaghan, N, 'Reconceptualising good character' [2015] 19(3) *International Journal of Evidence & Proof* 190

Munday, R, 'Good character directions in criminal trials: an exercise in containment' (2015) *Cambridge Law Journal* 388

Ormerod, D & Perry, D (eds), *Blackstone's Criminal Practice 2018* (Oxford University Press, 2017)

Ormerod, D & Laird, K, *Smith & Hogan Criminal Law*, 14th edn (Oxford University Press, 2015)

Ormerod, D, 'Criminalising Lying' [2007] *Criminal Law Review* 193

Quirk, H, 'Identifying miscarriages of justice: why innocence in the UK is not the answer' (2007) 70(5) *Modern Law Review* 765

Redmayne, M, *Character in the Criminal Trial* (Oxford University Press, 2015)

Smith, JC, *Buzalek and Schiffer* [1991] *Criminal Law Review* 116

Steyn, J, 'Does legal formalism hold sway in England?' (1996) 49(1) *Current Legal Problems* 43

Tur, RHS, 'Defeasibilism' (2001) 21(2) *Oxford Journal of Legal Studies* 355
Tur, RHS, 'Legislative technique and human rights: the sad case of assisted suicide' [2003]
   Criminal Law Review 3
Twining, W & Miers, D, 'How to do Things with Rules', 4th edn (Butterworths, 1999)
UK Government, *Fraud Review Final Report* (25 July 2006)

Index

Page references in bold indicate tables; 'n' indicates chapter notes.

Printed in Great Britain
by Amazon